THE BIG BOOK OF CLUBBELL TRAINING

2nd EDITION

by Scott Sonnon

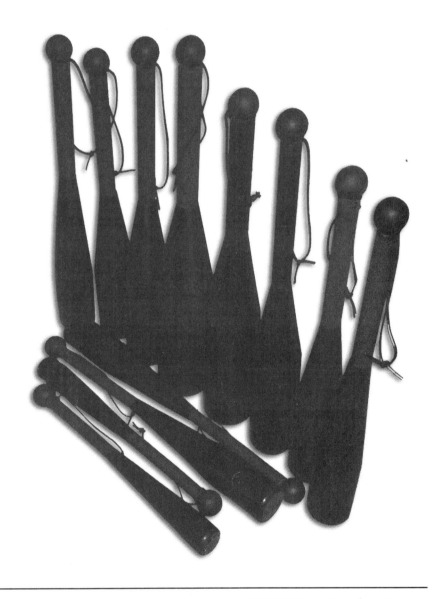

RMAX.tv Productions
Copyright 2006 by RMAX.tv Productions
All rights reserved

Printed in the United States of America. No part of this book may be used or reproduced in any manner whatsoever without written permission except in the case of brief quotations embodied in critical articles and reviews.
ISBN: 0-9763560-6-6

For information address:
RMAX.tv Productions
P.O. Box 501388
Atlanta, GA 31150
Website: www.RMAXINTERNATIONAL.com
Email comments and questions to: info@RMAXINTERNATIONAL.com

Circular Strength Training® and Clubbell® are registered trademarks.

Credits:
Editing: Ryan Murdock
Design and Layout: Wade Munson • www.wadeincreativity.com
Photography: Amanda Folsom, Shutterdog Media • www.shutterdogmedia.com
Brad Kenyon, Aurora Films, Inc. • www.aurorafilms.com
Additional Photo Contributions: Chris Beltrante, Carol Britton & Will Chung, D. Cody Fielding & Wesley Buckingham, Ryan Hurst, Jarlo Ilano, Gary Morozov, and Wade Munson.

DISCLAIMER:
The information in this book is presented in good faith, but no warranty is given, nor results guaranteed. Since we have no control over physical conditions surrounding the application of information in this book, the author and publisher disclaim any liability for untoward results including (but not limited to) any injuries or damages arising out of any person's attempt to rely upon any information herein contained. The exercises described in this book are for informational purposes only, and may be too strenuous or even dangerous for some people. The reader should consult a physician before starting the Clubbell® training or any other exercise programs.

LEGAL STATEMENT:
When purchasing equipment or other products from RMAX.tv Productions, the purchaser understands the risk associated with using this type of equipment. The purchaser also understands the risk associated with following instructions from other products, and agrees not to hold RMAX.tv Productions, its officers, members, employees, assistants, affiliates, volunteers, assignees, or agents of any type whatsoever acting on behalf of the aforementioned entities or persons responsible for injuries.

ATTENTION:
Nothing within this information intends to constitute an explanation of the use of any product or the carrying out of any procedure or process introduced by or within any material. RMAX.tv Productions as well as any of its officers, members, employees, assistants, affiliates, volunteers, assignees, or agents of any type whatsoever acting on behalf of the aforementioned entities and persons accept no responsibility for any liability, injuries or damages arising out of any person's attempt to rely upon any information contained herein. Consult your doctor before using this or any other exercise device. Do not use if you have an injury, or are experiencing pain or inflammation in your hands, wrists, forearms, elbows, or shoulders without first consulting your doctor. Use this product at your own risk. Failure to follow instructions and/or using this product in any way other than its intended use could result in injury.

IMPORTANT:
Please be sure to thoroughly read the instructions for all exercises in this book, paying particular attention to all cautions and warnings shown for the Clubbell® equipment.

SPECIAL THANKS

My wife Jodie for her patience, support and wisdom.

Nikolay Travkin for making it all happen.

Sara Good for demonstrating that beauty
and power are synonymous.

Dan Chomycia for taking it to the extremes by example.

Brandon Jones for his hellfire integrity, like it or not.

Michael Gannon for his Zen wit and tenacious compassion.

Joseph Wilson for his organizational genius for keeping it real.

Ryan Murdock for bringing literally a world of experience.

Doug Szolek for pioneering two-handed training
for the big man in all of us.

Connie Brown for cutting to the basic heart of the matter.

The entire Tribe for embracing personal mastery in order to empathize
with how damn hard it is to transcend oneself.

OUR CREDO

"I believe in the sanctity of the human body."

"I believe in the divine right of every being to possess a body that is strong and beautiful and radiant with energy."

"I believe that the care of the body is a sacred responsibility — the first we accept and the last we lay down."

"I believe Nature is the great physician and health is the inevitable reward of those who sit at her feet and learn her ways."

"I believe that sickness is the offspring of ignorance, and that the greatest teacher of mankind is he who bears the flaming torch of right living to those who dwell in darkness."

"I believe that in the true art of healing there is no mystery and no vagueness, and that he only can help the sufferer who faithfully interprets the methods of Nature."

"I believe that physical betterment and morale welfare go hand in hand."

– *Max Unger (aka "Lionel Strongfort") 1928*

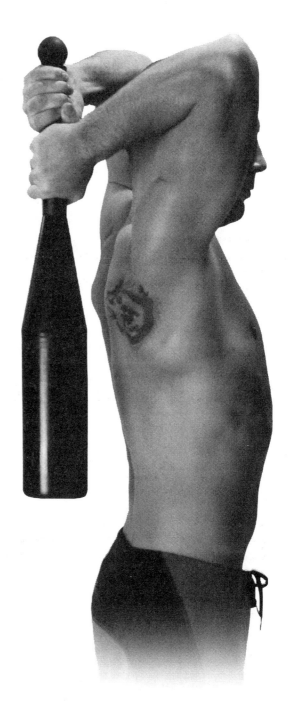

THE BIG BOOK OF CLUBBELL TRAINING

Table of Contents

Forward i
Introduction v

What is Fitness? 1
CST Fitness Standard #1: 2
CST Fitness Standard #2: 3
CST Fitness Standard #3: 4
Fitness and Wellness 4

What is Flow in Fitness? 5
What is the Goal of Fit-ness? 6
What is the Purpose of Work in Fit-ness? 6
Two Types of Forces: Driving and Restrictive 7
Tabula Rasa: Removing Restrictive Forces 7
What is The Ultimate Physical Expression of Fitness? 8
Flow Under Resistance: Adding the Driving Forces 9

What is the CST System? 11

What is the CST College? 13
The 3 Courses of CST System 14
The CST Coaching Development Program 15
CST Level Overview Expanded 16
How do RMAX Martial Art Systems Fit In? 16

How is CST Organized as a System? 17
Principles of Physical Development 18
Growth is a Universal, Predictable Process 18
Each Individual Progresses with Unique Timing 18
Simple to Complex — General to Specific 19
Head Downwards — Center Outwards 19
Fitness Value Hierarchy 20

Our Evolution: from Ancient Tool to Modern Athlete 23
Russian Bulava 24
Iranian Meel 27
Indian Gada, Jori, Karela, Ekka 30
British Club Swinging 33
American Club Swinging 34
20th Century Strongman Club Swinging 36

The Birth of Three Dimensional Training — 45

- Russian SAMBO 46
- Performance Diagnostic Trinity™ 49
- Training Hierarchy Pyramid™ 51
- General Physical Preparedness 52
- Specific Physical Preparedness 52
- Three Dimensional Performance Pyramid™ 53
- Experimenting with Designs 57
- The 4 Intentions of Combat Sport SPP 58

Tabula Rasa — Clean the Slate — 61

- The Site is not the Source 62
- Learning to Clean the Slate 63
- Cleaning the Slate 63
- Cycle, Circuit but Don't Cocktail 64
- How Do You Plan? 64
- Short-term Success vs. Long-lasting Development 65
- Avoiding the Immediate Results — Eventual Injury Loop 65

Intuitive Training — 67

- Resolving the Pain through Mobility Drills 68
- Sometimes No Pain Means No Gain! 68
- How do You Design RPE into Your Program Assessment? 69
- How does Recording Your RPE Help your Program? 69
- So All I Need is My RPE to Use My Intuition in Training? 70
- So How Can Intuitive Training Help You Assess Form? 70
- The Problem with Guys 71
- The Problem with Gals 72
- Diagnostics and Assessment 72
- Cycle or Circuit, but do not Cocktail 73

The Golden Ratio of Fitness — 75

- The Fibonacci Sequence and the Golden Mean 76
- Intuitive Training meets the Fibonacci Wave 76
- Energy Levels and the Fibonacci Sequence 76
- Tapering to Peak Performance 77

Clubbell® Training Mechanics — 79

- Safety Strap 80
- Approach 80
- Aligning your Spine 81
- Confirming Your Grip 82
  - *Micro-loading Grip Choke Depth* 82
  - *Right and Left Grip* 83
  - *Split Grip* 83
  - *Complimentary Grip* 84

Intelligent Grip 84
Leverage Grip 85
Packing Your Shoulders 85
Practicing the Shoulder Pack with a Basic Swing 86
Two-Handed Clubbell® Exercise and Shoulder Pack 86
Locking Your Arms 86
Elbow Pit Rotation 86
Short and Long Arms 87
Wrist Alignment 88
Activating Your Core 88
Fear and Anger Level Breathing 88
Discipline Level Breathing 88
Flow Level Breathing 89
Breath Development is Specific! 89
Recruiting Your Hips 89
Hip Snap 90
Side Hip Snap 90
Hip Sit-Back 91
Hip Sway 91
Hip Root 92
Driving Your Legs 93
Shock Absorption 93
Rock-It Drill 95

Clubbell® Basic Positions — 97

Floor Park 99
Ready Position — The Silverback 99
Shoulder Park 100
Chest Park 101
Arm Stop 101
Order Position 102
Two-Handed Order Position 102
Guard Position 103
Flag Position 103
Two-Handed Flag Position 104
Torch Position 104
Two-Handed Torch Position 104
Back Position 105
Two-Handed Back Position 106

Clubbell® Exercises — 107

Equipment Substitutes 108

Swings — 109

- Front Swing 110
- Two-Handed Front Swing 112
- Side Swing 113
- Side Semi Circle Swing 114
- Pirouette Swing 115

Pendulums — 117

- Front Pendulum 118
- Two-Handed Front Pendulum 120
- Inside Pendulum 121
- Double Side Pendulum 122
- Two-Handed Guard Inside Pendulum 123
- Outside Pendulum 124
- Two-Handed Guard Outside Pendulum 125
- Lunge-Step Pendulum 126
- Two-Handed Guard Lunge-Step Pendulum 127
- Side-Step Pendulum 128
- Two-Handed Guard Side-Step Pendulum 129

Circles — 131

- Front Circle 132
- Back Circle 134
- Inside Circle 135
- Outside Circle 136
- Two-Handed Side Circle 137
- Alternating Circles: Front Stroke and Backstroke 138

Cleans — 139

- Front Clean to Order Position 140
- Two-Handed Front Clean to Order Position 142
- Front Clean to Shoulder Park 143
- Two-Handed Front Clean to Shoulder Park 144
- Front Clean to Flag Position 145
- Two-Handed Front Clean to Flag Position 146
- Front Clean to Back Position 147
- Two-Handed Front Clean to Back Position 148
- Side Clean to Guard Position 149
- Side Clean to Shoulder Park 150
- Side Clean to Back Position 151
- Side Clean to Side Flag 152

Jerks — 153

- Front Torch Jerk 154
- Two-Handed Front Torch Jerk 155
- Front Jerk 156

Two-Handed Front Jerk 157
Shoulder Park Front Jerk 158
Two-Handed Shoulder Park Front Jerk 159
Front Clean + Jerk 160
Side Torch Jerk 161
Side Jerk 162
Shoulder Park Side Jerk 163
Side Clean + Jerk 164

Snatches — 165

Front Torch Snatch 166
Two-Handed Front Torch Snatch.. 168
Front Snatch 169
Two-Handed Front Snatch.. 170
Side Torch Snatch 171
Side Snatch 172

Presses — 173

Torch Press 174
Two-Handed Torch Press 175
Front Press 176
Two-Handed Front Press 177
Flag Press 178
Two-Handed Flag Press 179
Side Torch Press 180
Side Press 181
Side Flag Press 182
Clean and Press 183

Casts — 185

Wrist Cast 186
Two Handed Wrist Cast — The Crowbar 187
Arm Cast 188
Alternating Arm Cast — Drumming Cast 190
Two-Handed Arm Cast — The Gama Cast 191
Two-Handed Arm Cast Circular Pivot 193
Two-Handed Arm Cast to Flag Position — The Barbarian 194
Shoulder Cast... 195
Two-Handed Shoulder Cast 196
Shoulder Cast to Side Flag Position — The Muscle Out 197
Double Shoulder Cast — The Crucifix 198
Alternating Shoulder Cast — The Kodo Cast 199
Head Cast 200
Shoulder Cast Leverage Hold Variation 202
Alternating Head Cast – The See-Saw 203

Two-Handed Head Cast 204
Shield Cast 205
Two-Handed Shield Cast 206
Parry Cast 207
Reverse Parry Cast 209
Two-Handed Parry Cast 211

Clubbell® Superiority — 213

Constant Center of Mass 214
Dangers of the Shifting Center of Mass in Plate and Shot Loaded Tools 215
Dangers of the Contour of Plate-Loaded Tools 216
Protective Coating of the Clubbell® 216
Dangers of Cast and Lathed Designs 216
Knob Design 217
Dangers of Collar Failure in Plate Loaded Tools 217
More Collar Dangers 218
Choosing Metal over Wood 218

Frequently Asked Questions — 221

What are the advantages of using Clubbells for CST? 222
What are the differences between traditional antique clubs and modern Clubbells? 223
Which sports have been improved by the use of Clubbells? 223
With which Clubbell® weight should I begin? 224
Which should I purchase next? 224
What about the 45-lb Clubbells? 225
Should I purchase the entire Clubbell® PRO Gym immediately? 225

Safety Guidelines — 227

Sample Programs — 231

Basic types of Work 232
Longevity Program Guidance 232

Basic Strength Conditioning — 235

Dense Strength...236
Swing Power...236
Neural Strength..236
Club Mass 237
Power Plant 237
Functional Hypertrophy..238

Ladder Training — 239

Linear (Geometric) Ladder 240
Wave Ladder 240
Competitive Ladder 240
Step (Exponential) Ladder 240

Ratchet Ladder..241
Choking Ladder..241
Control Pause Ladder...241

Century Training — 243
Double Century Training..246

Phi Century Ratchet Sequencing — 249

Youth Clubbell® Classes — 253
Youth Athletic Training Guidelines 254

International Clubbell® Sport — 257
ICS Rules and Regulations 258
    2005 Women's Qualifications 260
    2005 Men's Qualifications 260
    ICS Ratings 261

Sport-Specific Program Examples — 263
Basketball Teams..264
Baseball Swinging..264
Baseball Pitching 265
Football Quarterbacks..265
Soccer Goalies 266
Tennis Players 266
Field Hockey Teams 267
Volleyball Players 267
Golf Players 268

Bibliography — 269

Contributed by Jarlo Ilano

FORWARD

By Marty Gallagher, author of over 200 fitness and training columns for washingtonpost.com, a feature writer for some of the nation's top fitness magazines for the past thirty years, and star of the soon to be released fitness reality show *60 Day Makeover*, created with seven-time Emmy Award winning producer Mark Hammond. Gallagher won five world and eight national championships as a master powerlifter and was co-coach of the 1991 world champion U.S. powerlifting squad.

Scott Sonnon's approach to fitness is unique and hard to encapsulate; part flexibility, part progressive resistance, part cardiovascular. The totality of Sonnon's system is impressive, effective and totally unlike anything I've encountered in my 42-years involved with athletics and fitness-related activities.

Scott Sonnon exasperates the hell out of people. Ours is an age of yawning predictability, and standard operating procedure is to completely commercialize and dumb-down all things fitness-related. Scott Sonnon is opaque, obtuse, obstinate and passionate. He doesn't spoon feed folks fitness, and that exasperates them to no end. People have a tough time getting their arms around the totality of his approach, and this confuses those used to having their fitness served up in user-friendly fashion.

Simpleton solutions are all the rage and laughable transparency is the name of the fitness game, so a philosophic approach as dense and multi-layered as the one Sonnon promotes is bound to have a tough go of it. John Q. Public desperately wants to believe that their favorite, user-friendly infomercial fitness guru is telling the truth when they convincingly exclaim how easy and effortless the process of physical transformation is. Like a classical contrarian, Sonnon rightly insists just the opposite: the process of physical transformation is difficult and arduous, and transforming from who you are into who you want to be will be a long and protracted battle. Meanwhile the blissfully ignorant, taking their cues from fitness shuck-and-jive artists, bounce from one miracle product to the next, each in turn offering a shortcut for a price and none ever delivering on anything.

Sonnon stands apart and alone, a crazed fitness saint speaking in tongues, offering up an exasperating cold-truth message in obstinate, no-compromise language that leaves no wiggle room. Gadflies, muckrakers, revolutionaries and true innovators exasperate the hell out of ordinary folk and poke sharp sticks at the defenders of the status quo. They force us to think and question and reevaluate and recalibrate our own quest. Normal folks don't really want to devote themselves to the degree necessary to trigger true transformation and would prefer someone sell them renovation in a bottle.

Sonnon's approach doesn't come in a container and could be called a *thinking man's approach to fitness*. His system questions long-held basic assumptions about what fitness is, what the goals should be, and offers a unique and iconoclastic methodology as the vehicle to the destination.

Scott has successfully morphed both his physique and his mind. Scott is his own best example and finest sales tool. Scott not only talks the talk, but walks the walk. With most fitness 'experts' the more you learn of them and their methodology the less impressed you are. With Scott the opposite is true: the more you are exposed to his unique approach the more you want to know.

How do you recognize a real transformation expert? There's no pat answer to that one. Sonny Barger was once asked how they selected Hell's Angels. He replied, *"We don't select 'em, we recognize 'em!"* And so it is among elite fitness professionals. They don't hold auditions, they recognize obvious talent. When discussion turns to the new breed of fitness innovators, Sonnon's name is continually brought up. Real experts recognize real talent.

Cast a wide net and you can discover a plethora of amazingly diverse, varied, effective and unusual approaches to physique renovation. One of the most interesting and effective is the resurgence of old time tools and modes that have been resurrected and swung back into action (literally) as Clubbells. These ancient tools, thought passé, have been resurrected and updated for modern times by the "fitness heretic" Scott Sonnon.

Through the iron grapevine I became aware of an American martial artist who had relocated to Russia to immerse himself in the specifics of Russian Sambo, a brutal combat fighting style. The American "went native" and began deep study of a mysterious, quasi-mystical ethnic health system that top Sambo men swore fanatical allegiance to. Eventually he ended up studying with the inner-circles of elite Sambo masters. Scott soaked it all up like a dry sponge held underwater.

That was a decade ago. Since then Sonnon relocated to Washington State and in the intervening years has redefined, refined and polished all that he had learned. His articles began to appear in magazines and were always well-written. I took note of the luminaries Sonnon was rubbing elbows with, and I began to investigate more.

I contacted Scott for a Washington Post.com interview and found him refreshingly lucid and possessed of an amazing tale and a unique multilevel methodology. His gregarious business partner Nikolay Travkin sent me the basics on CST. The individual postures, movements, and the breathing techniques were sequenced in such a way as to achieve the ultra-subtle link between brain and body. Not yoga, not martial arts, not dance, not a lot of things. His approach borrowed from everywhere but ended up resembling nothing I'd ever come across. His final finished product is unlike anything you've ever been exposed to.

His approach could be called holistic: he incorporates flexibility drills that meld mind and body with harsh Clubbell® training that stresses flow and precision. Various weighted Clubbells are maneuvered in a wide variety of patterns and motor-pathways to trigger varying effects: heavy Clubbells trigger muscle hypertrophy while lighter ones are swung to promote cardiovascular effect.

He couples his Prasara™ yoga body weight conditioning exercise and Intu-Flow™ dynamic joint mobility exercise with Clubbell® exercises to produce a strangely effective amalgamation of power and subtlety. I arrived at his seminar in Philadelphia to find that his instructors were quite impressive, displaying great power and awesome flexibility. The individuals gathered for the certification seminar underwent a rigorous program that made no allowances for poseurs or the faint of heart.

His Circular Strength Training® System delves into diverse inter-related and inter-dependant aspects. His is truly the thinking man's approach to unorthodox fitness. Many roads lead to Fitness Rome. If you are a serious student of fitness and burn for physical transformation, check out Mr. Sonnon and his amazing fitness menu.

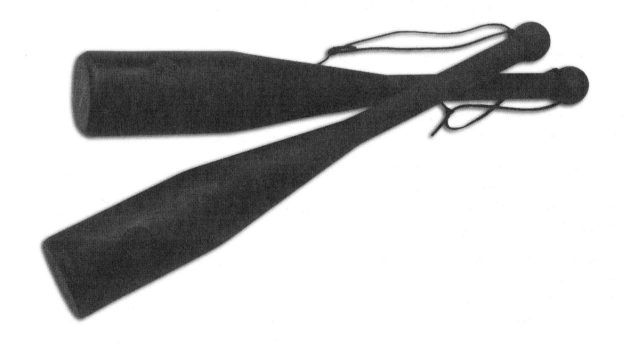

Contributed by Ryan Hurst

INTRODUCTION

Congratulations on entering the world of **Circular Strength Training® (CST)**.

I'd like to begin with a word about the language used in this book. There's a rule of thumb that applies to communication of sports and combat athletics instruction: athletes need to experience the instruction and teachers need to provide it in a language that the athletes understand, whether that's words or drills. You'll get both here.

Some of you may already be very familiar with terms that are used in scientific or instructional materials for either exercise or physiology. Others of you may not.

Everywhere that I introduced a technical or scientific term, one that is part of the exercise physiology or sport psychology lexicon, I've tried to explain it such that the general reader will understand it, without surrendering the precision of the science or losing those who care more about the practice than the underlying principles or theories.

It is also important to note that my coaching involves symbolism. Symbols embody deep and complex imagery and communicate empowering dimensions beyond cold, sterile terms. I use symbols deliberately because we think in images and not in elaborate strings of scientific terminology. Talk to a quantum physicist and to a Zen Monk and you may have a very similar, if not identical, dialogue. Language is a means to an end. Symbolism accelerates communication and amplifies understanding.

If you have a question, please ask it on our forum at WWW.RMAXINTERNATIONAL.COM. The only dumb question is the one that you don't ask. An entire 'tribe' of athletes, instructors and coaches is at your disposal 24 hours a day.

To begin the practice of the material in this book you'll need at least one pair of authentic, patented Clubbells, and the Clubbell® Training Basics DVDs.

I want CST to be the most satisfying fitness experience you've ever had, and I want to provide you with the tools that you need to surpass your goals. It's my hope that this book will give you both.

**Chief Operations Officer
RMAX.tv Productions**

Contributed by Jarlo Ilano

WHAT IS FITNESS?

The first step in establishing a dialogue is to define terms. The first term that we must define here is what it means to be 'fit.' What is our 'fit-ness' definition?

CST FITNESS STANDARD #1:
WORK CAPACITY TO SOPHISTICATION TO SPECIFICITY TO FLOW

Unlike conventional fitness definitions that only regard the bottom-level attributes of endurance, strength, stamina, flexibility and power, which come from training, CST includes the critical elements of coordination, body control, agility, balance, accuracy, timing, rhythm and sensitivity, which come from practice. CST measures fitness as the ability to recruit maximal multi-joint efficiency to move through multiple planes of motion with greater and greater ease compared to previous attempts.

CST's model of physical development progresses upward through cycles of incremental sophistication, like a pyramid built from a base up to a point. Effortless performance — known as peak performance, the optimal performance zone, or flow-state — is CST's primary goal, and it is deliberately built from attributes to abilities to skills to flow.

Included in this development is the facing of chaos. In order to develop fully one must feel the external and internal resistance of competitive forces. Competition IS a cooperative game. The recent trend to vilify competition is due to an etiological misunderstanding. Competition derives from the Latin roots *con* and *petire,* which in unison mean *to seek together.* Could there be any better definition of co-operation? The goal of competition is to co-create the transformative element of resistance or pressure. Without this transformative element of competition one can stand at the door of flow-state but it will remain locked. The transcendent possibilities that occur during competition change the individual on a fundamental cellular level.

CST FITNESS STANDARD #2:

EXPEDIENT ABILITY TO ACQUIRE EFFICIENCY IN NEW SKILLS, AND MORE IMPORTANTLY TO INNOVATIVELY CREATE NEW SKILLS.

'Skill' is used here to refer to a physical motoric, structural and respiratory tool which accomplishes a task. Traditional fitness standards base fitness solely on the amount of work that can be produced and not on the effortlessness with which the athlete can perform the skill. A skill is not merely a physical event but is also a mental and emotional one. Developing the appropriate physical, mental and emotional integration determines the efficacy of a skill. Understanding this 'Gestalt' perspective (that skill is the inextricably intertwined tapestry of mental, emotional and physical components) of skill acquisition allows one to <u>develop the driving forces as well as to remove the restrictive forces</u> so that one can expediently, if not immediately, absorb new skills.

In contrast to conventional fitness standards which state that mere repetition, volume, load, intensity, frequency, et cetera of a 'rote' skill determines one's fitness, CST posits that it is the traditionally elusive role of innovation, adaptation and improvisation which affords victory in any task.

Zwischenzug is a German chess term used to describe *"an in between move which is an unexpected reply, tossed in the middle of an expected sequence of moves."* In theater, martial arts, dance, athletics and comedy, as well as in life, *Zwischenzug* awes and inspires us.

Every skill was once spontaneously evolved from the performance of an innovative athlete. Every new barrier has always been overcome through the innovative creativity of an athlete performing outside of the 'box' of a known/expected skill set. CST's secondary goal is to tap the idiosyncratic genius of each individual's physical expression of fitness.

CST FITNESS STANDARD #3:
EFFECTIVE RATIO OF RESTORATIVE FORCES TO WORK FORCES

As opposed to conventional fitness standards, which are based upon one's performance when situations are at their best, CST defines fitness as one's ability to perform a task at any particular time, including the most suboptimal periods. By conventional standards you are only fit to the degree that you can maintain your best condition. However, that is a fleeting period, and the greater the intensity of your training the longer the recovery period demanded by the activity — in which case you become 'unfit' until restored to normal performance.

CST defines fitness as your ability to perform at any time. It approaches training and practice with pre-incorporated restorative methods so that 'down time' is minimized, if not negated. In other words, your daily activities themselves become an extension of your training and practice.

Moreover, CST endorses an approach that sees nutritional, meditative, attentional, and emotional (biochemical) behavior as a bidirectional feedback system. How and what you eat, how you recover your mental space, how you focus your mental energy, and how you address your emotional arousal and discharge emotional energy directly impacts your fitness, just as your training and practice impact them.

CST uses the perennial model of the Golden Mean (or Fibonacci Sequence) and the vehicle of Intuitive Assessment to guide effective, daily balancing of activities to coordinate with one's ever-changing biorhythm.

FITNESS AND WELLNESS

Under conventional fitness standards fitness is not synonymous with wellness. One can be fit for a task but not well (healthy). According to CST's above three canons of fitness, one must be well in order to be fit, and fit in order to be well.

Pursuing an athletic career of 10 years from the age of 15 to 25 with the result that one becomes so physically decrepit as to be invalid does not make one fit. Further, one cannot be a slave to junk foods, belligerent temperament, sexual excess, substance debauchery, and so on, and be deemed 'fit'.

The definition of fitness must be expanded to every activity of one's life, at any moment of one's life, for the duration of one's life. Fitness must also extend (or at least not shorten) one's life.

WHAT IS FLOW IN FITNESS?

I shall expand upon what specifically is this elusive virtue of *flow* in fitness, why we give it the highest premium in CST, and why CST stands unique in that flow remains the primary agenda and goal.

WHAT IS THE GOAL OF FIT-NESS?

Most, if not all, fitness systems intend to provide superior results in General Physical Preparedness (GPP). When I say "if not all" it's because I recognize that there may be fitness systems out there that are like CST, but I am not aware of them. GPP holds as its exclusive goal *the capacity to do work*. GPP asks how much you can do, how fast you can do it, for how long and how often.

GPP is a subset of CST. GPP is only the beginning step, one unnecessarily and deleteriously fixated upon by most, if not all, fitness systems. GPP is only the base level of CST's *Training Hierarchy Pyramid*™.

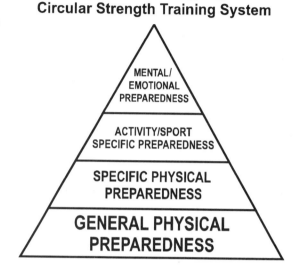

To offer a simple introduction, **GPP** deals with *work capacity;* **SPP** deals with *work sophistication;* **A/SSP** regards *work specificity;* and **MEP** regards *work flow*. Understanding this graduation of work refinement requires extensive seminaring, studying and practice to internalize. This chapter is meant to provide you with an overview of what is contained in CST's "black box".

To understand the upwardly sophisticating nature of *work* we need to define its true place in fitness.

WHAT IS THE PURPOSE OF WORK IN FIT-NESS?

This question must be asked and answered in order for a fitness system to mature its organization, content and programming. Most, if not all, fitness systems define fitness as the ability to do **work:**

$$work = force \times distance$$

In other words most, if not all, fitness systems define fitness as being synonymous with GPP. Moreover most, if not all, fitness systems place the highest premium on **power**, which is *work divided by time*, or more specifically:

$$power = (force \times distance) / time$$

However work only defines GPP. Since GPP is only a subset of CST's *Training Hierarchy Pyramid*™, power is a necessary but insufficient quality of fitness.

Power does not define fitness. Efficiency defines fitness.

$$efficiency = useful\ work / total\ work$$

Efficiency asks how much of the force that you exert actually contributes effectively to the task objective. More importantly, efficiency asks how little total work you must perform to accomplish the most towards the task objective. In other words, the more useful the work you do, and the less you must exert yourself to do it, the more fit you are. Ultimately isn't this what we all want out of fitness?

Think of it this way: the person who can accomplish a life task while conserving the largest amount of energy is the most "fit" for the task. But general fitness systems attempt to define fitness as the ability to perform more work, faster, for longer duration, and more often.

To further obscure the ultimate aim of fitness most, if not all, fitness systems have created 'tests' to assess your fitness level based upon their definition of fitness as work (and power). This is akin to defining the best 'fit' automobile as the one that can accelerate the fastest and pull the most weight the longest. A more accurate definition of automobile 'fitness' emphasizes fuel efficiency, handling and maneuverability, reliability, longevity, and ('pain-free') ease of travel. None of those examples are addressed by mere work capacity (quantity), but rather by the **quality** of work.

TWO TYPES OF FORCES: DRIVING AND RESTRICTIVE

This brings us to another very important point which is rarely, if ever, addressed by fitness systems. If it's addressed at all it's mentioned only in passing, as an afterthought.

There are two different goals of force production: the generation of driving forces and the removal of restrictive forces. Most, if not all, fitness systems only seek to apply more force. However, all actions yield more efficient task achievement by removing internal blockages, impediments and pre-conditions which stop (or at least inhibit) your ability to apply force.

Worse still, if you do not remove the restrictive forces then adding driving forces reinforces, strengthens and increases these restrictive forces in a downward spiral that leads to total debilitation.

TABULA RASA: REMOVING RESTRICTIVE FORCES

Our point of departure in CST is *Tabula Rasa* (a Latin phrase which means "to Clean the Slate") — removing the restrictive forces that inhibit your ability to perform efficiently. You must first remove the problematic limitations to your physical life in order to reap 100% of the benefit of any additional driving forces generated by fitness systems. Moreover, you must continually recycle back into Tabula Rasa to remove the painful performance impediments which limit your fitness.

As a result of this understanding the first sub-system in CST involves the use of an assessment process and pre-incorporated physical recovery practice called *Intu-Flow*™ to continually remove restrictive forces. *Tabula Rasa* is Phase I of CST. Building upon this phase of removing restrictive forces is CST's unique approach to generating driving forces.

WHAT IS THE ULTIMATE PHYSICAL EXPRESSION OF FITNESS?

As we've noted above, most fitness systems attempt to define fitness as work capacity. However, work capacity is only a necessary but an insufficient aspect of fitness, and only a sub-set of the *Training Hierarchy Pyramid*™.

The ultimate expression of fitness is **flow:** *the ability to efficiently accomplish a life task.* Accomplishing a task does not mean merely the rote repetition of some standard set of physical skills. That is only fit-ness to perform those static skills. Life is dynamic and requires you to constantly improvise, innovate and adapt. There's no User's Guide in existence that tells you exactly how to lead a physical life.

If you fall down a set of stairs then gymnastics tumbling, pushups and sprinting may help you indirectly. But perhaps attempting to perform those skills may bring more harm, since they ignore the dangers that are actually present as you fall. Perhaps the impediments from repeated performance of those skills may lead you to become injured more from the fall than you otherwise might have had you not practiced them at all. Addressing a life event like a fall, moving furniture, or lifting an injured child involves the ability to improvise an efficient physical skill to meet the dynamic task at hand.

Flow is what we mean when we say that someone has a "knack" for picking up new skills. *Knack* is not some genetic anomaly. We all have the capability for *knack* due to our neurological, biochemical, myofascial, and vestibular programming. How we practice determines our "knack capacity."

Flow is the ability for someone to create new, idiosyncratic solutions to sudden, dynamic life tasks and to seamlessly respond to those tasks with timing, accuracy, coordination, rhythm and ease.

FLOW UNDER RESISTANCE: ADDING THE DRIVING FORCES

This basic notion of flow spawned the two physical expressions of flow in CST: *the ability to flow under both external and internal resistance.*

In CST the ability to flow with **external resistance** requires that the body be caused to move in the most efficient manner possible. As a result, the most dynamic moving tool (and hence the "least efficient" tool as compared to the high efficiency of machines, cables and pulleys) is the Clubbell®.

To effortlessly absorb and smoothly retranslate the incredibly high forces produced by the special combination of torque, leverage disadvantage and traction grip of the Clubbell® is an obvious expression of masterful flow. Further, in CST the goal is to be able to create new movement connections once basic movements have been mastered, fostering those ineffable qualities of improvisation, innovation and adaptation that are the ultimate virtues of fit-ness.

In CST the ability to flow with **internal resistance** requires that one's own bodyweight be moved in increasingly more challenging patterns. To absorb and retranslate force through ever-sophisticating, idiosyncratic and innovative movements is the ultimate expression of flow in bodyweight mastery. This is *Prasara*™ and its precursor, *Body-Flow Biomechanical Exercise*™.

Flow under resistance requires that you shift your focus from the quantity of work output to the **quality** of work that you perform over the course of your progression up the *Training Hierarchy Pyramid*™.

How can one person be ?more fit? for one's life than another? Doing more pullups, more squats, running faster or longer, these things do not define fitness. You must ask yourself the question, "How can I be ?more fit? for my life?" Therein lies the only true answer to your fit-ness.

We must always return to the very sobering and very authentic question: What are you in need of being fit for? Everyone wants to be fit for their individual lives. Work is only a subset of life. Flowing with what happens in dynamic reality is what gives us authentic life fitness.

Go for the flow.

Contributed by Carol Britton and Will Chung

WHAT IS THE CST SYSTEM?

CST is an exciting alternative to the dead end of linear training. Humans are three-dimensional beings; linear movement is a mistaken notion. CST prepares you for when movements deviate from the expected.

The term "circular strength" refers to the infinite multi-planar degrees of freedom that multiple joints own when allowed to work together synergistically.

With CST joints are strengthened throughout their entire range of motion. The benefits include increased stability, injury prevention, and an increase in force production. Its byproduct is the fully functional opposite of a puffed-up dysfunctional "gym body."

The key tenet of CST is "mobility first." You must first recover your true range of motion. You can then coordinate it with adjacent joints, refine the movement so that it regains full integration with the entire body, and finally add resistance to that refined range of motion to strengthen it.

The Clubbell® was designed and patented to be the weighted component of CST; the logical extension of pain-free dynamic mobility. The Clubbell® has been called "the most inefficient tool," meaning that it demands the most personal physical efficiency and skill to move it gracefully. The Clubbell® has its roots in traditional club swinging: the oldest method of strength and conditioning known to humanity, and a former Olympic Sport. Club swinging existed for centuries in ancient Persia, India and Burma. CST lifted the archaic techniques of "fancy" traditional club swinging, combined it with an incrementally progressive system of joint mobility, and systematized it through modern sport science. Clubbell® Training is simply the most sophisticated, fun and creative vehicle for strength and conditioning ever conceived.

Prasara Body-Flow™ is a synergistic physical practice which at first glance can appear to incorporate aspects of yoga, martial arts, acrobatics, break-dance and gymnastics. *Prasara* — Sanskrit for "Flow without thought" — transforms the self through a uniquely powerful approach to integrating breathing with movement and structure to unlock "flow-state." *Body-Flow* is a system of somatic engineering to release bound flow. Flow lies beneath the rusty armor of fear, anxiety and trauma that our ego carries around like so much luggage. Prasara Body-Flow™ is a physical practice of discharging fear, anxiety and trauma, which in turn restores one's natural state of Grace, or Flow.

Intu-Flow™ — a combination of the phrase "Intuitive Flow" — refers to the fact that our bodymind knows precisely what it needs for pain-free health and longevity. Intu-Flow, as a result, is an incrementally progressive system of dynamic joint mobility exercise designed to release stored tension and break up calcium deposits, connective tissue adhesions and fascial density. Getting Intu-Flow™ restores energy by washing our entire matrix of connective tissue in nutrition and lubrication, which in turn vitalizes one's health, removes pain, and promotes longevity, because *"We are as old as our connective tissue."*

WHAT IS THE CST COLLEGE?

In 2005 I restructured the rapidly expanding curriculum of certifying CST Instructors and Coaches. Under the prior intensive certification process some candidates were becoming too cerebral, and as a result lacked necessary and sufficient CST athleticism themselves. In the prior model there was no way to ensure enough focused time on the basics. Yet it is the basics which make all of us strong, healthy, fluid, and most importantly truly able to grasp the entire breadth of the CST System.

The CST Coaching Development Program was not created to divide people but to concentrate attention. Certain trainees were trying to understand the impact of one movement somewhere else in the body before they were able to perform even the most basic exercise with proper form. Other trainees were trying to perform client assessment and specific program design before they had even performed their first kinetic chain.

This worked itself out for the people who continued to attend CST seminars after earning their initial instructor certification. But most people stop at the minimum, riding out their certification, waiting only to attend again for mandatory recertification near the end of their valid term. Those who continued got a chance to see deeper into the material presentation of coaching development. For those who didn't continue this insight was unlikely, unless they were fortunate enough to have some other professional training and experience with common source principles.

Throwing improvisational demands at the instructor candidates ostracized about 85% of the student body. It's just too overwhelming for most people. I felt it my responsibility to administratively screen this out of the coaching development program to the extent that it is possible. I structured the revised program based upon the academic model of prerequisite information: basic exercises on the first level; kinetic chains on the second level (though they are obviously still doing and teaching the basics); and improvisational movement on the third level (though they are obviously still doing and teaching basic exercises and chains).

After evaluating the trainees in the program I observed that, *whether they intended to or not,* each individual followed this developmental progression. *If they stuck with it,* this is how each and every person evolved. The intention of the coaching development program is to give **every** individual **equal** access to that progression in a deliberate, orderly and consistent fashion.

THE 3 COURSES OF CST SYSTEM

The material content of the CST System continues not only to refine but to expand. Over the years I have continued to produce more and more refined presentations of the system, and I have expanded its scope as various amateur and professional sports teams have embraced CST, and as hundreds of thousands of people around the world have come to demand access to CST for themselves.

The only way to focus on the basics is to ensure sufficient coverage of the material content of the three basic directions of CST:

1. Weighted strength and conditioning
2. Bodyweight agility and coordination
3. Dynamic, pain-free range of motion / mobility training

Since CST is an integrated system, these basic directions heavily (if not totally) overlap one another. However, the entry level athlete doesn't understand this and cannot be force-fed it. Further, some people felt overwhelmed by having to "study it all" when they initially only wanted to taste their specific interest. As a result, CST certification has been broken into 3 different courses: Clubbell® Training, Intu-Flow™ and Prasara Body-Flow™.

People may choose to pursue any particular concentration and not pursue full CST certification. For instance, a yogi interested in Prasara Body-Flow™ Certification need not enroll in Clubbell® Training or Intu-Flow™. A chiropractor or physical therapist, or even just an aging individual, interested in connective tissue health and longevity may pursue Intu-Flow™ Certification without enrolling in Body-Flow™ or Clubbell® training. A strength coach, athlete, or individual who solely wishes to be strong and fit through Clubbell® Training need not enroll in Prasara Body-Flow™ or Intu-Flow™.

I encourage CST athletes to first certify in Level I and practice for at least 3–6 months before enrolling to certify in Level II, though some CST athletes who have rigorously practiced Intu-Flow, Prasara and Clubbell® Training in advance can take all 6 courses on consecutive days (as scheduled annually). Individual courses not passed can be retaken in a future quarter.

Although everyone (Athletes, Candidates, Instructors, Coaches and Head Coaches) participates in the same seminar, they are being evaluated under different criteria depending upon their "Level".

THE CST COACHING DEVELOPMENT PROGRAM

I've expanded this into a very succinct, digestible chart. The chart is based upon an understanding of what specifically the different levels (Instructor, Coach and Head Coach) should be concentrating upon with regard to the three primary virtues of physical culture: Movement, Breathing and Structure.

	Movement	Breathing	Structure
CST Athlete	Practicing basic exercises to learn movement, breathing and structure		
CST Instructor	Expanding range of motion	Discipline	Integrity/ Platform
CST Coach	Absorb and retranslate force	Flow	Compensatory Movement
CST Head Coach	Store and release energy	Mastery	Intuitive Improvisation

CST LEVEL OVERVIEW EXPANDED

CST Athlete (Level 0): practices the basic exercises in order to have an experiential template for understanding the integration of breathing, movement and structure.

CST Instructor (Level I): teaches and practices expanding range of motion, disciplining the ('performance') breath, and integrating an effective structural platform for absorbing and retranslating force.

CST Coach (Level II): teaches and practices absorbing and retranslating force, allowing the breath to flow ('Be Breathed™'), and compensating for preconditions ('that which has already been specifically conditioned') throughout the structure.

CST Head Coach (Level III): teaches and practices the storing and releasing of energy (sensory motor amnesia, fear-reactivity, residual tension, myofascial density), mastering the breath ('control pause'), and intuitively assessing the fluctuating structural state and its relationship to the environment of forces while spontaneously improvising a response to that state.

We will be introducing codified basic exercises and stock combination routines / kinetic chains for CST Athletes organized into rating levels: CST Athlete Level 3, Level 2, Level 1, and CST Instructor Candidate. CST Athletes will be evaluated based upon gymnastics competition standards. CST teachers (and only <u>certified</u> CST's!) may examine CST Athletes at their own gyms.

For 2006 CST certification will automatically include subcertification in Intu-Flow™, Prasara Body-Flow™ and Clubbell® Training. From 2007 they will be separate courses, the details of which will be scheduled and released publicly in late 2006. All certification courses are conducted throughout the year. Schedules, times, and registration details can be found online at www.rmaxinternational.com

HOW DO RMAX MARTIAL ART SYSTEMS FIT IN?

It is impossible for someone to understand the martial art aspect of RMAX without sustained, daily deepening of CST personal practice. CST "is" the martial art of RMAX. I selected FlowFighting™ as the name of our martial art because "Softwork" represents only one pole of the Work Continuum.

As a result, if one seeks Certification in FlowFighting™ then one must have the prerequisite courses in CST. For instance, if one wants FlowFighting™ Instructor Certification then one must first be a certified CST Instructor. If one seeks FlowFighting™ Coach Certification, one must first be a certified CST Coach. FlowFighting™ Head Coach assumes CST Head Coach Certification. This is the only fair, consistent and verifiable means of quality control of coaching competencies in the martial art.

FlowFighting™ will not be included in CST Certification Seminars, and certification to teach CST <u>does not include</u> certification to teach FlowFighting™. (Read that again to avoid swift and severe administrative intervention in the future!) CST and FlowFighting™ certification will remain separate seminars. The certification standards for FlowFighting™ are forthcoming.

CST Instructors, Coaches and Head Coaches <u>are not required</u> to participate in FlowFighting™, though obviously it's an easy transition.

HOW IS CST ORGANIZED AS A SYSTEM?

CST is a complete system unto itself. You cannot remove a portion from a circle and still have a circle; to remain a 'holistic' approach, you must have a whole. The micro of the macro is that the body is not composed of hundreds of individual muscles, but of one muscular sack of bioelectric jelly with hundreds of sets of insertions. Nothing in isolation. Everything a complete whole, a perfect circle.

Many people have asked why I constructed CST in the manner in which I did. They ask this, as you might, to understand how to properly fit CST into their lives. Let me first explain the developmental principles that I observed in order to create CST, and then explain options for how you can tailor your personal practice to meet your needs and demands.

PRINCIPLES OF PHYSICAL DEVELOPMENT

As we develop from infant to child to adolescent to adult to old age we experience a complex process of perpetual refinement of skills. Each period in the development of these abilities is punctuated by a short and rocky regression. We undergo four general developmental principles in the first few years of our life, and understanding these helps create a template for development in later stages. It is from these four principles that I forged the format of CST.

GROWTH IS A UNIVERSAL, PREDICTABLE PROCESS

We can generally predict the sequence of development in all areas: physical, emotional, mental, social and verbal. For example, locomotion proceeds from sitting, crawling, and standing to walking. As a result, I orchestrated CST to progress according to the simple rubrics of each joint's movement (flex, extend, rotate) and formatted an incrementally progressive, step-by-step advancement of recovery to coordination to refinement. Simply stated, I constructed CST to be **"Incrementally Progressive."**

EACH INDIVIDUAL PROGRESSES WITH UNIQUE TIMING

Although this may appear to contradict Principle 1, each of us progress through the generally universal and predictable sequence in our own unique time. For example, some of you may recover full elbow range of motion within 3 months and full knee range of motion within 6 months, while others may experience the reverse. However, in general for all people, shoulder range must improve before elbow, and hip before knee.

SIMPLE TO COMPLEX — GENERAL TO SPECIFIC

I constructed CST to progress with **"Increasing Sophistication."** (I use the term *Sophistication* to refer to both increasing complexity and increasing potential specificity.) Simple movements must come before and must be built off of complex skills. This is why children first eat with their fingers before learning how to use a utensil. As a result, I crafted CST to progress from simple range to circles to infinities (first cardinal, then diagonal) to clover leaves to waves.

HEAD DOWNWARDS — CENTER OUTWARDS

During the first few years of our development we experience what is called the *Cephalocaudal-Proximodistal Trend:* we develop from the head downwards and from the center outwards. This is evident in the shape of a baby, with its large head and torso compared to its small arms and legs. Each of us experiences our own unique pace through this sequence as per Principle 1. However, in general, the sequence is consistently and repeatedly verifiable empirically.

CST was created to take into account the way we universally and predictably develop in our own unique timing sequence from infant to adult: *Incrementally Progressing* with *Increasing Sophistication* from the *head to toe* and from the *core to periphery*. For optimum development it's best to follow that format, not because CST is "The One True Way" but because CST observes these and other important laws and principles.

CST is also highly adaptable to your needs and demands. Some CST is better than none. Based upon these laws, if for some reason you cannot afford to practice for 15–20 minutes in the morning, it's best to hit the neck, shoulders, spine and hips as primary. I would suggest that throughout the day you can fit in the rest 2–3 minutes at a time: elbows, knees, ankles, wrists, fingers and jaw.

This also assumes that you have no local inflammation. With local inflammation mobility is contraindicated. However, mobility is still indicated adjacent to the inflammation to carry away toxic byproducts and to restore nutritive and lubricative flow to the area.

Problem areas are not always the source of an issue and may be merely compensatory "sites" of tension — another argument for completing the full regime daily. However, if you find that local CST resolves your problems, then keep it up.

FITNESS VALUE HIERARCHY

To understand how to organize your personal practice you must first assess your personal value structure for training. The CST Value Hierarchy is:

1. Health
2. Mobility
3. Function
4. Attributes
5. Physique

CST states that you must first ensure that you are promoting what is healthiest for you. You must then ensure that you have full coordinated mobility; that you are able to move with complete, sophisticated freedom. Next, you must be able to function within tasks (rather than merely at the gym). Then you may be concerned with attributes (such as strength, endurance, flexibility, or agility) for their own sake. Lastly you may be concerned with your physical body's appearance (however, when following the CST Value Hierarchy, a beautiful, powerful physique is a natural by-product!).

The conventional "bodybuilding" model orders its value hierarchy in the following way:

1. Physique
2. Attributes
3. Function
4. Mobility
5. Health

The recent "functional training" vogue orders its values in this manner:

1. Attributes
2. Function
3. Physique
4. Mobility
5. Health

The conventional sports / martial art model holds this value hierarchy:

1. **Function**
2. **Mobility**
3. **Attributes**
4. **Health**
5. **Physique**

It can also be argued that recent bodybuilding and functional training influences may locally reorder values to meet their agendas, regardless of detriment to combat sport performance.

Concerning your fitness with appearance and attributes over function, mobility and health is like hauling your family around suburbia in a monster truck. Sure, you can get where you're going, but the excess is not only a danger to yourself but to your friends and family as well.

"Bigger, stronger and faster" is only good in so far as it is balanced and tempered with function, mobility and health. The primary emphasis of conventional fitness is upon the physical. It focuses somewhat upon the emotional, mental and spiritual components, and pays only lip service to the social implications of physical culture.

A balanced approach, as in Circular Strength Training®, uses the physical as a vehicle to emotional, mental and spiritual well-being. Implied within this use of the physical as a vehicle to intrapersonal transformation is, of course, dramatic social change.

We must help shift the paradigm back into balance. We do this in the most effective way possible: by focusing upon our daily personal practice in a balanced, compassionate, and patient manner; by concentrating on moderate, sustainable movement for pain-free health and longevity; and by shielding our right to exuberant play with our friends and family.

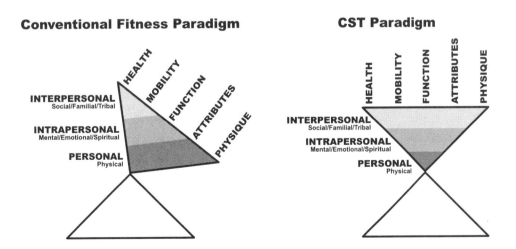

It is upon this core doctrine that CST is built.

It is up to you to arrange your hierarchy and then to program your training and organize your personal practice (if any) appropriate to your goals. However, if you wish to maximize your CST experience, then I urge you to seriously deliberate upon the balanced CST Value Hierarchy, as it is tailor fit for optimal living.

Contributed by Chris Beltrante

OUR EVOLUTION: FROM ANCIENT TOOL TO MODERN ATHLETE

The most ancient weapon, the club, evolved over millennia into a devastatingly effective martial arts tool. Cultural martial traditions across the planet utilized the club not just for combat but for restorative health, joint strength, grip development, and specific physical preparedness. We see examples of this in Japanese Judo, Okinawan Karate, Iranian Varzesh-e Pahlavani, Indian Kalaripayatu, Burmese Bando, and Filipino Kali.

David Webster, in <u>*Bodybuilding: An Illustrated History*</u> (New York: Arco Publishing, 1982; pages 123–124), explains that what began as a survival strategy and tool — the caveman's club — evolved into a highly sophisticated system of physical training that was passed from one generation to the next: club leverage lifting.

The history of CST encompasses various militaries, professional sports, and even the Olympics. But during the twentieth century functional training was slowly replaced by cosmetic fitness fads. As an outcast based on traditional martial and total-body strength practices, *Circular Strength Training* was relegated to the shadows, to lurking in basements, dungeons and lumber yards where heavy club leverage lifting was preserved by the old-time Strongman physical culture.

At the millennium, with international terrorism at its zenith, Americans turned their vision inward to revitalize timeless methods that had been proven to work for both physical preparedness and defensive readiness:

- Russian Bulava
- Iranian Meel
- Indian Gada, Jori, Karela and Ekka
- British Club Swinging
- American Club Swinging
- 20th Century Strongman Club Swinging

Club training can be traced to the strongman competitions of Ancient Persia. It created a definitive edge in strength and endurance training. During these times the weight lifter, wrestler or fighter was called a *Pahlavan,* or strongman.

RUSSIAN BULAVA

Contributed by Nikolay Travkin, CEO and President of RMAX.tv Productions
International Martial Arts Hall of Fame Inductee

Historically in Russia the *Bulava* was a symbol of great power.

Westerners know it more commonly as the "Mace." Celts had the mace as a weapon of Dagda, and it served as his symbolic possessor of life and death. In Greco-Roman history the mace was the symbol of Hercules. The mace was also the symbol of Gallic Sucellos — "Great Warrior."

Initially the *bulava* or mace was used as a bludgeoning weapon, a heavy medieval war club with a spiked or flanged metal head used to crush armor. Later it was primarily used by bodyguards, until it finally became a symbol of authority. In England the mace probably appeared in the British Parliament as early as the 14th century. Later the Mace became Parliament's symbol as well. The modern Mace thus represents the authority of parliament as well as that of the monarch.

Although the mace serves largely symbolic purposes in the West, in Russia the *bulava* is still being used. It was first mentioned in old legends, where a warrior would arm himself with a *bulava* and go off to defend his motherland.

The prototype of the *bulava* was a simple wooden mace. Initially large and spiked maces were used as weapons. The *bulava* began its transformation as different materials were used in its construction. *Bulavas* appeared with handles made of wood and tips made of stone. The stone was later replaced by iron. Handles were usually covered with notches or thick thread or cord to allow for a better grip.

Russian warriors successfully used this weapon against foreign troops. Having developed tremendous strength from training with the *bulava*, the warriors used them to strike the enemy's head and body. Russian warriors also threw *bulavas* (sometimes from very long distances) to attack their foes' head.

One *bulava* variation was a mace with a spiked ball secured to the handle by a chain. This device was known as a "Morning Star" in the West. Even given such innovations, Russian warriors preferred the traditional design. This weapon could easily crush and pierce an opponent's armor to cause serious injury, sometimes even grinding bones. The *bulava* could stun a warrior by hitting his helmet, or even totally destroy it.

Over the centuries the materials used for building *bulavas* changed. With iron, cast iron or bronze, *bulavas* could be made in different forms to turn them into even more effective weapons. The tips could be round or multi-angled.

During the middle ages, the *bulava* was equipped with sharp stakes in order to break through armor. To further increase the tip's impact the handle's length was altered as well. It could reach up to a meter in length. Long *Bulavas* with stakes sticking out of their sides were called *shestoper* or *pernach*.

Later, the *bulava* was made entirely of iron. The invention of new and sturdier armor contributed to and required a better design for the *bulava*. Making *bulavas* fully of iron increased their power and weight. The redesigned *bulavas* proved to be more effective than even swords in battle. Although *bulavas* were primarily used for striking the head, the heavier iron implements could easily break bones, even if the armor itself was not pierced.

The *Bulava* was one of the Russian warriors' most beloved weapons, and being very strong men they used all of its features to their advantage. Look at this photo of the famous painting *Tri Bogatyr* ("Three Great Warriors") by Victor Vasnetsov (1898), which hangs in the Tretyakov Gallery in Moscow. These three knights, Muromets, Dobrynya Nikitich and Aliosha Popovich – the heroes of many Russian legends — defended their Homeland from its enemies. Look closely at what Ilya Muromets (in the middle) has on his right hand —a *bulava*.

Tri Bogatyr ("Three Great Warriors") by Victor Vasnetsov 1898

Later, when the *bulava* became obsolete as a weapon, it was used as a commander's symbol of power and authority. Further refinement of the *bulava* as a weapon ceased at that time. However, even today it continues to be used as a weapon and as a symbol of authority by Cossack troops in Russia.

Not only is the *bulava* an ancient weapon and symbol of authority, it is also a critical tool for power training, fitness and health improvement. The narrow end serves as a handle while the other heavier end adds resistance such that the *bulava* can be used for exercises that would be impossible to perform using other equipment.

Circular motions develop the arms and shoulders. Vertical, horizontal and diagonal motions can be used not only for gaining physical strength, but also for improving balance, plasticity, flexibility, and dexterity.

The *bulava* also figures in Russian history as game equipment. It was used in throwing contests and to train Russian athletes and military personnel for power and strength, as historical documents attest. Schools and gymnasiums used the *bulava* for similar purposes.

During the Soviet era the *Bulava* was an important tool for military troops and for physical education in schools and universities. Anatoly Taras, former USSR Spetsnaz Hand-to-hand Combat Instructor and author of <u>Combat Machine</u>, recommends *bulava* training for all martial artists (Tsatsouline). In documentary films athletes marching in columns during parades and other celebrations can be seen holding bulavas.

"I remember hearing from my father that the bulava was standard equipment in Russian gyms up to the 1960's, when it was replaced with more sophisticated body-building oriented fitness devices. He told me that this was a mistake and that nothing could replace the specific features of the implement. He was talking specifically about boxing, for hooks and swinging power." – Oleg Yakimovich (ROSS System – Minsk, Belarus)

Once a part of the Olympic Games, the sport was excluded and, regretfully, the *bulava* faded away and has been undeservedly forgotten — until now.

Russian Olympic and National champions continue to use the *bulava* for strength and endurance training and conditioning. The light *bulava* is currently being used in Rhythmic gymnastics, which is an Olympic discipline, of which Russian athletes are leaders.

The *bulava* has been an unalienable part of Russia's history, and of her martial art and physical culture.

IRANIAN MEEL

Contributed by Farzad Nekoogar, a Pahlavani researcher for over 20 years
Author of Pahlavani.com, *and currently composing a book on the subject.*
Author of several technical books and lectures at the University of California Dept. of Electrical Engineering and Theoretical Physics
International Martial Arts Hall of Fame Inductee

During the Mongol invasion of Iran (1256 AD) many Iranian Pahlavans traveled to India and introduced some of the Pahlavani traditions and instruments to the Indian subcontinent. Among these were *Meels*, also known to the western world as *Indian Clubs*.

Pair of Iranian Meels

After many centuries, in which they traveled throughout the subcontinent, *Meels* took on different sizes and shapes in India and appeared under names such as *Ekka, Karela, Jori* and *Gada*. Some even have sharp nails or blades in the sides of the clubs to encourage wielders to avoid touching their bodies. These features cannot be found in the present form of the Iranian Meels. There is also evidence that Meels are occasionally called *Gavargah*, a Mongol word.

Among many Pahlavans who traveled to India during the thirteenth century were Pahlavan Bozorg Pouriyay-e Vali and Shirdel Kohneh Savar. Their journeys and the accounts of their wrestling matches are documented in Pahlavani books and have been passed from generation to generation in the form of oral history.

Centuries later the British brought the clubs to Europe and named them "Indian Clubs." The Clubs were eventually brought to the United States of America by European immigrants in the 1800s.

Meels come in different sizes and weights. Two factors that affect exercising with *Meels* are their height and weight. Light *Meels* usually weigh about 10–15 lbs. This type of *Meel* is good for improving one's stamina, and they can be used to do hundreds of repetitions. Pahlavan Bozorg Hassan Razaz reportedly swung the meel for thousands of repetitions as part of his daily exercise.

Heavy *Meels* are used to build strength and range in weight from 25-lbs to 60-lbs each. Their height can be as tall as 4.5 feet. The following picture (next page) shows Pahlavan Mustafa Toosi, in his later years, easily holding a pair of heavy Meels that weigh about 60-lbs each. He won the Pahlavani Armlet competition three years in succession, from 1944 to 1946.

Because *Meels* are very effective for developing one's upper body strength as well as stamina, many of today's wrestling champions in Iran practice with *Meels* and other Pahlavani instruments. *Meel* swinging builds shoulder muscles, grip strength, and overall upper body strength.

Pahlavan Mustafa Toosi holding a pair of heavy Meels

Jahan Pahlavan Takhti Olympic Gold Winner (1956), World Wrestling Champion (1959 and 61), winner of Pahlavani Armlet in 1957–59 practicing with a pair of light-weight Meels

Pictured bottom left is Jahan Pahlavan Takhti exercising with a typical lightweight pair of *Meels*.

Exercising with heavy *Meels* is part of a Pahlavani tournament that is held each year in Iran. As of 2002 the record lift is 50 repetitions of a 63.5 kg (140-lbs) *Meel*.

Meels are produced with walnut wood for its heavy weight. To make it even heavier *Meel* makers add lead to the bottom, but this has to be done with care in order to ensure the symmetry of the *Meel* as well as its center of gravity.

The illustration "Meel Exercise in 3 Steps" (next page) provides some insight into *Meel* practice. Whenever possible, the *Meels* must not touch the body. The fingers should hold the head of the *Meel* where it is shaped into a hand holder. The small finger should grasp the bottom of the hand holder.

When holding the *Meels* the practitioner's forearm and upper arm must form an angle of about 100°. In Step 1 the practitioner holds both *Meels* vertically in front of his chest and positions himself in the starting point.

In Step 2 he swings one hand, normally the left, to the back while keeping the other *Meel* straight in front in a static position. From the back the *Meel* is returned to the starting position using the shoulder muscles.

In Step 3 left hand is brought forward and the right hand then swings the *Meel* to the back as explained in Step 2.

One cycle of Steps 1 through 3 is considered "one set" of *Meel* swinging. Each swing cycle normally takes 3–4 seconds. After some practice the athlete is able to swing the *Meels* in a rhythmic fashion guided by the drum of the Morshed in Zoorkhaneh.

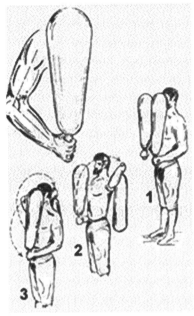

Meel Exercise in 3 Steps

Meel Exercise, Step 2

A unique *Meel* tradition calls for the practitioner to follow the music of the Morshed, who sets the pace with chants and drums inside the Zoorkhaneh, or "House of Power," where practice takes place. Almost all Pahlavani exercises are accompanied by rhythmic music.

Because *Meel* swinging is a group exercise, the music coordinates both the individual moves and those of the group. Secondly, the Morshed's rate of playing the drum will determine the rate of swinging. As he drums faster, the swings become faster.

Juggling lightweight *Meels* is a form of theatrical entertainment that is not a part of Pahlavani tradition and has no Pahlavani characteristics. It became popular over the last 70 years in many Zoorkhanehs in Iran. In recent years the Pahlavani Federation of Iran has discouraged juggling with *Meels* in Zoorkhanehs.

Reference: www.Pahlavani.com

Group Exercising with Meels

Meel Juggling:
not part of Pahlavani tradition

INDIAN GADA, JORI, KARELA, EKKA

Indian Strongman with Gada courtesy of Roger Fillary and Sandow Website

The most popular traditional antecessor of *Circular Strength Training*® arose in India, although the "clubs" themselves were derived from Persian predecessors as Iranian and Indian wrestlers competed with one another.

Indian strongmen and wrestlers use four implements for combat athletics: *Gada* (mace), *Jori* (cylindrical "popsicle" clubs), *Karela* (rounded "bowling pin" clubs) and *Ekka* (massive wrestling pillars). Combat athletes used these implements to develop grip strength and muscular arms and shoulders, as well as the back, chest and legs. Each implement existed in progressive weights and trainers deployed them incrementally to enhance combat-specific strength and endurance (Mujumdar, <u>Encyclopedia of Indian Physical Culture</u>).

Scholars find mention of these implements in depictions of Hindu religion and comment that Vishnu, as well as nearly every other deity, often wielded the gada (or war mace) in pictures and statues. As with the Russian *bulava*, wielding the *gada* bestows great honor upon warriors. Rajput rulers and Muslim sultans during the Islamic Period publicly honored warriors for mastering the art of the *gada* (Hoffman 1996, p.6). In fact, so-called "Indian" wrestlers were generally Muslim, not Hindu. The research of some historians has therefore been criticized for failing to make proper distinctions.

Daily practice with any implement will lead to improved performance. These heavy weapons provided significant resistance training in the exact range, depth and scope of the intended activity. Improvements in performance would therefore be noted due to sustained and/or intensified practice. Regardless of the popularity of the implement as a weapon of choice and esteem, the *gada* naturally evolved into a first-rate tool for physical preparedness.

Decorative Gada courtesy of Roger Fillary and Sandow Website

Practice, Stone Gada courtesy of Roger Fillary and Sandow Website

The *gada* used for training and the gada used for ceremony look dramatically different. The training *gada* looks more like a giant lollipop — a large round rock attached to the end of a stick. Rocks could weigh from 10 to 80 kg (22 to 176-lbs). This weight required incredible strength to move, considering that it is attached to the end of a meter-long staff, often made of bamboo.

Indian Strongmen with Jori courtesy of Roger Fillary and Sandow Website

In contrast to the *jori,* which were used in pairs, *gada* were used singularly with either one hand or two hands. Swings begin in *Shoulder Park* (see Exercise Section) and carry through large motions, halting momentarily in *Top Position* (see Exercise Section) until returning to the opposite Shoulder Park.

Indian Wrestlers such as the world famous "Great Gama" practiced in special private gymnasiums called *Akharas*. In these training halls wrestlers invested intense study time into the use of the *jori,* a visually unmistakable twin to the Iranian meel. The Indian wrestlers, long known for their incredible strength and endurance, used *jori* for both physical exercise and as an artistic discipline of choreographed programs. The extent that wrestlers use *jori* varies from one gym to the next, but the tool can be found in nearly all *Akharas*.

Joris are swung in pairs beginning in *Order Position:* an inverted position in where the weight is held balanced over the handles in front of the user. They are then swung from back to front in long alternating arcs, as in the *Arm-Pit Cast Drumming* exercise (see Exercise Section). Due to their popular use throughout India, athletes from one gym competed against one another as a sport as well as a form of exercise. They competed for grace of execution, for maximum volume of swings, for speed of completing a set volume of swings, for maximum weight of *joris,* and for combinations of these protocols. To add to the complexity, Indian wrestlers pounded nails and blades into the *jori* to ensure that proper form — not allowing the *jori* to touch the body — was observed.

Spiked Jori for perfect technique courtesy of Roger Fillary and Sandow Website

Due to the need for specific muscular endurance in grappling, Indian wrestlers placed a higher premium on mid-range weight swung for higher volume in exercises approximating wrestling maneuvers. Heavier *jori* were used only infrequently, and for maximal attempts, to avoid rigidifying wrestling technique.

This type of circular strength training resulted in the development of coordination and agility through precision timing. However, *jori* training also produced great strength. Joseph Alter, in <u>The Wrestler's Body: Identity and Ideology in North India</u>, examined the discipline in exhaustive detail and personally observed a wrestler leverage-lift two eighty kilogram (176 pound) *joris* — a VERY heavy weight.

Two pair of heavy Jori courtesy of Roger Fillary and Sandow Website

Where the rather blandly dressed *jori* holds little decoration, the *gada* shines with ornate silver and gold carvings. The opulent design of the *gada* apparently made it an appropriate devotional item for Hindu deities. Rulers often bestowed intricately designed *gada* to champion wrestlers, such as the 85-lbs Golden *Gada* presented by the Maharajah to the "Great Gama" in 1928, on his return from defeating World Wrestling Champion Stanley Zbyszco in a mere 42 seconds! (Zbyszco was 50-lbs heavier and several inches taller than Gama, who was 50 years old at the time of their bout!) With the gift of the famous Golden *Gada,* the Great Gama was made the protégé of the Maharaja of Patiala.

Karela and *jori* were often used interchangeably; their use was strictly a matter of preference of the Akhara in which they were swung. The British adopted the *karela*-shaped implement over all others, which is why the *karela* is the most widely recognized of the traditional antecessors to CST — the so-called "Indian club."

Karela, jori and *gada* trainers counted repetitions in *hands:* one full movement from starting position, through the motion, ending in starting position. For *gada* this means one pass to the opposite shoulder. For *jori,* both right and left need to complete the motion to count as one *hand.*

As in Soviet strength conditioning, Indian wrestlers considered the total tonnage of greater importance than the number of repetitions: they preferred to move heavier weight through an exercise fewer times.

Heavy Karela courtesy of Roger Fillary and Sandow Website

The British largely ignored this when they adopted lightweight Circular Strength Training as a fitness vogue. In *"Bodybuilding and Muscle Control in India"* (*Eugene Sandow and the Golden Age of Iron Men*), Roger Fillary and Gil Waldron note as a result that, *"It is often considered that the British Rule in India started a period of decline in Physical Culture and general health amongst the Indian population."*

Ekka were slightly less popular for strength training than *karela, jori,* and *gada* due to the sheer size of the implement. These stone pillars were scaled rather than swung. An entire gymnastic routine developed for wrestlers called *Mallakhamb,* or "The pillar of the strongman."

BRITISH CLUB SWINGING

In the late 18th Century foreign missionaries, merchants and British military personnel were awed by the physical prowess of the Indian Slaves and policemen. Inquiry led to the Indians' admission that their muscularity and strength resulted from the systematic use of wooden clubs. After this initial exposure in India, a new fitness vogue was imported to Britain.

Sim Kehoe recorded one report by a British offer in Indian Club Exercise (1866, Page 6):

"The wonderful club exercise is one of the most effectual kinds of athletic training known anywhere, in common use throughout India. The clubs are of wood, varying in weight according to the strength of the person using them, and in length about two feet and a half, and some six or seven inches in diameter at the base, which is level, so as to admit of their standing firmly when placed on the ground, and thus affording great convenience for using them in the swinging positions. The exercise is in great repute among the native Slavey, police and others whose caste renders them liable to emergencies where great strength of muscle is desirable. The evolutions which the clubs are made to perform, in the hands of one accustomed to their use are exceedingly graceful and they vary almost without limit. Beside the great recommendation of simplicity, Indian club practice possesses the essential property of expanding the chest and exercising every muscle in the body concurrently."

Donald Walker, the man responsible for introducing the traditional discipline to Europe and America, published in 1834 the book British Manly Exercises — considered the most influential book on physical exercise published in the 19th century.

Later, in 1835, Walker introduced 2 lb. ornamental "Indian Scepters" for women's fitness, accompanied by the release of his book, Exercises for Ladies Calculated to Preserve and Improve Beauty, calling them *"The most useful and beautiful exercises introduced into physical education.,"* He bravely stated that the scepters had *"vast advantages over dumbbells"* for women.

Walker received competition from a well-known London gymnastics teacher, Professor Harrison. Harrison published Indian Clubs, Dumb-bells and Sword Exercises, which featured extremely heavy club leverage lifting exercises. The August 14, 1852 issue of the Illustrated London News (Russell Trall's The Illustrated Family Gymnasium (1857, Page 58) reported:

"We learn that Mr. Harrison first began to use the clubs three year ago, at which time his muscular development was not regarded as being very great. His measurements being then: chest – 37 ½ inches, upper arms 13 ⅞ inches and forearms 13 ¼ inches. The clubs with which Mr. Harrison commenced weighed about seven pounds each. He has advanced progressively until he can now wield with perfect ease two clubs, each weighing 37 pounds, and his heaviest weighs 47 pounds. The effect of this exercise on the wielder's measurements is as follows: chest 42 ½ inches, upper arms 15 inches, and forearms 14 inches. At the same time his shoulders have increased immensely, and the muscles of his loins, which were weak when he first used the clubs, are now largely developed and powerful. In short, all the muscles of the trunk have been much improved by this exercise."

Professor Harrison's accomplishments in Circular Strength Training received such acclaim that he gained an audience with Queen Victoria (see the Preface of Harrison's *Indian Clubs*).

The British Army, despite Professor Harrison's arguments, incorporated only lightweight versions into its training doctrine and neglected to include heavyweight training as part of their physical conditioning doctrine. As a result of the "trickle down" effect, lightweight club swinging gained great popularity with the English public as well.

AMERICAN CLUB SWINGING

In 1861 Professor Harrison met Sim Kehoe, a New York manufacturer of fitness equipment, who was so enthralled by Harrison's strength and *"use of the mammoth war clubs"* that he *"vowed to return to the United States to introduce heavy club swinging to Americans"* (Todd, *Iron Game History*).

Sim D. Kehoe brought the tradition to the US from Britain. In 1862 he opened a New York shop to manufacture clubs. To spread the word, he sent free samples of his clubs to prominent individuals in the hope of securing endorsements.

One of these endorsements came from the famous Civil War era boxer John Heenan, who wrote him that, *"As an assistant for training purposes, and imparting strength to the muscles of the arms, wrists, and hands, together in fact with the whole muscular system, I do not know of their equal. They will become one of the institutions in America."*

Another endorsement arrived from Washington from President Ulysses S. Grant, who wrote to thank Kehoe for the clubs: *"Please accept my thanks for thus remembering me, and particularly my boys, who I know will take great delight as well as receive benefit from using them."*

In 1866 Kehoe published *Indian Club Exercise*, a beautifully illustrated book showing the benefits of HEAVY club swinging. Kehoe's book is significant for two reasons. Firstly, he drew a distinction between Indian club swinging and the short, lightweight "bat" — a one to four pound club used in the popular Don Walker and Dio Lewis' calisthenic drills. Secondly, Kehoe drew attention to "Proper Club" or heavy club leverage lifting. Kehoe stated in his book that a beginner could start with 10-lb. clubs.

Todd, in *Iron Game History*, further details club competition and exhibition:

"On 1 May 1866, a solid gold medal cast by the Tiffany Company was presented to J. Edward Russel of New York. According to Kehoe, a panel of judges found Russell to be the best club swinger at a gymnastics competition at Irving Hall. In another event, Kehoe reported, Charles Bennett, the 'California Hercules' gave an exhibition in which he used twenty pound clubs 'in a variety of movements and held 52-pound clubs in each hand at arms length, with ease.' A drawing of Bennett, 'copied from a photograph,' gives some indication of how such feats might be possible. The heavy, defined musculature of his upper body is unusual for the mid-nineteenth century."

Dr. Jan Todd, Ph.D. notes that lightweight club swinging was used primarily for flexibility and quickness, and heavyweight club swinging for strength and muscularity (Todd, Page 8).

In 1887 William Dick published *Dick's Dumb-bell and Indian Club Exercises* in which he explained:

"The advantages gained by the proper use of Dumb-Bells and Indian Clubs are too well appreciated to be disputed. Both of these simple implements of exercise have been in constant use for years, and still hold a prominent place among the methods of Gymnastic training. The principal objects for which they are designed may be briefly summed up: They strengthen the muscles of the arms, and, incidentally, those of the body and legs; they expand the chest and induce full and regular respiration; they impart firmness of balance and grace of motion. The Indian Clubs are the most effective for giving grace, ease, and accuracy of movement, and, when skillfully used, they present a very attractive appearance."

M. Bornstein in 1889 stated in his book *Manual of Instruction in the Use of Dumb-bell, Indian club, and Other Athletic Exercise* that Clubs were *"the most universal method of developing the muscular anatomy of the human body. Schools, colleges and even theological seminaries have adopted their use in their respective institutions with the most beneficial results. For keeping the body in a healthy and vigorous condition there has as yet been nothing invented, which for its simplicity and gracefulness can be favorably compared with club exercises."*

Fitness guru and gymnastics teacher Dr. Dio Lewis, MD, in *Exercises with Clubs* (1882), noted that club swinging would *"cultivate patience and endurance, and operate happily upon the longitudinal muscles of the back and shoulders, thus tending to correct the habit of stooping."*

Lightweight bats became the Ivy-league vogue in popular Victorian culture in the late 19th Century, becoming attached to the then popular "Muscular Christianity Movement" which linked physicality to moral and spiritual development.

Swedish Slave and physical educator Baron Nils Posse came to America to propagate his system of Swedish Military Gymnastics. In 1894 he wrote that the club was *"the oldest known implement for military gymnastics."* In this book he was the first to introduce the distinction between linear strength training with dumbbells and barbells and *Circular Strength Training* with leverage lifting.

The US Army eventually implemented club swinging in the military physical training program. In 1914 the US Army Manual of Physical Training illustrated many required exercises, and explained that *Circular Strength Training* would *"supple the muscles and articulations of shoulders, upper-arms, forearms and wrist. They are indicated in cases where there is a tendency toward what is known as 'muscle bound.'"*

Club swinging became an Olympic Sport called *"Rhythmic Gymnastics"* in 1904 (St. Louis, USA), in which Americans won in all divisions. It endured until 1932 (Los Angeles, USA), where the Americans swept up all the medals again. Club swinging is still considered Olympic in Russia, where it is used by various Olympic and National sports teams for physical conditioning.

In Carnivals, Music Halls, and Wrestling Gymnasiums, club swinging met its hallmark in the Strongman physical culture.

20TH CENTURY STRONGMAN CLUB SWINGING

Many historical physical culturists preferred the challenges of heavy leverage lifting to the lightweight "fancy swinging" adopted by the British Army. **Arthur Saxon** echoed these words in his book <u>The Development of Physical Power</u>. He wrote that it was *"a form of light exercise which is of no use to the would-be strongman, as it stretches and makes supple the muscles rather than develops them with increased contractile power."*

Many turn-of-the-20th-Century strongmen used heavy club swinging for the cultivation of unique strength advantages. The following list is not in chronological order.

The Great Gama with his Golden Gada

Mian Ghulum Mohammed Born in 1878 and died in 1960, he was later named "The Great Gama" Baksh. At the apex of his career Baksh measured 5 feet 7 inches and weighed 260-lbs and was the world's most renowned Indian wrestler. When he was six years old Gama's father, a very famous court wrestler, died suddenly. Gama was told that his father wanted him to become the world's greatest wrestler, and that "he could keep his father alive through disciplined training" (Alter, <u>Iron Game History</u>).

John Jesse notes in <u>Wrestling Physical Conditioning Encyclopedia</u> (1970) that Gama *"developed a 56 inch chest and 31 inch thighs by performing 4,000 one and two legged squats, including 700 jumping squats and 2,000 one and two hand pushups, running 4 to 5 miles and wrestling 3–4 hours every day of training."*

<u>Black Belt Magazine</u> (Summer 1963) tells of Gama's famous match against Roller, where Gama threw the American champion in one minute and pinned him in less than 10 minutes, breaking his opponent's ribs in this process. In 1928, at the ripe age of 50, in a match lasting all of 42 seconds, Gama beat the World Wrestling Champion Stanley Zbyszco (who outclassed Gama by 50-lbs and several inches)! Gama returned to India where he received a hero's welcome and was made the protégé of the Maharaja of Patiala.

George Jowett: Born in 1891 in Bradford, Yorkshire, England, this "Lord of Leverage Lifting" began life with challenges caused when his mother accidentally dropped him on an iron furnace. Doctors believed his case to be hopeless, and he was ridiculed by classmates for his slight build. Inspired at an early age after watching Eugene Sandow perform, Jowett dedicated his life to increased strength and athleticism. His fame grew after he moved with his family to Canada, especially after he lifted a 168-lb anvil by the horn and pressed in it one hand (in street clothes!). Kathleen Lawry, great, great, grandniece of Jowett, provided the following account of his prowess (Fillary and Waldron):

George Jowett and the Fulcrum Bells courtesy of Gordon Anderson

"Men from miles around came to the gymnasium above the shop where George gave lessons in wrestling, weight-lifting, and judo. He also loved to entertain at the local fairs — straightening out horseshoes, snapping chains around his body, lifting 550-lb barbells off the ground with one finger, and one-handing 160-lb anvils above his head. To Phyllis, all this seemed normal. During these years, George continued to train and build. At 154 pounds, lifting 310-lbs, he became the first man in America to lift double his body weight. At 176 pound, he lifted 340-lbs in a clean and jerk. At 192 pounds he became the first North American to one-arm swing more than his own weight, pulling up 210-lbs. In Chicago he won the title "World's Best Developed Body". Over the course of his lifetime he was to win some 300 medals in all."

Jowett founded the ACWLA (American Continental Weight Lifters Association), the father of the present day AAU and the first of its kind in North America. He started the famous Jowett Institute of Physical Culture, a mail-order instructional course on strength training.

Furthermore, he invented the famous club swinging innovation called **Fulcrum Bells,** which he marketed through American Athletic Appliance Co., one of the largest companies of its kind at that time.

In his Magnum Opus <u>Muscle Building and Physical Culture</u> (1927), Jowett wrote:

Illustration of Jowett's Fulcrum Bell exercise, courtesy of Gordon Anderson

"It is a fact that you can lift more with a barbell, BUT where is the man that can lift a two hundred pound barbell overhead who can lift two Fulcrum Bells separately of the total weight? THERE IS THE VALUE! Besides they take away the danger of heavy weights. For muscle building and strength creation purposes the Fulcrum Bells are far the best. They open a broader field of exercise to you, which provides an avenue for greater results. Then, who wants to be bothered by heavy weights all the time? They are hard to handle, almost impossible to store in the house, or the average bedroom. On the other hand, why do all the strongest and best-built men in the world favor Fulcrum Bells? Because they have better muscle and strength building principles. Used on the scale of progression I give they have a greater value, which is the reason why every leading body builder and strongman says that Fulcrum Bells are THE BEST!"

In his book *Molding a Mighty Grip*, Jowett provided us with one of the most quoted insights into the Iron Game: *"The grip is the barometer of physical strength and the energy you possess."*

Bob Hoffman: One of the fathers of the American Iron Game, creator of the York Barbell Company, and publisher of *Muscular Health Magazine and Strength and Health Magazine,* Hoffman received great "industry" criticism over the years. Born in Georgia in 1898, his Strongman father became Hoffman's inspiration for muscular development. A WWI hero whose decorations include the Purple Heart, Hoffman held Physical Culture to be paramount to a man's personal readiness to fight, and for his longevity.

In 1943 Bob Hoffman wrote the *Simplified System of Swing Bar Training*, a unique look into the world of club swinging. Despite criticism from competitors and industry fans, Hoffman persisted in authoring several other books that greatly influenced the growth and overall popularity of the Iron Game in the United States.

Paul Von Boeckmann was born in January 1871 and was known for his tremendous grip strength. A lost relic of the Iron Game is Boeckmann's Iron Indian club, said to have tipped the scales between 80 and 85-lbs and standing approximately 20 inches high.

Willoughby, in *The Super Athletes*, describes how Boeckman grasped *"this club at the small end with his hands close together (in baseball bat style), and could readily lever it up and over his shoulder."* He challenged many a strongman to lift the club. Eugene Sandow, the man who had inspired Nordquest's teacher George Jowett, tried the club but failed to make the lift. Charles Atlas, with great effort, managed to lift it slightly once. Boeckman also claimed to be able to chin himself for three reps using only the middle finger of his right hand. Von Boeckman died November 7, 1944.

Joe Nordquest: In 1916 Nordquest, a Jowett prodigy, performed a one finger curl and holdout with a 70-lb dumbbell. He was noted as the only other man to have shouldered Von Boeckmann's monstrous iron Indian club by lifting it strictly parallel from the floor and onto his shoulder.

David Willoughby, in *The Super Athletes* (Page 262), writes that Nordquest could do a one-hand handstand with a 100-lb dumbbell in the other hand. Nordquest barbell bridged 388-lbs without using a belly toss, surpassing Arthur Saxon's record of 386-lbs.

Staff Sergeant Alfred Moss was a British Army Gymnastics champion in 1900, having fought in WWI where he earned his *"Staff Sergeant"* rank. In 1902 he contended in the British preliminaries for Bernarr Macfadden's "Most Perfectly Developed Man" event, held in the UK and USA. His tattoos gained him a disqualification, though he had been considered an easy win for the event. After retiring from a career as a Professional Strongman he wrote and published a postal course on Physical Culture featuring different types of gymnastics, including club swinging. He wrote of club swinging, in his book *Simple Indian Club Exercises;*

"The majority of people always appear to have their lower limbs in a more vigorous state than the arms or chest. And here again a good reason for the adoption of club swinging manifests itself. It is the upper parts of the body that need all the auxiliary exercise. The lower parts will look after themselves. Most of the vital organs of the body are above the waist. Indeed, the state of health of the upper part of the body may be taken as a criterion of the health of the whole. And it is for this reason more than any other that I would urge club-swinging as the most efficient means of keeping the body thoroughly fit on all counts."

Staff Sgt. Moss with Heavy Club courtesy of Roger Fillary and Sandow Website

George Russell Weaver popularized the wrist leverage test in Manhattan, NY in 1945. Weaver recently wrote <u>The Enrichment of Life</u>, which discusses his design. The Weaver Stick became used in a competitive sport for the *United States All-Round Weightlifting Association* (WWW.USAWA.COM):

*"**F9. Weaver Stick Lift:** Stick dimensions: 42 inches long. At one end, place a notch ½ inch from end. The weight will be placed in notch. Thirty-six (36) inches from center of notch, mark a line on stick. This will be the foremost position of the hand. Place some sort of bracket (angle brackets will work) at this point, leaving 5 ½ inches for the gripping surface. The gripping surface may be taped, for thickness, with non-stick tape. Place the stick on a surface, even with the lifter's hand when hanging straight down. The stick must be lifted approximately parallel to the floor. The stick must be lifted straight up from the lifting surface, with no rocking of the stick prior to lifting. The lifting hand and arm must remain free of the body, and the heel of the hand must remain on the top of the stick. If the hand twists around the stick, the lift is not allowed. The entire weight must be free of the surface and under control. The lift ends on command. The lift may also be made by reversing the grip and grasping the stick with the little finger towards the weight, instead of the thumb towards the weight. The body may be bent during this method of lift."*

How tough is it to lift a Weaver Stick? Warren Travis, a former world champion (Back and Harness Lifting), managed a mere 4.25-lb forward lift with the Weaver Stick.

John Grimek was born in 1910 and lived to be 88 years old. Many consider him "The Legend of the Iron Game." Grimek was also the only man to win the Mr. America title twice, was a member of the 1936 US Olympic weightlifting team (that went to Berlin), and won the Mr. Universe in 1948 and the Mr. USA in 1949.

In addition to this he was an expert swimmer, diver, acrobat and muscle control expert. *"The all-prevalent muscle-bound myths of the day were largely dispelled and reversed by his awesome demonstrations of flexibility, grace and speed,"* writes Bob Whelan in his article, *"John Grimek was the Man"* (Hardgainer Magazine 1999).

Grimek's strength gained legendary status when, at 185-lbs and 5 foot 8 inches, he could perform a 400-lb jerk. Historians contest that at a challenge match in 1941 with San Francisco strongman Karl Norberg, Grimek curled and military pressed 285-lbs. That same year he performed a 10-lb Weaver Stick leverage lift with his left hand, and 11¾-lbs in his right hand.

George Hackenschmidt with sledgehammer

George Hackenschmidt, of Swedish descent, was born in 1878 of in Dorpat, Estonia. At the Golden Age of his career he stood 5 foot 9 inches and weighed 200-lbs, yet he demonstrated feats still unrivaled. A prize-winning gymnast, broad jumper and cyclist, his father convinced him to enter weight lifting. His neck became so strong that he performed the wrestler's bridge and pressed a 311-lb barbell for two repetitions, a feat that remained unmatched for 50 years (until Jack Walsh beat the record in 1950). At age 18 he did a single-hand overhead press of 200-lbs, and in 1899 he even surpassed Eugene Sandow's one arm lift of 255-lbs by pressing 279-lbs.

While in St. Petersburg, Russia, Hack lived under the tutelage of the Russian Tsar's physician, Dr. Von Krajewski, a millionaire bachelor who had a penchant for wrestling. Hack won the European Greco-Roman Championships in 1898 – the same year that he won the Russian weight lifting championships!

Other feats of strength that he performed include a single-handed deadlift of a 660-lb stone, and lifting and carrying a fully grown horse. Hack won the 1901 World Greco-Roman Championships. He placed 3rd in the World Weight Lifting Championships the following year. He is best known in weight lifting circles for "developing" the Hack-Squat, in which he performed an amazing 50 reps with 110.25-lbs. He also performed a static crucifix with a 90.25-lb dumbbell in his right hand and an 89⅛-lb dumbbell in his left hand.

Undefeated in a total of 3000 catch-wrestling fights from 1889 to 1908, Hack became famous throughout the World and took his place in fighting arts history as THE RUSSIAN LION.

In *The Way to Live*, Hack wrote, "*Throughout my whole career I have never bothered as to whether I was a Champion or not. The only title I have desired to be known by is simply my name, George Hackenschmidt.*"

Note the implements with which Hack poses in this photograph: a Keg for lifting and a hammer for levering. Hack lived to be 90 years old (he died 1968), and much like The Mighty Atom, he performed feats of strength well into old age.

Arthur Dandurand, a renowned Canadian light heavyweight strongman, at the age of 50 and 185-lbs (5 foot 8 inches tall), held in each hand 12-lb sledgehammers that were 36 inches in length. He would then hold them at arms length in front of him. The strain produced equates to approximately 9-lbs on the Weaver Stick, but held at arms length!

Murl Mitchell placed second in the 1945 Sr. National Weightlifting Championship in the 123-lb weight class. Mitchell would grab two 25-lb sledgehammers at the end of their 30 inch handles. He would then hold them directly out from his shoulders, in front of him, vertical to the floor and, bending his wrists slowly, yield them to touch his eye glasses. Truly this man was the precursor to the most famous of Sledgehammer men, Slim Farman.

"Slim the Hammerman" Farman, was a protégé of the Mighty Atom, Joseph Greenstein. Ed Spielman, in *The Spiritual Journey of Joseph Greenstein*, writes that Farman was the "Spiritual offspring" of the Mighty Atom. The first issue of *Milo* lists his world record at 62.5-lbs total (two 31.25-lb sledgehammers) levered over his head, though it's stated that he's now actually working with 56-lb sledgehammers. Farman levers the handles until they are perpendicular to the ground and then lowers them down to his nose and back, as detailed in Spielman's book, *"slowly, without moving an arm or bending an elbow."*

John Brookfield, grip guru and Clubbell® athlete, in his book *Mastery of Hand Strength*, cleans the beastly 80-lb Challenge Clubbell® in one hand to Order Position:

Dr. Mike Hartle, D.C., is a powerful mastodon with a LOT of grey matter. Dr. Hartle believes that sledgehammer training increases rotational and angular/diagonal "core strength," and also increases the strength, size and muscular reactivity of the arms. He writes in his installment article on "Sledgehammer GPP" (June 04, 2002) about the value of this type of leverage swinging for sports performance:

John Brookfield cleans the beastly 80lbs Clubbell® in one hand to Order Position.

"A hockey player can power clean 110 kg [242.5-lbs] for 5 reps. A very good weight for anyone. Now, when he gets on the ice he is able to use this added strength to check harder and skate faster. However, when it comes time to hit the puck as hard and with as much finesse as he can, he is not able to transfer all that added strength to hitting the puck. Why? In this example, his prime mover muscles are strong, but his rotary and angular/diagonal muscles are not as functional. When it came time to utilize his new strength, there was a loss of power transfer to the puck since his trunk stabilizers and movers were not as strong, thereby not allowing the prime movers of his body to put forth all of their power. If these trunk stabilizers and movers were stronger and more functional, there would be less power loss during transfer of the energy created by the prime movers to the rotary and angular/diagonal muscles, thereby creating a more powerful slapshot!"

Steve Justa, backyard strongman extraordinaire, in his book <u>Rock, Iron, Steel: The Book of Strength</u> (Pages 70–73), describes what he calls the "King of all lifts," the **Shovel Lift** as "an awkward weight, or any weight that is away or far away from the spinal column, because it puts maximum stress on the muscles from severe angles." He explains that this exercise is:

"…awesome because it works so many muscles. When the weight is in front of your body, it stresses all the muscles on your back side, it hits all your side muscles — side waist, thigh and hip; and when the weight is behind you it works all your front muscles, front stomach, front shin, front thigh, front chest. When you raise the weight to head high or overhead, it hits all your upper body muscles. And when you swing the weight from front to back and to the front, you're working all your sideways twisting muscles — muscles that 99% of today's lifters neglect. These sideways rotator muscles are truly powerful muscles when developed. This would be a great lift for any athlete in any sport, and it is truly a great lift for the person interested in developing super strength and super coordination and stamina."

Brooks Kubik, in his supreme strength-training manifesto <u>Dinosaur Training: Lost Secrets of Strength and Development</u>, wrote that *"Lever bar movements are an essential part of advanced grip training because they hit your wrists harder than anything else you can do."*

Yasuhiro Yamashita, the greatest Japanese Judo champion of all time, is pictured in <u>The Fighting Spirit of Judo</u> see-saw pressing *Chashi,* an old Japanese strength training device that came in two forms: one that was similar to a kettlebell and another that was similar to a Clubbell®.

Many top boxers, such as the famous Jack Dempsey in *"How I Got and Keep My Fighting Muscles"* (Muscle Builder, 1925), touted wood chopping for Circular Strength Training. Even today modern boxers such as Oscar De la Hoya and George Foreman use wood chopping as a major part of their conditioning routine. <u>Men's Health</u> reported that chopping wood burns 23 calories per minute and is the best overall conditioner and endurance builder.

Jake Shannon, historian, athlete and author of <u>The Handbook of Authentic Indian Club Swinging</u> (WWW.SCIENTIFICWRESTLING.COM) wrote: *"Scott Sonnon has pulled off a Promethean feat: he has successfully revamped the brutal Indian Club, making Club Swinging relevant and fun for both contemporary athletes and general fitness enthusiasts alike. The Clubbell® and the Circular Strength*

Training® curriculum have turned this well-respected former Olympic sport (with its deep roots in ancient Hindu/Middle Eastern wrestling and martial arts conditioning) into a comprehensive athletic 'plug-and-play' system for the modern age that is as flexible as it is rigorous. Scott's approach has truly taken the 'work' out of 'workout' and replaced it with <u>play</u>!"

Willoughby wrote over 30 years ago in his tome of strength, <u>THE SUPER ATHLETES</u>, *"One would suppose that thick wrists and tight wrist ligaments would be of great assistance in the [leverage] lift; yet actually some strong-men who possessed these attributes did very badly on the Weaver Stick, while others, who had more slender wrists and limber wrist joints, did unexpectedly well."*

What special knowledge and unique training methods allowed such tremendous feats of strength? Don't do as they did. Seek what they sought — and found!

Photographer: Wesley Buckingham • Contributed by D. Cody Fielding

THE BIRTH OF THREE DIMENSIONAL TRAINING

I am simply an Athlete. I view Coaching as the onus one carries forward to share the benefits reaped from an Athletic life. For me this holds deep spiritual connotations. From a young age I held athletics to be a moral responsibility for character development.

Strength includes but transcends the physical — strength of character, strength of will, strength of spirit, strength of resolve. To me it embodies what martial artists aspire to, what athletes cultivate, and what our heroes personify. Bernarr Macfadden, the Father of Physical Culture, wrote many decades ago that *"Weakness — a crime."* I agree with him, but rather than persecute the aspiring strongman I would say: *Strength is a duty.*

When insidious threats imperil our social fabric, strength holds us together. When any needy or threatened compatriot extends a hand for help, let our hand channel strength enough to aid and protect. When men of nefarious intent enter our vicinity, let them do so with hesitation and doubt because of the preparedness every citizen quietly wields. *Here be Dragons.*

I was very fortunate to encounter monumental figures in my life, coaches and mentors who groomed me. They did so without trying to usher me through, allowing me to make the choice to enter the hallowed corridors of hard work, persistence, and discipline upon which USA was founded and now shines.

RUSSIAN SAMBO

After seven years of competitive football I began a competitive career in single combat sports: folk style wrestling, kickboxing and Sambo.

SAMBO, the Russian national combat sport and the 3rd style of international wrestling recognized by FILA (*International Amateur Wrestling Federation*), is actually an acronym for *"Unarmed Self-defense."* The Soviets developed an amazing discipline that extended beyond a set of skills and a competitive outlet. Sambo comprised an integrated training philosophy of combat specific attribute development.

Sambo became a fierce passion for me because of its comprehensiveness, because of my background in folk style wrestling, and because of my love of combat sports in general. To aid my passion I spent eight years at university studying philosophy and sport psychology, which provided me with the opportunity to delve deeply into Soviet sport science. The USSR recognized Sambo as an Olympic sport. Therefore, Soviet sport physiology and psychology research found a testing ground in this combative discipline. Over 10 years ago not only was there nothing available on Sambo, but investigation met with some curious door slamming by the former USSR.

The USA Sambo Coach at the time, himself a consummate athlete, asked me to join him on the USA National Coaching Staff, to which I agreed. He honored me with this position. As a National Coach I enjoyed great opportunities to go abroad and study the other two aspects of Sambo (the first being Sport Sambo): Combat Sambo and Specialized Sambo.

Combat Sambo can be understood as the skills needed for more complex combat engagements, such as counter-terrorism, hostile subject control, close-quarters combat, and executive protection. Combat Sambo developed the skills and Sport Sambo tested the metal in the forge of fierce opponents.

But the Trinity contains another element. Specialized Sambo is a specialized exercise syllabus for the purposes of elite combative readiness. The government classified Specialized Sambo "Absolute Secrecy," and delegated the training exclusively to Soviet Special Operations Units (SOU), called "Spetsnaz." Spetsnaz dubbed it "Combat Sambo Spetsnaz" during the lifetime of the Soviet Union.

I was a successful competitor in Sport Sambo, having won gold medals in the Capital Games, the AAU (*Amateur Athletic Union*) Grand National Championships, and the Pan-American Games, as well as a silver medal at the World University Games.

I was a highly accomplished Combat Sambo instructor, in which I served several appointments. I was elected President of the association responsible for the Combat SOMBO division of the USSA (*United States SOMBO Association*). Dr. Leonid Polyakov, AASF President and FIAS Vice-President, appointed me Chairman of the Combat Sambo Committee, and later Vice-President of the AASF (*American Amateur Sambo Federation*). Mikhail Tikhomirov, FIAS President, appointed me Chairman of the International Combat Sambo Commission for FIAS (*International Amateur Sambo Federation* — the world governing body for Sambo). I also served multiple times as the US Coach and as an International Category Referee, officiating (while also coaching and competing) at international FIAS tournaments. For my contributions to the sport and for my international achievements I was awarded the Distinguished Masters of Sport in Sambo.

In spite of all of these achievements I realized that there was a large empty space in my education. No one in the West had experience with the Soviet approach to sport physiology and sport psychology in the realm of combat athletics — Combat Sambo Spetsnaz. My intuition guided me to complete the trinity of experience in Sambo.

In 1996 I received two offers within the same month: one an invitation to formally intern for Sport Sambo at SAMBO-70, the largest Sambo academy in the world; and the other from Coach Alexander Retuinskih to become the first foreigner to study the updated version of the old "Combat Sambo Spetsnaz" with the National and Olympic coaches and SOU PT instructors.

Training with Mr. Retuinskih completed my experience of the trinity of this discipline. He advised me, as the first foreigner to train behind the former "Iron Curtain," to take the ROSS Training System and adapt it to best help my people, the Americans. Nothing else. No agenda. He is a true visionary, that man. He said that athleticism is stronger than any diplomacy. Truer words have rarely been spoken.

The years that I spent with my Russian coaches had a unique impact on me. Their format impressed me as a blueprint for what I hoped to achieve. I wanted to build a UNIVERSAL tradition with a strong moral foundation. That was my goal.

I consider myself an ambassador of combat athleticism. As such, I slowly and carefully unveiled my approach and began sharing my training methods with anyone dedicated enough to look critically at their performance and work hard to fill those gaps. To help me assess my clients, I created tools to determine the precise location where individual combat athletes were hemorrhaging their performance.

I was not a strength dominant fighter in my competitive years. I had to get by on finesse of skill alone. With one exception, I lost the few matches that I did due to inferior strength and conditioning. The exception? I lost because I refused to tap. My Russian opponent broke my arm in the World Games. I had only my ego to blame. I believed that having my arm broken would be an acceptable sacrifice. (I would lose less team points for USA if I did not submit.) Call it national pride or personal prerogative intensified by the needs of the "tribe," in this case the national team. I call it immaturity and ego.

However, I am very thankful for this lesson, which helped me to realize that skill alone was insufficient. An athlete needs superior technique, superior conditioning and superior mental toughness (including lack of ego). This realization was instrumental in the eventual formulation of my sport psychology tool for combat athletes: _Flow-Fighting_ and the _Flow-State Performance Spiral_. The *Performance Diagnostic Trinity* encapsulates most of what I contribute to combat athletics.

PERFORMANCE DIAGNOSTIC TRINITY™

I developed the *Performance Diagnostic Trinity*™, an assessment approach, with the intention of improving results in athletics. The PDT advocates the position that an athlete with superior conditioning and toughness can over come one of superior skills; one of superior toughness and skills can overcome one of superior conditioning; and one of superior skills and conditioning can overcome one of superior toughness.

Coach Sonnon's Performance Diagnostic Trinity™

While conducting sport psychology and performance enhancement seminars for athletic gyms and martial art schools internationally I came to learn that old-school hardcore traditional Japanese martial art training once embraced a similar concept to the PDT, known as the Red Triangle in Shotokan Karate.

Gichin Funakoshi, the founder, wrote that three aspects must be balanced in martial art education: *kata, kumite,* and *kihon. Kata* practices one's techniques; *kumite* allows one to compete against resistant opponents; and *kihon* conditions mind, spirit and body. It's refreshing and reassuring to know that my conclusions echoed similar realizations of noteworthy physical culturalists of the past.

My Sambo experience helped me to gestate the PDT concept. Think of Sport Sambo, Combat Sambo and Specialized Sambo as Competition, Practice and Training, respectively. From SAMBO and my research, the defining mosaic of my philosophy finally gained clarity: *Mind, body and spirit united through practice, training and competition honing skills, attributes and toughness to assist family and friends (and ultimately everyone who enters my sphere).*

While continuing to assess performance and researching methods to improve it, I ultimately opened the door of *Circular Strength Training*®.

As a former international champion and USA National SAMBO Coach, I had a vested interest in tweaking athletic performance through any and all means possible. This included the creation of CST. I didn't invent "club swinging." It has been done for centuries by various cultures, as you have already read. I brought together this discipline in a cohesive, sophisticated, and tested proprietary system through personal experimentation and the evolving design of Clubbell®.

I developed CST as a natural progression of wanting to make specific conditioning gains for athletes. I experimented by tinkering to arrive at solutions. I did not create a hypothesis and attempt to prove my theory. I cite Roger von Oech's comment: *"Necessity may be the mother of invention, but **play** is certainly the father."* Let me begin by sharing some other notable statements that have influenced me over the years and have helped to shape my concentration upon combat athletic conditioning.

These represent the most potent:

"Conditioning is the greatest hold." **Clarence Ecklund**

"Fatigue makes cowards of us all." **Vince Lombardi**

"Weakness is a crime." **Bernarr Macfadden**

Action guy guru Mike Gillette once told me, *"You can't take someone where you haven't been, and you can't give someone something that you don't have."* As such, I concentrate on efficiency and effectiveness for athletes.

People ask me why I train military and law enforcement personnel, and why I have trained with some of the finest special operations personnel in the world. From my experience, combat and sports share the same bed, a love affair encapsulated by MacArthur's opinion of athletics: *"On the fields of friendly strife are sown the seeds that on other fields, on other days, will bear the fruits of victory."*

The USSR mirrored this sentiment, and considered physical culture a political platform. Marshal Konyev, a Soviet commander, wrote, *"Only physically fit people can stand the strain of heavy fighting, can march long distances under heavy bombardment, and quite often must start fighting at the end of a long march. We owe it primarily to the sports organizations that Soviet people were training and had imparted to them such qualities as courage, persistence, will-power, endurance and patriotism."* (Tsatsouline, <u>Power to the People</u>)

Because much of my training took me through the former Soviet Union countries working with national and Olympic coaches, as well as training with various military SOU trainers, I was greatly influenced by a spectrum of different sources. This experience focused and congealed into the Training Hierarchy Pyramid™.

TRAINING HIERARCHY PYRAMID™

The model of training that I developed is really not that challenging to grasp. When I met Iron Game Legend Dave Draper, he said something that struck home: *"Training is simple to understand, but difficult to achieve."* I agree with him.

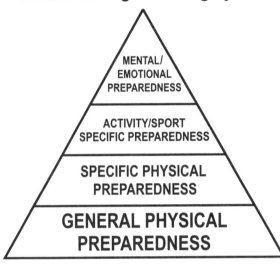

My model is comprised of just four elements: basic, fundamental work; specific work; physical skills; and psychological skills. My views show the influence of Dr. Tudor Bompa. My model, however, departs from his work in structure and content. The THP can be understood as a pyramid with *General Physical Preparedness* (GPP) on the bottom, *Specific Physical Preparedness* (SPP) next, *Activity/Sport Specific Preparedness* (SSP) on the third rung, and *Mental/Emotional Preparedness* (MEP) on the top.

It's important to state that these steps should be made so gradually, so incrementally, that the shift between levels should be nearly imperceptible to the athlete. Furthermore, when intuitively progressing through the model yourself, you should feel compelled to move to the next step rather than scheduled to move. In other words, your mental, emotional and physical state should crave the move to a higher increment up the THP. Listen to and trust your intuition.

Let's assign some general concepts to each of the THP steps:

- GPP creates **work capacity**, which refers to developing the energy system utilized.
- SPP creates **work sophistication**, which refers to developing the range and depth of the skills to be prepared, as well as the "safety valve" of training slightly outside the scope of the activity.
- SSP creates **work specificity**, which refers to the deconstruction of the target skill into its elementary components, their practice, and the practice of the transitional movements between these components.
- MEP creates **work flow**, which refers to developing the neural drive (or "nerve force," in old strongman speak) and disinhibition, stabilization of autonomic and hormonal arousal (aka "emotional control"), and attentional strength and stamina (known in pop culture as "mental toughness").

I structure this as a pyramid and not a block because each lower level requires a more substantial foundation than the one above in order for the higher levels to concretely hold. For instance, the greatest amount of time is dedicated to GPP, next to SPP, and so on. But these are not clear distinctions: strictly GPP, then a new program of SPP, then a new program... Rather, this pyramid contains a very gradual transition from one to the next, so subtle as to be unnoticed by the combat athlete. The subtle gradation of bottom to top reflects the fact that *advanced training is a refinement of basic training.*

GENERAL PHYSICAL PREPAREDNESS

The primary goal of GPP, irrespective of activity or sport, is enhanced working capacity. If work capacity increases, combat athletes will adapt more readily to sustained increases in mental and physical demands. GPP holds priority as the BASE of all solid programming because, without this level of readiness, the mind and body cannot effectively absorb specificity. My theory is much like Maslow's Pyramid, meaning that one cannot effectively address higher levels of training without the lower level's fulfillment. One can practice MES, but without GPP it's a house built on quicksand.

SPECIFIC PHYSICAL PREPAREDNESS

Next up on the pyramid is SPP, sport-specific exercises to transform GPP into increased performance for specific skills. From my experience in the former Eastern Block countries, I discovered that the Soviets generously developed and successfully applied a VAST array of exercises and apparati to augment attributes within the contexts of specific sports.

Further, former Eastern Block trainers put their athletes through their paces as frequently and as freshly as possible (Zatsiorsky: *Science and Practice of Strength Training*). SPP builds upon the GPP foundation by furthering development in the exact characteristics of the intended activity or sport. Victory is predicated upon specialization, which further increases work capacity while decreasing recovery time.

What I have done with my clients is to approximate their skills through GPP. I trained attributes and simultaneously developed and integrated specific skills. Therefore, I began to fill the gap between GPP and Activity/Sport Specific Preparedness. Pavel Tsatsouline, in *"Grease the Groove for Strength"* (*Milo*), stated simply: **Specificity + Frequent Practice = Success.**

Dr. Hartle distinguished between GPP and SPP work in an illuminating manner in his article "Sledgehammer GPP" (*Intensity Magazine*):

"Most weight programs focus on the big lifts to enhance their athletes' sports performance and decrease incidence of injury: squat, bench press, deadlift, power clean, etc. While these lifts will enhance an athlete's performance on the field, they are all done essentially in a singular plane aspect. They will allow an athlete to jump higher, run faster, hit harder, etc., but ALL sports will require the athlete during practice/competition to utilize their body in one, two or all three planes of motion at the same time. This means the athlete needs to have the motor units of the rotary and angular/diagonal muscles ready to assist the prime movers as they function in a near-maximal or maximal state and are ready to function when called upon."

Without fulfilling the SPP level, SSP and MEP lay on a weak foundation with limited potential. As one of the world's most renowned coaches, Fred Hatfield, wrote, "Optimal physical conditioning provides the platform from which the skills can be used." (Sportscience News). Hatfield goes on to provide an excellent example of the need for personalized training standards:

"Fighters possess unique styles that create specific physical demands. Some rely on explosive strength ("power"), for others it's starting strength ("speed"), and for most a combination of the two ("speed-strength"). True champions alter their style in a way that will make them more able to attack the weaknesses of any given opponent. Improvements in specific capacities can be made, but they are only helpful if integrated into the fighter's style. For example, extensive footwork exercises may not benefit the power puncher who fights stationary and looks to deliver a blow that starts with the legs and drives right through the opponent (and wins that way). Similarly, a fighter who relies on punching speed and fast footwork should not put all his training hours into heavy bag work and muscle mass development. So, the program designed must not only be specific to boxing, but also specific to the boxer."

THREE DIMENSIONAL PERFORMANCE PYRAMID™

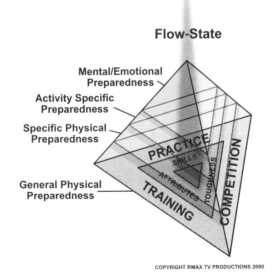

There are three aspects to physical culture: training attributes, practicing skills and competing against failure.

The latter is most often misunderstood. Competition derives from the Latin roots con and petire, meaning "to seek together." In other words, competition refers to **work against a resistant partner for mutual benefit.**

Competition is typically (and incorrectly) interchanged with a winning/losing paradigm. One can compete in a drill, but people view this as competing against the opponent. You compete WITH the opponent, but you compete **together AGAINST failure.** You seek to create the most challenging environment possible (within the parameters of the exercise, drill, game or event) for you **and** your partner(s) to recover from and to resist failure. In sport psychology this is called mental toughness — the ability to recover from and resist failure.

Too many people blind themselves to this ultimate goal of athletics. "Good sportsmanship" is based upon this understanding, which is why a "good sport" appreciates his "losses" as much as his "wins." The goal is about something more visceral, something deeper — the struggle against the *Inner Foe*, striving to become a better, more sophisticated human being.

As a result, a good athlete is a good person. Such a simple statement couldn't hold more weight. Everything that's admirable in athletics can be found in developing a healthy athletic lifestyle: the raw effort to challenge one's attributes, the diligent attention to refine one's skills, and the sheer persistence to resist failure.

Moreover, 'good' athletes seek these virtues **alone together** by giving their absolute best on the field of competition. Athletics holds winning and losing as secondary to creating the most challenging environment possible for all participants to have the opportunity to grow, improve and develop.

This is not a popular idea in the ego-driven mania of the "sport industry." The self-proclaimed "professionals" promote a fixation upon winning at all costs, rather than upon the lifestyle and ideals of physical culture.

Often these "professionals" have never actually won anything substantial in their lives (or if having done so view their sport as the only way to personal mastery). When you've never "significantly" won in a sport, or you've competed in only one sport, you tend to still romanticize about being THE best instead of constantly doing YOUR best — and more importantly, giving your best so that ALL of the participants have a chance to shine.

For these trophy-hunters, a sport is still about them and their 'important' little world. Typically they've never coached a team of athletes, or they would assign collective athletic development as the primary goal, and would truly realize the perpetually echoing impact that athletics has upon our world.

Many people neglect or totally ignore the *Performance Diagnostic Trinity*™ (PDT) in their training, and as a result never truly rise above mediocrity. They neglect it or do not understand that it is not two dimensional. It is not a flat diagram composed of three different agendas in athletics. They hit the gym, they work on their skills on the field, and they scrimmage. This is the conventional, compartmentalized view of the PDT.

But the PDT is only the **top view** of the model. It actually has height, depth, and width. The PDT has a **side view,** which I called in my first book the *Training Hierarchy Pyramid*™.

Improving Sophistication serves as one of the two primary principles at play in the model. In other words, the objective is to improve the quality rather than the volume, intensity or frequency of one's abilities.

Incremental Progression, often referred to as Errorless Learning (a phrase which I no longer espouse), became the protocol of the model, giving it graduated height. The two principles merge to create an upwardly moving and inwardly refining step-by-step process of development — in other words, a three-sided pyramid.

This 3D Model (combining the PDT and the THP) is what we need to grasp. In **Flow-Fighting,** what stands at the center of the PDT? **Flow-State** — the ability to remain indistractible despite resistance, despite error, despite unexpected events.

Three Dimensional Performance Pyramid™

And what is the top eschelon of "work" concentrated upon in the THP? That's right: **Mental/Emotional Preparedness** — in other sport psychology speak, mental toughness training.

What is the ultimate significance of the THP and the PDT being merged into a 3-Dimensional Model of Performance?

When we bring the PDT and the THP together, we discover that *Training, Practice* and *Competition* **merge** in an upwardly progressing refinement from general to specific physical development, towards mental and emotional development. In other words:

You need Mental Toughness to enter and maintain Flow-State.

I recently provided an example of this development in response to a question regarding high school athletic programming:

"At a General Physical Preparedness (GPP) level, you'll be helping them regain their capacity to "work." Complex movement patterns overwhelm clients at this point in their development. Stick to simple movements. Simple *Biomechanical Exercise*™ movements can be used at this point to increase work capacity.

I like to apply a strategy that is summed up in a word that I coined: DeSISSifying. It refers to my acronym *Stuck In Simplistic Stupidity,* which speaks to the hazards of sustained KISS (Keep It Simple Stupid) training.

Take a conventional calisthenic. Train the client with it until you see sufficient GPP (work capacity) gains. Then "sophisticate" the movement. Done correctly, the client doesn't realize the increasing sophistication of the movements **because the increments progress so gradually,** though it is rapid enough to keep pace with challenging the client and preventing boredom.

Since you propose high school athletics, let me throw in an example for high school football, in particular for offensive linemen.

The beginning of the season would focus on GPP conditioning exercises like burpees and pushups, and games like wheelbarrow races and frog leap races. You're creating a **bridge** for the athletes to cross into their potential sophistication. One's unlimited potential is initially inconceivable for most people. You need to walk slowly with them, allowing them to own their discoveries of their innate talent.

The rest of the sessions would focus upon skill development, game play and scrimmaging.

As soon as an athlete achieves a predetermined work capacity, the conditioning would sophisticate into SPP.

For example, the burpees would evolve into spinal waves with pelvic pop-ups; the pushups would evolve into quad hops (with a hand position emulating hand-blocking configuration); wheel barrow races sophisticate into block-hops (again emulating hand-block configuration); frog leaps evolve into high amplitude frontal ground engagement drills off another players back, immediately followed by leg threading rolling laterally, then explosive pelvic pop-up (then repeat down the field).

Once you gauge the athletes to have gained sufficient competency in the above SPP, move on to the Activity Specific Preparedness portion of the THP.

For example, the last DeSISSified frog leap sophisticates into emulating offensive line play. Three athletes per squad move down the field in the training exercise. Two athletes role play the defensive line face, one role plays the offensive lineman.

Emulating the physiological profile of the SPP exercise (the "DeSISSified frog leap"), offense must absorb the collision with one player across the line upon whistle blow. He must absorb and redirect, then immediately spin (thread) the opposite direction to impact the rushing 2nd defensive player with sufficient force to knock him off course.

As the squad gets the groove of the training exercise, add another player into each squad as a role-played ball-carrier with whom the offensive lineman must coordinate timing, replicating actual game realism more closely. The stress involved in this coordination helps the (offensive) athlete render the Mental/Emotional Preparedness of the top of the THP.

Coaches can prime the (offensive) athlete with what I've called *Performance Mantras* to focus and concentrate the attention of the athlete upon the TRUE performance goals (so as to increase indistractibility).

The above is by no means carved in stone, and it does not consider the actual play template of the head coach's team strategy. However, I hope that this provides a clear example of how to implement the model into a high school athletic program format.

Extrapolating this into the format of the general health/fitness client requires us to look at the model as the coupling of two critical principles: Increasing Sophistication and Incremental Progression."

We know that the primary principle of the PDT is the merging of training, practice and competition towards the ability to flow. When we combine this with the two principles of the THP, Increasing Sophistication and Incremental Progression, we create a new understanding about the role of athletics in personal development and we gain a deeper appreciation for the **lifestyle of physical culture.**

Misunderstanding this, most people become overwhelmed by the conventional notion of **more**: higher intensity, greater volume, shorter frequency, and greater number of exercises, skills, and competitive events. They do *too much* and burn-out, or they become overwhelmed at the misinformed belief that they must do *so much* and they quit.

This confusion derives from a basic lack of systematic programming of **Flow-State** within Physical Education, or as it is now known, Human Kinetics. The conventional goal remains *doing more* and *winning more* rather than *performing better.*

There is a great deal of ego blocking most people here. Many experience knee-jerk *Fear-Reactivity* about 'not losing' and the 'need for winning.' They cry desperately that there's nothing wrong with holding victory as the goal. That's fine.

Victory is the goal — but they compete against the wrong opponent. Having only indirectly engaged (if at all) their ego, this *Inner Foe* to which every coach in every sport in every culture speaks, they may win an event but unless they reprioritize their athletic goals they will never taste true victory, which is growth.

Performance-based athletic programs begin and end with **growth**: the upward mobility expressed by the *Training Hierarchy Pyramid* merged with the fused refinement of the *Performance Diagnostic Trinity*.

EXPERIMENTING WITH DESIGNS

When you lack a convincing theory you must depend upon the odd mixture of experience and intuition, experimentation and logic. In my case I relied on my intention to utilize exercises and methods of SPP for combat athletics. I intended to intensify the grooved-in development of my clients in the shortest time possible, while guaranteeing the greatest longevity of health and pain-free performance. I always experiment on myself first, so…

I began with conventional equipment, such as barbells and dumbbells, in odd exercises that most closely approximated the range, scope and depth of motion of the activities of combat athletics. When I determined that these apparati were too bulky and awkward, unsuited to dynamic motion, I moved on to kettlebells, having first been exposed to this manner of training in Russia. I was later instructed by Pavel Tsatsouline, Master of Sport in Kettlebell Lifting and Physical Training Instructor of the former USSR Spetsnaz — the man responsible for revitalizing kettlebell lifting in the USA. He appeared at one of my seminars to learn more about my approach. I learned some solid theories from Pavel, and he has incorporated much of my work as well.

I began to make modifications to equipment, understanding that I did so at my own risk, and I did not ask any of my clients to follow suit. I grafted and edited whatever I could, until my Frankenstein inventions were more readily crafted from junkyard reconnoitering. I used old church curtain weights equipped with karabiners to load plates, lead shot filled aluminum baseball bats, sledgehammer heads on steel poles, and axes. I couldn't afford the risk of exposing my clients to homemade versions. Do not try these experiments at home or anywhere else, please! I still shudder at some of the property damage that could have been flesh. This impossible design slowly evolved, with a lot of "play-time" spent between the beginning of the journey and the final prototype. To understand how it evolved I'll share the thought-process of my investigation.

THE 4 INTENTIONS OF COMBAT SPORT SPP

I had four intentions that **needed** to be fulfilled in my experiments. These intentions molded the design, rather than some prefabricated mental blueprint.

Firstly, combat athletes dedicate themselves to weight restrictions and often cannot sustain immense nutritional intake while competing or operating. Further, in fighting larger is not necessarily better. Limited muscle reactivity and mobility means limited options and decreased reaction time. Therefore my clients seldom possessed the option of increased bulk. I needed to develop methods that would enhance attributes such as strength without necessarily adding mass or reducing mobility.

Secondly, one of the single most defining characteristics of combative efficacy is grip strength. The ability to boldly adhere (and the first one to do so) to an opponent generally determines the outcome of the conflict. This is certainly true of grappling. The ability to crush grip an opponent very often overrides any counter-defense. As Dr. Ken Leistner states, *"Success in sport is often determined by how well one wields the implements of the sport"* (The Steel Tip). Dr. Leistner wrote that Kim Wood, Strength Coach of the Cincinnati Bengals, made three points to him during a conversation on grip strength:

"Hand and forearm training is usually the most overlooked aspect of any conditioning program. The potential strength in the hands and forearms is great for most athletes. As muscle and connective tissue mass in the hands increase, the size and density of the hand increases, making it a more efficient and hitting tool."

The wheels began to turn when I read that Dr. Leistner advised (in the same article) that *"leverage exercises using broomsticks, dumbbell bars or ax handles (I recommend removing the cutting blade for the sake of safety) give added variety and stimulation to your workouts."*

Next, I intended to maximize the physical ability to resist, stop and overcome the application of submission holds, joint manipulations and hold-downs in fighting. I intended to create equipment that would allow me to build combat specific strength under what I named the *Yield-Halt-Overcome* protocol. Ballistic motion needed to be slowed (eccentrically), stopped or statically held (isometrically), and reversed (concentrically) when the arm was taken out of its normal functional range. The equipment needed to be able to address this *Yield-Halt-Overcome* protocol in dynamic ranges of motion.

The intent of submission holds in fighting is to bring a joint to extreme range of motion until either the athlete receives so much pain that he concedes the win to the opponent or his joint breaks and he loses the match. I began to use my devices in ranges of motion that most closely approximated the range, scope and depth of various holds. I would add inertia to the pendulum, slow the device as rapidly as possible, stop it "on a dime" and instantly reverse the motion, or send it to an angle that countered the visualized attempt.

The equipment needed to function even at extreme ranges of motion where holds are typically final. I gained insight from the sport science of the former Soviet Union and its concept of *Dynamic Flexibility*. Their Olympic Coaches had their athletes train slightly outside the range, scope and depth of the ranges of motion "expected" to be found in their sport. They did this so that, WHEN the movements of the athletes deviated from expected ranges of motion, they would effectively possess a "safety valve" to prevent injury (Yessis). This notion of dynamic flexibility, exhibiting both the characteristics of strength and flexibility-enhancing properties, became an invaluable standard that influenced the design evolution of what would become the Clubbell®.

Finally, I intended to cultivate EXPLOSIVE throws and takedowns through superior conditioning. Throwing or taking an opponent to the ground requires a special combination of three characteristics:

1. Kinesthetic sensitivity to balance and tension,
2. Specialized skills and tactics, and
3. Physical attributes.

I believe that physical attributes are the most important because, at all competitive levels, superior conditioning becomes a measuring stick of success. Jesse, in _Wrestling Physical Conditioning Encyclopedia_ (Page 23), states, *"Between two wrestlers having comparable experience and skill, all other factors being equal, the stronger (strength and endurance) wrestler will win."* SPP is the EDGE over the competition. SPP is the gap between GPP and Sport Specific, Mental and Emotional Preparedness — a gap that's too substantial and neglected in most sports and combative training.

I intended to research and develop equipment that could most closely approximate the range, scope and depth of motion of throws. Most throws occur at extreme ranges of motion. The strength required must explode over a fulcrum, like one's shoulder or hip, and happen at the earliest portion in the range of motion, as depicted in a "shoulder throw" or a "hip toss." For example, power generation in a shoulder throw requires forward explosion from one arm where the hand is positioned behind one's head and the elbow pointed skyward. The other arm begins across one's body fully extended, gripping the opponent's sleeve, and must explosively rip the jacket around in front circularly. Not only did I require explosion from "fit-in" positions, I needed the strength to continue to ACCELERATE throughout the movements of each throwing technique.

I concocted many devices, such as ropes on pulleys with nets containing varying amounts of stones, rubber strands attached to dumbbells, and medicine balls attached to ropes and belts. These devices slightly improved the performance that my clients specifically required, so I continued with R&D in this direction. I honestly had no idea that these four intentions would result in CST and would evolve into a singular piece of equipment — the Clubbell®.

Experience with fighters from other cultures and training with Olympic and National Team coaches from different countries allowed me to uncover this rarely known artifact of old-time strongman physical culture. This method forged a long history of success in physical conditioning for combat specific strength, power, speed-strength, endurance, agility, coordination and flexibility. My research and experiences with CST produced the final genesis of the Clubbell®.

It should come as no surprise to anyone that the Clubbell® resulted from the singular intent of gaining superior physical advantage over opponents in hand to hand fighting and combat sports. I believe that the Clubbell® — what I have named the standard of CST — IDEALLY suits performance enhancement in combat athletics. I believe so simply because I journeyed through this evolution and arrived at the final design rather than thinking of a hypothesis, creating some invention, and hoping to "test" its merit.

I have been very fortunate with our clients, and their success has been outstanding: they've been world champions and national coaches in various martial art styles and combat sports, including boxing, kickboxing, judo, Sambo, wrestling, karate, jiu-jitsu and no-holds-barred fighting. The list goes on. I consider myself blessed to have such fine American men and women call me "Coach." It's what I have lived my life to do. It is all I ever want — to help, to contribute, to coach. My success has only come from standing on the giant shoulders of my clients.

What follows is a map to navigate CST. It is not a HOW-TO, though there are adequate and exhaustive instructions. I do not throw you a fish, but rather teach you how to fish for yourself. I challenge you to open the doors to your full potential in combat athletics. Take this map with you on your journey.

I'll now discuss the primary principles of Clubbell® Training.

TABULA RASA — CLEAN THE SLATE

Most people have a fitness destination in mind when they begin their journey. Some do not. All fitness books focus on telling you how to get to those purported fitness 'ideals' that the public is led to believe in. However, like any journey, your point of departure and your mode of transportation determine your course, and more importantly so do the challenges you will encounter along the way. The primary issue for empowering your lifetime fitness development is not where you are going, but where you are coming from — where you are right now, physically, mentally and emotionally.

We all have baggage when we begin our fitness journey. We're overburdened and even debilitated by the weight of that baggage. Worse still, we increase the amount of baggage that we carry as we muddle our way through the choking volume of fitness information available in the digital age. Our baggage of course comprises a host of painful, limited mobility, residual tension, injuries, anxiety, trauma, and fear-reactivity.

If you want to expedite your fitness journey you must choose to set down this baggage. Who wouldn't choose pain-free mobility and lifelong vibrant health and fitness? Beginning is the most difficult task because you must create new, healthy patterns in your life. Those harmful, painful patterns can grow roots and, no matter how much better the quality of life you could be having, it will require dedication, persistence and faith not to fall back into those negative patterns.

Your goal is to begin with a clean slate, the cleanest possible, so that you minimize the restrictive forces that imperil your personal development.

THE SITE IS NOT THE SOURCE

Many years ago I suffered a horrible back injury in Russia from deadlifting. Early in 2004 I lost 80% of the strength in my left shoulder.

My intuition connected the two absolutely. The defensive bracing that was protecting my lower back (the Source) predisposed me to an overtraining injury in my shoulder (the Site).

Before my shoulder injury I had introduced goofy-foot specialized long-board skating into my regime for several months, and as a result I developed a kinetic chain of tension: muscles activated along the length of the body from repetition and adaptation to a specific demand. I didn't think to compensate for this activity at the time, since I considered it 'merely' recreational.

This kinetic chain resulted from pumping with my left leg while stabilizing with my right, creating an isometric chain of tension that ran up from the hyperstabilized right leg to the bound defensive bracing at the lower back.

Then, one day, add a strength test with the dumbbell bench press. Voila. TWANG! The encounter of a kinetic chain with the bound tension of my lower back fired upward and across (since we function symmetrically) to my left shoulder under the load of the exercise. I lost almost all the strength in my shoulder within a few days.

I underwent several months of self-rehab through Prasara yoga. It was a textbook case, and it was instrumental in teaching me how to 'see' the necessity of "cleaning the slate" in others.

LEARNING TO CLEAN THE SLATE

It has taken me many years to develop CST, with one of the major stimuli being healing my back. I rehabilitated it through a program that I developed called Be Breathed™, and I developed Warrior Wellness™ to improve the dynamic mobility of my spine and all of my other joints. I've been working since then to release some deep residual muscular tension, presumably intersegmental musculature, that is the final remains of that very old injury and the emotional issues that it anchored.

I chart my progress photographically, but I could sense releases rather dramatically, sometimes through a POP and other times through a soft melting away of tension, but always progressing by one baby step at a time. I had been locked up in the thoracic and the pelvic regions. First the thoracic released and then the pelvic. There are attached 'emotional' issues anchored to each 'bound' area.

CLEANING THE SLATE

I find myself telling people to clean the slate more and more, in different words. So many people have gotten on the CST craze that they want to jump into the deep end of the pool without first taking off all of the rusty armor that they've been carrying around for years. Even though you may feel accustomed to carrying and wearing that armor, it still puts you on the express route to the bottom when you jump in the water.

I hear many people say that they're just starting CST by 'cleaning the slate,' and that the only precondition they suffer from is less than ideal mobility/flexibility. Well, who doesn't? That's the whole point of CST. It's like saying that the only thing wrong with your nutrition is that you don't eat regular meals and don't monitor your food choices. There's a lot more going on than you may know at this time.

I've been teaching the first CST Maxim so often now that it's becoming a household phrase: **If you want consistent, long-lasting progress, you must clean the slate... and do so daily!** *And there isn't one person who has a clean slate!*

Not only must you resolve the submerged chains of tension created over the years, but you must also offset the effects of daily stresses which will embed if not discharged immediately. Cleaning the Slate is the goal of <u>Deepening your Daily Personal Practice</u>.

Yes, it's possible to train specific goals concurrent with 'cleaning the slate,' since through journaling your training you can monitor, assess and address resulting interference from preconditions. However, if you compound preconditions with "cocktailing," then by definition you won't be able to clean the slate. As a result neither your short nor your long-term performance will improve to optimum.

CYCLE, CIRCUIT BUT DON'T COCKTAIL

It's the primary CST protocol generator: **cycle** a training program towards achieving a specific physiological goal (endurance, strength, speed, flexibility, mobility, et cetera) with one or two specific exercises over a specific time period to adapt and progress (and craft a scheme appropriately); or create a **circuit** of exercises performed to tap a particular energy system (in other words, all exercises are performed towards one physiological goal).

However, don't create a **'cocktail'** of haphazardly (or fad-determined) exercises with differing (contradictory) physiological goals. In other words, training with no goal in mind gets you nowhere fast. (Caveat: exploration and fun are valid goals so long as they are 'checked' to prevent overtraining, but you still need 'planned' exploration and 'structured' fun.)

HOW DO YOU PLAN?

What is the progression scheme over what period of time to accomplish what goals? If you're just lifting for 'general fitness,' then realize that none of this work contributes to the energy system of your events. General Physical Preparedness increases your work capacity in your target activity. Random, unplanned 'work' will compete and interfere with the development of specific physical preparedness for your events. If you cocktail you will squander precious training time and energy, and you will accumulate overtraining trauma resulting in serious injuries.

Further, even if you're doing multiple activities that tap the same energy system they'll do this in different patterns through the body. The skills differ so the musculature activated differs, so the Specific Physical Preparedness will differ — in the same way that racquetball and tennis differ dramatically.

You CAN perform your sports or recreational activities concurrently. I do many activities throughout the day — BUT I don't 'train' for them. This is why you need to state specific goals and then concentrate on 'training' for them exclusively. If you're training for two different activities you need two different sets of goals.

At times two different goals may be integrated, but for the most part if you intend to benefit from both goals you must create a PLAN of progressive cycles that culminate in an event or a long term goal. This plan will move from General to Specific Physical Preparedness, to Sport Specific Training to Mental/Emotional Training (discussed later).

Begin by asking yourself this question, and answer it honestly: "HOW specifically do I clean the slate, and towards what end?" I've provided extensive guidance on how to do this within this book.

You want to prepare for your events and do your best. It's my honor to help you avoid the same mistakes millions of athletes make every day. Unplanned training not only COMPETES with your performance, it directly leads to overtraining. **You can't keep doodling on the chalkboard if you want to clean the slate.**

SHORT-TERM SUCCESS VS. LONG-LASTING DEVELOPMENT

People are in such a rush for immediate results that they're even willing to sacrifice their health and longevity to achieve them. What few realize is that, if you follow the CST Maxim of Incremental Progression, not only will you achieve your goals with long lasting success, but you will surpass them in ways that you couldn't ever have predicted or dared hope for!

This is what Active Recovery regards — cleaning the slate. If you shorten or neglect Active Recovery then slight overtraining effects accumulate rapidly. If you continue to ignore the apparently scattered aches, pains and twinges, you will land yourself in a chronic injury.

This is how most people live their lives: **hurry up** and get quick results (at a cost), **and wait** for the injuries to heal. Don't get stuck in, and do get out of immediately, the cycle of pursuing immediate results and regressing while your injuries heal. How many of you have said to yourself the following: *"I feel like I finally get the results that I want and then WHAM I get hit with another injury. I must be injury-prone or something."*

As you get older it becomes increasingly unlikely that you'll be able to recover from this cycle. This is why for most people injuries happen more often as they age. You can't escape your own folly.

AVOIDING THE IMMEDIATE RESULTS — EVENTUAL INJURY LOOP

That's the purpose of our online *FORUM*. You need to JOURNAL your CST PERSONAL TRAINING PROGRAM. This allows you to monitor when and how you need to 'clean the slate' every day. It allows you to reassess your plan and to adjust your approach so that you meet and exceed your goals. It guarantees that you'll be able to set your near-, short- and long-term goals. It also gives you the opportunity to receive feedback for FREE from certified coaches, as well as other enthusiasts.

Most important of all, journaling your training commits you to transforming your PLAN into a REALITY! Why do plans fail? There are many reasons, and journaling commits you to monitoring and regulating those reasons and to redefining your goals so that you do achieve them. Journaling forces you to exercise the most difficult thing of all: restraint.

You can't ignore what you've written. You've tracked your progress and you've committed to your goals. When a behavior doesn't support your achievement of those goals then you need to change that behavior. The world is full of chronic over-trainers, but you won't find any of them keeping a CST journal!

I'm honored to invest the time and energy to help you prepare for and achieve your goals. But if you want my help, then you need to listen carefully to the suggestions that I offer. There's a process. It begins with a plan, and with a commitment to recording your daily cleaning of the slate.

INTUITIVE TRAINING

Differentiate form, exertion and discomfort subjectively.

RESOLVING THE PAIN THROUGH MOBILITY DRILLS

One solution to chronic pain and *Fear-Reactivity* involves distracting the CNS through specialized Joint Mobility Drills (as seen in Warrior Wellness™ and its successor Intu-Flow™). This controlled conservative approach to pain helps foster the physiological environment critical for allowing the body to heal.

SOMETIMES NO PAIN MEANS NO GAIN!

Immobility often involves progressive stiffness. As you avoid painful movement, your body adapts to the tension by 'protecting' the area from the painful movement. It then progresses and 'develops strength' in that immobilized state. Therefore, you must sometimes move through a range of motion as long as you can tolerate the pain. You must do so in a CONTROLLED MANNER! For chronic lower back pain, it often requires at least two weeks of this exercise before pain begins to resolve. On a scale of 1–10 (1 being mild annoyance, 10 being intolerable agony), don't go farther than a 5 (tightness) or 6 (uncomfortable) in joint mobility exercise.

Sometimes you get the bear and sometimes it gets you. Same bear, different outcomes. Sometimes your program says you should be having a moderate workout and it feels like it's a hellacious maximal effort. Why does this happen? I'll give you some information and then make some suggestions to help you get in tune with your true training condition, because our workouts often look much better on paper than in reality.

So often the field of strength and conditioning remains enslaved to a highly mechanistic approach to training goals. However, we live in a subjective world, flooded with changing emotions, fluctuating energy levels, "mysterious" pains, and surprise stressors.

Everyone has at some time in their lives experienced fluctuations of some kind among common variables: lifting the same weight twice can seem heavier, running the same distance can seem longer, resting for the same duration can seem shorter, et cetera. The subjective experience of training differs from the numbers we etch into our training journals.

RATE OF PERCEIVED EXERTION (RPE) — how maximal you perceive your session's training load to be. Listing your RPE in your journal gives a more accurate assessment of your progress, and it may enable you to modify your program to better accomplish your goals.

If you want to prevent burn-out, over-training and injuries, and if you want to continue to create positive results indefinitely, your RPE should be one of the key factors in your program assessment.

HOW DO YOU DESIGN RPE INTO YOUR PROGRAM ASSESSMENT?

If you have a set/rep/time scheme, add RPE to your after-action report. You can do this with a basic light-moderate-heavy reference, a five-star system (5 being max), or you can fine tune it to a 10 point scale (10 being max) as suggested in this book.

Rather than trying to remember the perceived effort of each repetition, draw your RPE from the overall set experience, then average the entire session. If you don't want to record the RPE of each set, just pick out the hardest sets of the entire session. Record that RPE as your total experience of the session.

HOW DOES RECORDING YOUR RPE HELP YOUR PROGRAM?

Are you interested in achieving your program's projected results, or are you interested in achieving your true potential? Say your program has you listed to hit the same numbers over 4 sessions before increasing the intensity. The target for the session is actually supposed to be 70%RM (85% of the weight you could lift for one repetition). The objective 70%RM should conceivably pair up with your subjective 7 RPE (if on a 1–10 scale). However, at the 2nd session you realize that you're cruising through the exercise with an RPE of 4. Do you need to continue or do you alter your session to meet your current potential?

Say your program has you consistently going up in reps or weight over each session. However, each session you're being outstripped and fall farther and farther behind. Do you change your program, or struggle to put out the numbers?

Intuitive Training uses your RPE as a means of plugging in to the most elusive characteristic in physical training: your constantly changing biorhythm. Traditional strength and conditioning presumes that you can apply its numbered goals to any time of the day, any day of the week, any season of the year, any temperature, air pressure, weather condition, humidity level, etc... However, some times are better for you than they are for others. Add your emotional climate to the mix and you have a highly personalized pattern to assess and reassess.

A few "professionals" out there demand that you must see some increase in each training session. Linear progression looks great on paper, but it just isn't accurate neurologically when some aspects of development take longer to latch-on than others. Rigid number fixation cannot accommodate the impact that your sport and your life in general have upon the time that you devote to strength and conditioning.

For example, if the one-rep maximum that you attempted felt very demanding (a 9 to 10 RPE on a 1–10 scale), you may decrease the load by 20-lbs and do a few more sets of 2 reps each. You might then increase the load by 10-lbs for another few single rep sets. The same example can apply to timed running, to volume lifting and to rest period compression.

SO ALL I NEED IS MY RPE TO USE MY INTUITION IN TRAINING?

No. What happens when you push beyond your threshold? Your technique deteriorates. Your goal must always be to stop at the last repetition that you can do with proper form. Why?

If you force a fluid through a hose it comes out the end in a forceful stream. Now, take an ice pick and poke holes in the hose. Bend the hose in kinks. Place heavy objects at different places on the hose. Finally, wind and wrap the hose around a few obstacles. What's the water pressure like now? Dribbles, I'm sure. If the hose were sentient it would probably think to itself, "The pressure inside me is so great, but what I'm producing is terribly small." This is how many people train.

Watch the grimacing gym rats who scream through sloppy form. They'll tell you that it's the effort that counts. How often are they riddled with injuries, covered with straps, wraps and belts? How often do they complain of aches and pains? And most obviously, how far have they actually progressed in physical development over the years of this "method" of work? Effort without technique cannot sustain progression. You burn out or break down without fanatical ascription to form.

SO HOW CAN INTUITIVE TRAINING HELP YOU ASSESS FORM?

Alongside RPE, maintain a record of your **RATE OF PERCEIVED TECHNIQUE** (RPT) — the "Effective Efficiency" of the form you use for your exercises. Concentrate your actions on the actual performance goals of the exercise, and maintain vigilance against superfluous tension and movements. The accuracy of your technique is in direct proportion to the results that you create. Like the analogy of the hose, proper form focuses your effort into a high-pressure stream. The greater that focus the more significant your results, while minimizing any break-down in the container (the hose — in this case YOU!)

Form loss is most generally connected to overtraining or deficient training, but in most cases is attributed to lack of monitoring technique. Consider that Rating of Technique relates to the notion of making your training into "practice." At every training session you should focus on refining your skills.

Exercise selection should be varied too, but in balance. 'Serial monogamy' with your programs in 4–6 week blocks works well to balance the *Law of Adaptation* with the necessity of variety. Volume, intensity, frequency/density, exercise selection, form variations, and time under tension should change every session. Most of the variables should change every 4–6 weeks. More advanced athletes adapt much more rapidly, and programming must change accordingly.

One's subjective experience of the technique can vary from one session to the next, so it's periodically beneficial to videotape yourself to objectively evaluate your form. Compare your RPE with the objective accuracy of your form. *Intuitive Training* will help you balance the subjective experience (RPE) with the objective framework (RT).

Your RPT will also help you determine if you're prepared for a more sophisticated exercise. Only progress to more challenging skills when you've stabilized above 70–80% in your RPT (*Zone-by-Zone Mastering of Intensity* Matveyev, 1977). Do otherwise and you'll be building your house on sand. Refine your current skill before sophisticating it.

Your RPT will also communicate the reliability of your technique. If you're smart you're not just training. You also either enter competitions or set personal records that you must break under certain conditions. If your competitive RT is lower than your training RT then you may need to explore methods of controlling your emotional arousal and increasing your mental toughness. Here are a few suggestions:

- Remove factors that distract you from learning and refining your technique (such as mirrors, music and people)
- Prevent yourself from moving prematurely into more sophisticated skills
- Master mental toughness and emotional control in the tasks that bring you the greatest challenge and fear

This approach actually involves three values — Rating of Perceived Exertion (RPE), Rating of Perceived Discomfort (RPD) and Rating of Perceived Technique (RPT). Solely by differentiating between exertion, technique and discomfort, one develops an incredibly powerful perception, but this goes much, much deeper.

THE PROBLEM WITH GUYS

In general (and this is only a generalization!), men have great difficulty differentiating between **effort and technique.** Before CST, most of them didn't even have the memetic concept structure to support understanding the difference.

Men love exertion (a fact that I suspect relates to testosterone). As a result, *men often perceive more effort to be 'better,' even if good form is sacrificed during exercise.* They experience great difficulty in taking the time to PRACTICE SKILLS, and instead rush to brute effort.

For the early stages of a skill, say the first 2–3 years, exertion and technique are inversely proportional: as you increase exertion, technique goes downhill. This is typically why men often injure themselves within the first 2–3 years, need to take time off to recover, then start again and injure themselves again within another 2–3 years. It's a cycle that I've seen among men so often that I recognized the pattern before I understood the cause.

When men begin with CST they must learn to assign and OBSERVE the value of their perceived exertion and technique. Daily practice makes obvious that, as exertion numbers go up, technique goes down. This is also why I've given them a governor: they can only increase variables (intensity, volume, density, velocity, etc.) if they have a consistent RPE of 6 or less (on a scale of 1–10, 10 being the greatest effort) and a consistent RPT of 8 or higher in a particular exercise (exercise = a SKILL!). With this governor they most often regain the intuitive insight to responsibly control their own training load.

THE PROBLEM WITH GALS

With women (again — this is a generalization) I observe a different, though not necessarily opposite, phenomenon. Women reap the most benefit from learning the skill of assigning value to and observing the difference between **effort** and **discomfort.** Women seem to have no problem dedicating themselves to proper technique. They listen, ask questions and observe any changes in form. It's quite refreshing — except when it comes time to follow-through with consistently increasing levels of exertion.

When it comes to exerting themselves, in GENERAL, *women often associate increased exertion with increased discomfort.* This sets up dangerous patterns of failure and injury because, if they assume that exertion is (injurious) pain, they may CREATE injuries. I've seen this in women who become so afraid of exerting themselves that they end up hurting themselves because they feel out of control.

The other side of this regards their aversion to exertion, since it becomes associated with discomfort. This can set up negative patterns and a downward spiral of inactivity.

The very fact that women involved in CST learn to differentiate between values for exertion and discomfort reframes their entire approach to fitness (and more importantly, to life in general). The great thing about women is that, since they dedicate themselves to increasing form, they learn to apply force properly much faster than men. This is why I advise women, in general, to achieve an RPT of 8 or higher and RPD of 6 or lower before increasing RPE above 5. In this way the exertion takes on the shape of funneled technique — exertion through form — which is the most controlled effort.

It would be interesting to discuss the nature of these gender differences, but essentially it's a generalization. I've observed men who exhibit the effort-discomfort issue most common in women, and I've observed women who exhibit the effort-technique issue most common in men.

Regardless, the intuitive approach to health and fitness helps you to turn your focus and concentration where you need it, on the subjective experience of exercise, with the granularity of vision needed to gain the 3 C's: *confidence, competence* and *coordination.*

DIAGNOSTICS AND ASSESSMENT

Maximize your strengths and mitigate your weaknesses until those weaknesses become strengths. But you must address your weaknesses. Where are you weak? To determine the specificity of your training you must continually reassess your training program. Target your genetic weaknesses. If you have natural endurance, target strength or speed in creating your program cycle. Avoid working redundantly, which leads to overtraining. Work dissimilar movements that hit the intended sport specific conditioning from as many angles as possible (while still closely approximating the range, depth and scope of the activity). Further, assess your entire program for integration. If you already work long endurance sessions within your activity or sport, do not work for endurance on the same day that you partake of your sport. Assess the entire impact of your cycle.

Although the greatest strength derives from grooved skills, new skills increase your sum total strength development. As you periodize your training programs, remember to add variety from one program to the next, and do so in relation to your ratio of strength to weakness.

Always keep a Training Journal. Record your exercises, times, reps, sets, and most importantly your Rate of Perceived Exertion. This will allow you to assess your progress and will give you the power to diagnose a new program and cycle. Establish and pursue clearly defined and realistic goals. Remember, you adapt to any event that you perform, and that event becomes more easily repeatable. The basic rule is this:

CYCLE OR CIRCUIT, BUT DO NOT COCKTAIL.

Cycle training allows you to work a solid foundation of GPP to SPP to Physical Skill to Mental/Emotional Skills (*Training Hierarchy Pyramid*™). However, if you are an athlete and time and energy become a premium, remember that Clubbell® Training is supplementary, not primary.

Circuit training employs a variety of exercises (such as bodyweight calisthenics, Clubbell®, rope, rings, dumbbell, sandbag, medicine ball, rubber strand, etc…). The *entire circuit* has a specifically focused intensity/volume protocol in mind. Results become clearly defined and approachable. Circuit protocol can be cycled.

Cocktail training (the term was coined by Dr. Tudor Bompa) refers to mixing various exercise programs together that have arbitrary and even contradicting goals. Basically, the bottom line can be understood as this: If you don't have clearly defined, realistic goals when you train, you will "go nowhere fast."

THE GOLDEN RATIO OF FITNESS

Training should be coordinated precisely with one's innate and idiosyncratic tendencies. With that in mind, CST incorporates a scientific approach to the optimal relationship between work and rest as it relates to the Golden Ratio (Robert Sandler and Dennis Lobstein, _Consistent Winning_, 1992).

When this approach was disclosed to me, I was surprised at how it consistently resonated with not only my personal history and personal training logs but with those of numerous clients.

THE FIBONACCI SEQUENCE AND THE GOLDEN MEAN

The theory is that the body follows a cycle of variation based on the Fibonacci tendency (the emphasis here is on <u>natural tendency</u> rather than exact law), which was named after the mathematician Leonardo Fibonacci. The "Fibonacci sequence" involves a continuous adding of the previous two numbers to get the next, i.e. 1, 2, 3, 5, 8, 13, 21, 34,…

The pattern relates to a natural phenomenon of sequence proportions of 1:1.618 or 0.618, often called the Golden Mean. Many natural phenomena adhere to this proportion, including the spacing of flower leaves, the design of shells, stock market fluctuations, and even (it is proposed) human development. I state that this is a pseudo scientific approach in that science can neither prove nor disprove this 'tendency.'

This tendency, upon reflection, appears throughout my training logs, in both the micro and macro cycling of my programs and in tapering to my event performance zone.

INTUITIVE TRAINING MEETS THE FIBONACCI WAVE

I have always organized training to reflect the organism's natural tendency to wave rest and work. Moreover, this is why I endorse Intuitive Training as holding priority over ANY specific program. The key is to tap into your idiosyncratic rhythm and to train appropriately.

I believe that the Fibonacci tendency most effectively explains how we can hope to proactively organize training to "peak" on any given event day. Basically, the underlying assumption is that, if we can render the Fibonacci sequence in a program, then our rhythm resonates with it, syncs up, and allows us to influence tapering to a specific time for peak performance.

The Fibonacci waving of rest and work operates on the premise of variable intensity: active recovery, light, moderate and heavy work. Each of these elements must be organized within each macro and micro cycle. Most people make the mistake of only organizing an active recovery day or cycle when they suffer an injury or when they overtrain. We must PLAN active recovery to PREVENT these occurrences.

ENERGY LEVELS AND THE FIBONACCI SEQUENCE

Many times in the past, when I structured a linear ladder in an attempt to peak, I would plan my day of rest for the day before the event. However, when the day of the event arrived, as often as not I found myself sluggish, and I experienced what I can only describe as energy 'jits' (I felt the biochemical 'rush' of the event but couldn't channel that energy into my performance). Moreover, I tended to have a high energy day a couple days after the event, when I took a day of rest prior to the event. Something was out of sync. I learned to pay close attention to these energy fluctuations. We must listen to ourselves and get in tune with our natural rhythm.

Many people push through low-energy days to their detriment. I'm not talking about days when you didn't effectively plan your nutrition and you experience wonky energy levels. I'm referring to days when you just feel low-speed, high-drag. Pushing through these membranes only causes performance to hemorrhage when the subsequent high-energy day would have happened.

Contrarily, during events when I planned (or accidentally experienced) low intensity prep several days before an event, I nailed a full-on high-energy yield day during the event. I recall experiencing optimal performance every time that I deliberately or inadvertently arranged my schedule in this way. I was as stunned by the Golden Mean approach as anyone when I saw how closely it matched my experience.

It seems that, across many sports, successful coaches produced winning athletes and teams by ending any training 5–7 days before an event, and varying light to moderate intensity over the final days prior to the event. The key to this approach is that *you may add more rest, but you may not add more work.*

TAPERING TO PEAK PERFORMANCE

Think of it as a ratchet. I've used this analogy for over a decade, and it works. You need to torque BACK in order to catapult ahead. To CREATE a peak day you need to begin by strategically planning a rest period FIRST. This torquing back relates to PHI (the Fibonacci sequence) — you only begin to benefit from rest 3 days afterwards.

I'll give you the 3-Day Peak process. Count backwards starting from the target peak day as Day 3, the day prior as Day 2, and the day before that as Day 1. Now count back 3 days from that. Those are your three days of rest (you can do active recovery on those days). You then ramp up to your peak day from days 1 and 2 to day 3.

3 DAY SEQUENCE

Active Recovery	Rest	Rest	Light	Moderate	PEAK
Day -3	Day -2	Day -1	Day 1	Day 2	Day 3

3 WEEK SEQUENCE

		Rest Day -5	Rest Day -4	Active Recovery Day -3	Rest Day -2	Rest Day -1
Train Day 1	Train Day 2	Train Day 3	Train Day 4	Train Day 5	Train Day 6	Train Day 7
Train Day 8	Train Day 9	Train Day 10	Train Day 11	Train Day 12	Train Day 13	Train Day 14
Train Day 15	Active Recovery Day -3	Rest Day -2	Rest Day -1	Light Day 1	Moderate Day 2	PEAK Day 3

3 MONTH SEQUENCE

	Rest Day -13	Rest Day -12	Active Recovery Day -11	Rest Day -10	Rest Day -9	Light Day -8
Light Day -7	Moderate Day -6	Rest Day -5	Rest Day -4	Active Recovery Day -3	Rest Day -2	Rest Day -1
Train Day 1	Train Day 2	Train Day 3	Train Day 4	Train Day 5	Train Day 6	Train Day 7
Train Day 8	Train Day 9	Train Day 10	Train Day 11	Train Day 12	Train Day 13	Train Day 14
Train Day 15	Train Day 16	Train Day 17	Train Day 18	Train Day 19	Train Day 20	Train Day 21
Active Recovery Day -3	Rest! Day -2	Rest Day -1	Train Day 1	Train Day 2	Train Day 3	Train Day 4
Train Day 5	Train Day 6	Train Day 7	Train Day 8	Train Day 9	Train Day 10	Train Day 11
Train Day 12	Train Day 13	Train Day 14	Train Day 15	Train Day 16	Train Day 17	Train Day 18
Train Day 19	Train Day 20	Train Day 21	Train Day 22	Train Day 23	Train Day 24	Train Day 25
Train Day 26	Train Day 27	Train Day 28	Train Day 29	Train Day 30	Train Day 31	Train Day 32
Train Day 33	Train Day 34	Rest Day -5	Rest Day -4	Active Recovery Day -3	Rest Day -2	Rest Day -1
Train Day 1	Train Day 2	Train Day 3	Train Day 4	Train Day 5	Train Day 6	Train Day 7
Train Day 8	Train Day 9	Train Day 10	Train Day 11	Train Day 12	Train Day 13	Train Day 14
Train Day 15	Active Recovery Day -3	Rest Day -2	Rest Day -1	Light Day 1	Moderate Day 2	PEAK Day 3

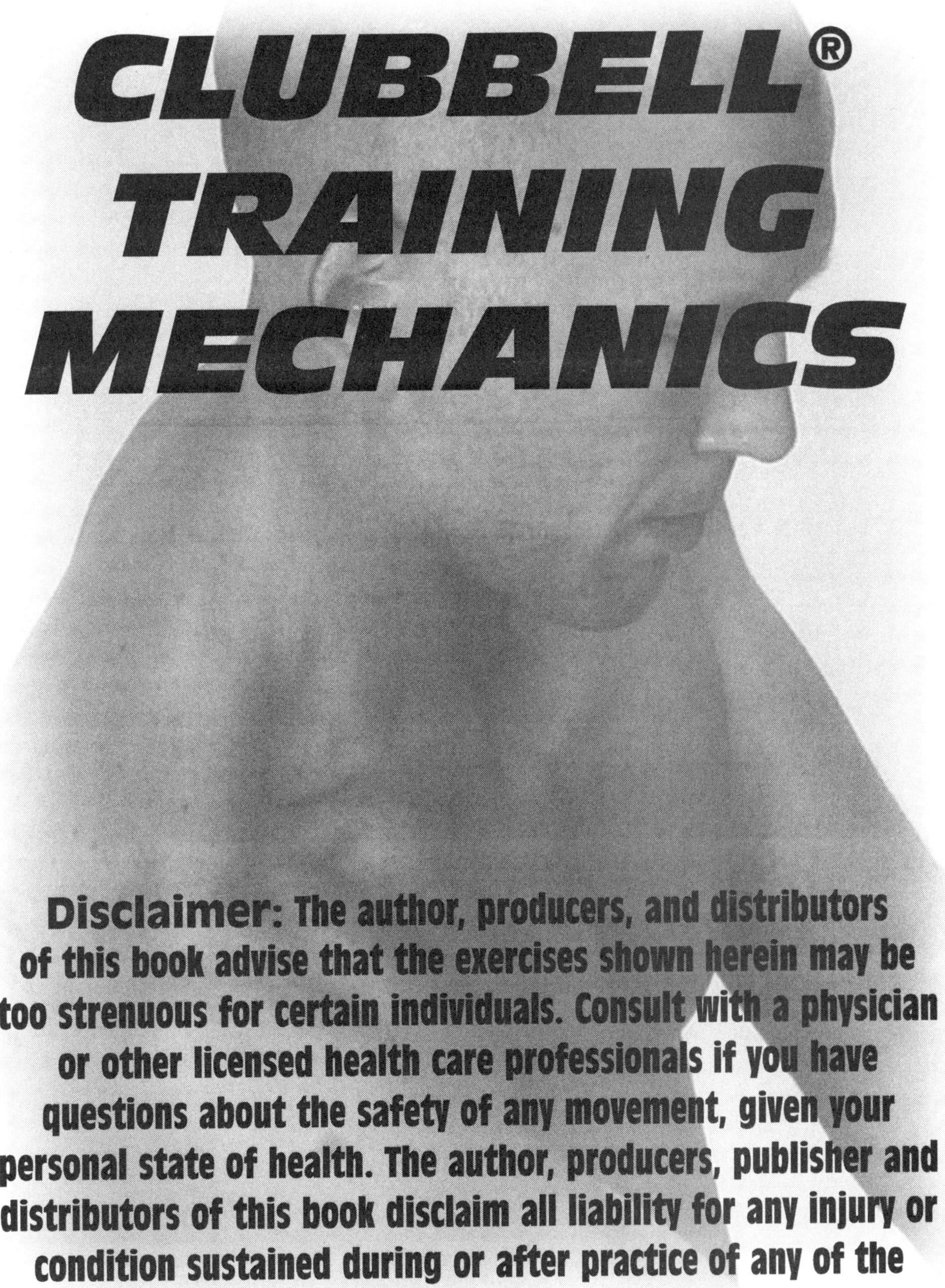

CLUBBELL® TRAINING MECHANICS

Disclaimer: The author, producers, and distributors of this book advise that the exercises shown herein may be too strenuous for certain individuals. Consult with a physician or other licensed health care professionals if you have questions about the safety of any movement, given your personal state of health. The author, producers, publisher and distributors of this book disclaim all liability for any injury or condition sustained during or after practice of any of the exercises demonstrated on this book.

All free weight exercises are inherently dangerous and could cause grave bodily injury if you use improper form or go to muscle failure. If during your exercise you lose control, something goes wrong in your technique, or you inappropriately go to failure, fatigue or exhaustion, let the equipment get to the floor in the safest route possible.

If you are in harm's way of Clubbells descent, push them out of your way to safety. Letting Clubbells drop may result in property damage, including damage to the Clubbells themselves. Furthermore, any person, any creature or thing in the vicinity may suffer damage or injury if you let the Clubbells fall or fly.

There are precautionary safety movements that you can use to minimize harm. Learn and practice these as skilled exercises in and of themselves before you practice or train any other movements!

SAFETY STRAP

You have another trainee safety design built into your Clubbells as "training wheels," to be used until you become competent in your practice: the wrist lanyard. This safety strap <u>does not prevent and only offers a chance to minimize damage or injury</u>. And, like an air bag or seat belt in a car, it may not minimize damage or injury at all. Use the safety strap for **emergency** braking only. Do not depend on the safety strap to save you. It cannot. Only you can prevent and minimize damage or injury. You must "put on the brakes" to engage the safety strap: this constitutes a flex of your wrist and forearm (as hard as you can) as a hook to snag the lanyard. If in an emergency you must abort the exercise and drop the Clubbells, you may also keep your fingers and wrist straight so that the lanyard slips off without snaring.

APPROACH

Always approach Clubbells in the parked position before a lift, and end each set in the parked position. Never hand Clubbells to other people. Park them and let the next athlete approach them, but only after proper instruction. Don't allow anyone to handle your Clubbells without proper instruction first.

It's imperative that these mechanics be understood and applied during all Clubbell® exercises to ensure the efficiency of the training method. Study and practice all of these BEFORE attempting any of the exercises outlined in the later chapters of this manual.

These are the key elements for attaching your Clubbells as a structural extension of your body such that you'll reap 100% of the health benefits from every exercise while protecting your body from injury:

1. Aligning your Spine
2. Confirming your Grip
3. Packing your Shoulders
4. Locking your Arms
5. Activating your Core
6. Recruiting your Hips
7. Driving your Legs

ALIGNING YOUR SPINE

Align your spine as though you were effortlessly balancing a large stack of heavy books on your head. Unless you have structural distortions due to overly dense connective tissue or vertebral damage, this visualization will help you to achieve proper long crown to coccyx spinal alignment.

Stand as if a string holds you from the crown of your head, dangling you like a marionette. Keep your mouth closed and your chin slightly tucked. Lift your heart without arching your spine. Allow a natural curve in your lower back, but avoid overdoing it (hyper-lordosis). Use core activation to ensure alignment generation from the core outwards. Keep your shoulders packed to maintain a compact, "springy" structure. Use hip recruitment and leg drive to stay under the primary control of your head, but allow yourself to "hang" from the head downwards.

Maintaining this spinal alignment gives you 100% of the health benefits of CST. Not maintaining proper alignment, especially under the load of progressive resistance training, can reinforce and create performance impediments, as well as potential injuries. Always establish proper crown to coccyx spinal alignment before adding any load to your structure, and maintain this alignment throughout every moment while under load.

CONFIRMING YOUR GRIP
Micro-loading Grip Choke Depth

Choose the distance between the knob and barrel head on the neck (handle) where you intend to grip. The closer to the barrel head and the farther away from the knob, the closer your grip is to the center of mass of the equipment. The closer your grip to the center of mass, the less leverage challenge and the easier it is to perform an exercise. Contrarily, the closer you are to the knob and the farther you are from the center of mass, the less leverage advantage you have and the greater the challenge of the exercise.

You adjust the intensity of the exercise by changing the relationship of your grip placement or "choke depth." *Full-choke* refers to gripping closest on the neck to the barrel head. *Zero-choke* refers to gripping closest on the neck to the knob.

Micro-loading is an incredibly innovative and internationally successful training phenomenon that allows you to adjust your grip depth in small increments so that you never become neurologically overwhelmed. With the unique length of the gripping area (neck, or handle) of the Clubbell®, you may adjust the leverage challenge by the tiniest of increments. Taking advantage of this powerful neuromuscular phenomenon and design innovation of the Clubbell® allows you to take your fitness to high levels in a short time span.

Right and Left Grip

These are the two grips that will be used in every two-handed exercise. The Right Grip refers to how a right-handed individual would hold a baseball bat or golf club, with the left hand nearest the end of the shaft and the right hand directly above it on the shaft. Left Grip, then, refers to how a "southpaw" would grip a baseball bat or golf club, with the right hand nearest the end of the shaft and the left above it for control.

Split Grip

Ty Cobb was known for this peculiar way of holding a bat, but it was Doug Szolek (author of the _Two Handed Clubbell Training_ DVD) who pioneered this technique in Clubbell® training.

Instead of gripping with both hands firmly near the end of the bat, Cobb would keep his controlling hand nearer the middle of the bat for added precision in his swing. The mechanical advantage of this half-choked grip is obvious. It is exactly what you'll need to know in order to increase your control of the Clubbell® in some of the more difficult lifts. Take advantage of the extra-long handle of the Clubbell® and notice that there is huge potential for incremental progression to a zero-choke grip.

Complimentary Grip

Complementary refers to the two independent but collaborative forces of your two hands, in other words the isometric action of each hand in controlling the Clubbell® when using two hands at once. The ***locking hand*** is at the end of the handle (the left hand in Right Grip) and the ***power transfer hand*** is the hand in the middle of the handle (the right hand in a Right Grip) as long as the head of the Clubbell® is down. Once the barrel head of the Clubbell® rises, the locking hand and power transfer hand trade roles. Clubbell® control and stabilization in two-handed exercise hinges upon on this mechanic.

Intelligent Grip

Because the muscles of the grip/forearm fatigue rapidly when applying maximal grip pressure, the Intelligent Grip Protocol was developed to actively relax the grip as the Clubbell passed through points of weightlessness in the Range of Motion (ROM) of a given exercise. This unique free weight grip developed to account for the circular trajectories of a tool that pulls THROUGH the hand (the swung Clubbell®) rather than against the fingers (the lifted dumbbell or barbell).

An Intelligent Grip permits periods of relaxation in the movement, so that blood flow through the muscle tissues can increase and can clean out the waste products of muscular contraction that lead to fatigue. The fingers intelligently and independently vary their grip intensity.

In general, the finger grip changes from a modified "OK" hand signal to the configuration of holding a funnel or ice-cream cone.

The mechanics differ slightly in two-handed exercises. In general during two-handed exercises, when one hand is tight the other is relaxed. To tell which one is which, look at the barrel head of your Clubbell®. When the barrel head hangs toward the ground, the hand nearest the knob should be crush-gripping while the other hand should be slightly relaxed for added sensitivity to control needs. When the head of the Clubbell® rises to point to the sky the grip protocol shifts. Now the upper hand must crush-grip the handle and the hand near the knob will relax and control the Clubbell®.

When you combine the mechanics of the Intelligent Grip with the Complementary Grip you maximize your efficiency at acquiring the skill of every exercise.

Leverage Grip

For maximum stability you would normally crush grip the handle. However, since the Clubbell® carries through circular motions, you need to allow for adequate mobility while maintaining control of the Clubbell®. The Leverage Grip is a very specific way of gripping the Clubbell® that will prevent you from incurring overuse injuries and from fatiguing too quickly.

Hold your left hand up so that your palm is facing you. Pretend that you hold a Clubbell® in that hand. In the Leverage Grip your pinky acts as the anchor against the center of mass prying out of your grasp. Look at the circle created by your thumb and index finger. They act as the fulcrum. The mechanics of using a can opener are identical to this grip. Take a look at the **Wrist Cast** and at the two-handed variant, the **Crow Bar,** to get an exercise visual on this mechanic.

PACKING YOUR SHOULDERS

This refers to keeping your shoulder joint closed and packed by locking your pecs and lats throughout the motion. Using a tight pec/lat lock to keep your shoulders firmly in joint is supremely important for maintaining and developing the health and strength of your shoulders.

As long as your shoulders are *"confirmed"* (in a 'closed and packed' position) the stress of the swinging Clubbell® transfers to your structure without excess strain to your soft connective tissue. However, if you let your shoulders fly loose through these movements, then the load placed on the connective tissues of the joint may lead to injury.

Sitting on your shins, confirm your shoulder by raising your arm in front of you with your elbow locked. Be sure that your chest is parallel to the floor, and lean into the floor with your thumb and pointer finger gripped as though you were holding a saber or a TV remote control. As your body weight pushes past your shoulder, roll your shoulder back and down so that it is locked in place. Now your shoulder is confirmed. This closed packed position is maintained throughout all exercises.

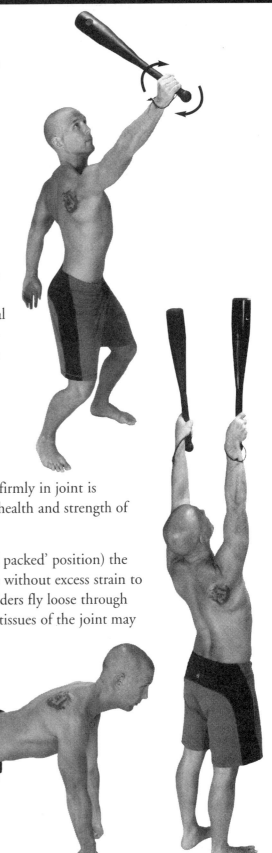

Practicing the Shoulder Pack with a Basic Swing

- This should be done only after you have reconditioned your breathing patterns by practicing **Disciplined Breathing** (reference the Breath Mastery Scale) with the **Basic Swing.**
- It will be helpful to have a mirror, or even better a partner present, to critique your shoulder position. You could also demonstrate to your partner what your shoulder looks like when it is in Closed/Packed Position.
- Begin by performing Basic Swings such that your **Disciplined Breathing** and **Intelligent Grip** Protocol are happening unconsciously.
- Swing through the arc maintaining a strong **Shoulder Pack** to keep your shoulder confirmed.
- When you are comfortable with this, take the swings all the way overhead to **Torch Position.** As you catch the weight in torch position, be sure that your shoulder has remained Closed and Packed throughout the arc.
- Have your partner critique your shoulder form while you are performing this exercise.

Initially it may seem like holding the **Shoulder Pack** will be draining to your strength, but as you practice it increases the efficiency, offsets the load bearing arm, and helps to groove the motions much faster.

Two-Handed Clubbell® Exercise and Shoulder Pack

Two-handed Clubbell® work adds another degree of difficulty to holding Shoulder Pack throughout an exercise because each shoulder travels through a different range of motion when both hands grip the same implement.

Pay extra attention to your shoulders until you develop the sensitivity to know when your shoulders are closed and packed and when they are not. It will help in the early stages to have a mirror or a training partner familiar with the proper form of the exercises that you're performing.

LOCKING YOUR ARMS

Arm Lock refers to making certain of proper wrist alignment, fully locked out elbows, and proper elbow rotation. You will need proper Arm Lock to tap 100% of the benefit of Clubbell® training and to prevent injuries such as tendonitis. You cannot establish proper Arm Lock without proper Shoulder Pack.

Elbow Pit Rotation

Throughout Clubbell® exercises rotate your elbow pits (the soft interior of your elbow joint which is hidden when the elbow joint is fully flexed) inside and upwards.

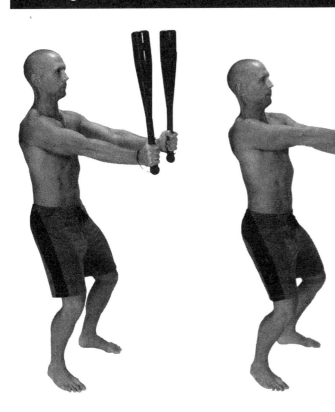

For example, the Flag Position demonstrates Shoulder Pack, locking the elbows (elbow 'pits' pointed toward the sky), and wrists properly tensed to fix them in place. Arm Lock allows you to make the Clubbell® an "extension of your body" rather than merely an implement that acts independently of your whole bodily motion.

Short and Long Arms

When grasping the Clubbell® handle with both hands at once, you need to pay extra attention to the Short and Long Arms of the given motion. This is of primary concern when swinging the Clubbell® in lower body ranges of motion. The Short Arm is the one nearest the knob and Long Arm is the one closer to the barrel head of the Clubbell®.

Throughout an exercise the **Long Arm** should be the primary load bearer, remaining straight and locked. The **Short Arm** acts to provide auxiliary guidance to the motion, staying bent but ready.

If you allow the Short Arm to bear too much of the load while it is bent it will develop residual tension in the wrist, elbow, and shoulder as soft tissues try to compensate for a lack of structural alignment. Building off of this is the likelihood that your upper spine will also be pulled out of alignment if you are not able to maintain closed packed shoulders throughout the exercise and straight locked arms at appropriate times in the exercises. Also notice that, even though the Long Arm is bearing most of the load, the Short Arm still maintains Shoulder Pack.

Wrist Alignment

Proper Wrist Alignment refers to having zero flexion or extension on the wrists when holding the Clubbell®. Make a fist with your palm pointed downwards. Lay a pencil on your forearm over your wrist so that half of the pencil lies on your hand. There should be no space between your wrist and the pencil. This will help you to establish and maintain proper wrist alignment so that you receive 100% of the health benefits of Clubbell® exercise.

ACTIVATING YOUR CORE

Much has been written above regarding the *Breath Mastery Scale*. Here is a synopsis of how to efficiently use your breathing to activate your core so that you gain 100% of the benefit of every exercise while protecting yourself from injury:

Fear and Anger Level Breathing

Unless you have practiced, when facing effort you will either inhale through exertion or you will inhale and hold your breath to exert yourself. You will either do this passively (Fear level breathing) or actively (Anger or Force level breathing). This is an inefficient exercise breathing pattern and a danger to health and longevity.

Discipline Level Breathing

In general, your default breathing practice should be to actively exhale on and through exertion. As you exhale, contract your abdominal wall as much as you can and hold it contracted through the entire movement. Activating your core through conscious exhalation and contraction is a skill that you will continue to develop with practice.

You don't need to worry about inhaling; it will happen naturally as a result of your deliberate exhalation through the effort phase of an exercise. As you practice you will discover a 'groove' for the breathing pattern, and you'll develop a highly efficient rhythm that is unique to you. This rhythm will be activated simply by consciously exhaling on effort. Everything else will take care of itself.

For example, the effort phase of the Basic Swing is on the up-swing of the Clubbells as they come out of the back-swing behind your knees. The effort continues until you complete the hip snap and dig into the ground, which sends the Clubbells on until they find free fall (where their upward momentum equals the force of gravity pulling them down). Disciplined Breathing exhales through this entire movement, from the Clubbells far behind your knees all the way up to hip snap. The inhalation sucks back in without your conscious intention as you allow the Clubbells to swing down and back into the ready "ski-jump" position.

Flow Level Breathing

As you develop your skill in a particular exercise you will suddenly realize that you have been breathing differently. You may 'forget' to actively exhale on effort (Disciplined Level Breathing). You'll realize that instead you're "being breathed" by the combination of the movement of the exercise and your structure compressing air out of your lungs.

For example, let's look again at the Basic Swing. As you develop your skill with a particular choke depth and specific weight you'll notice that you no longer need to exhale on the up-swing to put power into the Clubbells with your entire body. You'll discover that your skill allows you to relax into the exercise. As you compress your body down into the "ski jump" position with the Clubbells far behind your knees an exhalation pushes out of you as your torso and thighs approach each other. Complementing that motion you find that, when you fire your legs pushing through the ground to send the Clubbells into the up-swing, the air rushes back into your lungs as you decompress by moving your torso away from your thighs. Like a bellows, the air rushes out via the movement of your structure compressing your lungs and rushes back in as the movement allows your structure to decompress your lungs. You have then tapped into Flow Level Breathing.

Breath Development is Specific!

Every time you change a variable, the breathing may 'down-shift'. If you're performing the Basic Swing with 15-lbs. Clubbells and progress to Flow Breathing you may find that, when you grab your 25-lbs. Clubbells and perform the Basic Swing, your breathing may down-shift to Force Breathing. This will require you to actively apply Disciplined Breathing to groove the skill with the higher intensity. Down-shifting of the breath can occur when you change any variable, not just weight. Down-shifting can happen from decreasing your grip choke depth, from increasing the speed of your swing (causing more torque), from holding the Clubbells in a Leverage position (causing greater force production), from attempting a personal record in number of repetitions, from performing in public, at a competition or in front of a class, and of course from selecting a new exercise.

RECRUITING YOUR HIPS

Like *Securing your Grip, Packing your Shoulders, Locking your Arms,* and *Activating your Core*, the key to tying the Clubbell® to the body (and not merely the arms) is to *Recruit your Hips*. By doing so you tap into the incredibly strong anterior and posterior tension chains. The hips involve four actions: snap, sit-back, sway and root.

Hip Snap

To access 100% of the training effect of CST and to prevent injury you must move the Clubbells through their complete range of motion. This means that you must tie the Clubbells to the piston-like up and down motion of your body compressing and decompressing. When the hips are fully extended and locked forward, you access Hip Snap.

By using Hip Snap the positive stress induced by the Clubbell® passes to your structure without unnecessary strain transferring to your back and without undue shortening of your hip flexors from insufficient extension.

Side Hip Snap

In certain lateral and angular motions, such as the Side Swing and the Side Semi, one hip will lock out while the other remains flexed. To prepare for this, it's important to study and practice the other hip actions below (in particular the Hip Sway and Hip Root).

Hip Sit-Back

Without practice, most people confuse the Hip Sit-Back with bending over. Sitting-back refers to moving your bottom back onto an imaginary chair while keeping your back straight, not rounded over.

Your shoulders, knees, and feet should be in vertical alignment, with your feet pointed absolutely forward as though you were standing on railroad tracks.

When you're in the Sit-Back with Clubbells in front of you counter-balancing, your weight will be predominantly mid-foot to resting on your heels (as in the Rock-it Drill). When you're also folding at the hips, torso to thighs (as in the Basic Swing), your weight lies from mid-foot to ball-of-foot.

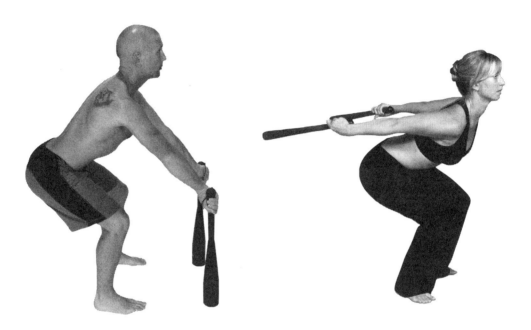

Hip Sway

Hip Sway laterally transfers your weight from one hip to the next in an effort to counter balance the swinging Clubbell®. You can also use the Hip Sway to accelerate the Clubbell® as it swings by you. Dip your knee to use more of your body to move the Clubbell®.

For maximum explosiveness, practice and develop your Side Hip Snap out of Hip Sway. Your far heel lifts as your near hip snaps and locks out directly to the side.

Keep your arms locked and your shoulders packed to cause the most energy transfer of this side Hip Snap to the Clubbell®.

Hip Root

Hip Root involves two methods, depending upon whether you are supporting weight directly overhead (through the Root Lock) or to one side (through the Side Hip Root).

Root Lock involves the grounding of overhead weight by tilting the pelvis and clenching your glutes, quads and calves with locked knees. It includes a sphincter lock and a urinary lock (imagine cutting off urination in mid-flow). Root Lock requires practice. Begin standing and place your arms overhead. Look upwards, tilt your pelvis forward and slightly upwards as you clench your glutes, contract your core and perform the sphincter and urinary lock. Then relax. Repeat this 15–25 times per day for a week and you'll have the technique primed for adding weight.

Side Hip Root refers to grounding your weight and the force of the Clubbell® into one hip and then straight into the ground. To get an idea of what I'm talking about, stand up and shift 90% of your body weight onto one leg. To do so you must center your pelvis over one leg. Next, push your hip even further to the side to create a shelf under your obliques. Finally, bend the knee over which you are centered. Your planted leg screws into the ground so that, if you were pushed from nearly any angle (particularly perpendicular to your pelvis), you feel immovable.

Once you're acquainted with the feeling of the Side Hip Root, practice with only about 50–60% of your weight shifted to the rooted leg. Stand with your feet a bit wider than shoulder width. Root over one hip as deeply as you can without removing the stability of the opposite leg. Your pelvis turns as it winds around your hip. Your core remains activated as you turn your trunk with it. Your hips and shoulders square in the same direction. Transfer to your other hip. Repeat this exercise back and forth several times while visualizing your legs as corkscrews drilling into the floor.

DRIVING YOUR LEGS

Understanding how to properly drive your legs into the ground gives you access to 100% of the health benefits of Clubbells. Driving the legs involves several key components: mid-foot press, toe grip, foot rock, and of course quad and glute contraction (which obviously connects into *Recruiting your Hip* and *Activating your Core*).

When people try to 'lift' weight they tend to tear down good structure and to use poor form to bear the load. For example, when performing a Clean, without practice of good form, people round their backs, shrug their shoulders, and fail to fully extend their legs and hips.

A proper Clean begins by gripping the ground with your toes and visualizing that you are explosively pushing the Earth away from the Clubbells. Simultaneous to this, the Clean rips the Clubbells off the ground, causing your weight to rock forward from mid-foot to ball of foot. Then, as you dip under the Clubbells, you rock back to a mid-foot / heel balance to absorb the shock of the weight in your frame.

Shock Absorption

Shock Absorption refers to the action of storing and releasing the rubber band-like energy of Clubbell® training. The body is built like Buckminster Fuller's Tensegrity Model — it is composed of hard compressive struts pushing outwards in a sea of continuous tension that is pulling inwards, finding the optimal balance to create the magical anti-gravitational act of human upright locomotion.

The human form is made up of one interconnected synergistic web of myofascia — or one muscle with hundreds of insertion points. We are actually a double-bag system. The inner bag contains hard tissue: *bones* and *cartilage*. Where it is cling-wrapped around the bones it is called *periosteum;* and where it wraps the ends of bones together it's called *joint capsule*. The outer bag contains an electric jelly that we call *muscle*. Where it wraps the muscle we call it *fascia*, and where it tacks down to the inner bag we call it *muscle attachment* or *insertion point*.

It is important to understand tensegrity somewhat so that we don't view the body as a brick wall upon which we place weight. Every weight that we place upon ourselves 'loads' us (through the principle of *Stored Elastic Energy* discussed earlier). This helps us to understand that we use good form in order to most efficiently absorb and retranslate force, like the steel springs of an older automobile suspension system.

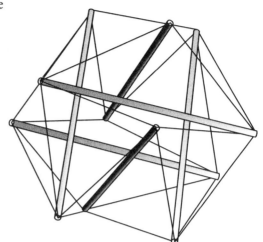

For example, combining the proper wrist position, elbow flexion, shoulder pack, crown to coccyx alignment, core activation, hip recruitment, and leg drive allows you to absorb the recovery of the Clubbells from the ballistic explosion of the Clean. In the Clean you dip your body underneath the upwardly traveling Clubbells that you ripped from the floor. Before the Clubbells begin their downward travel (and optimally during their free-fall when gravity zeros-out their ascent and they are, for a moment, weightless), you establish the platform of good form to absorb them into Order Position. This becomes increasingly more challenging in positions that have very slight deviation potential, such as Torch Position, and great leverage disadvantage, such as Flag Position.

Leg Drive and Shock Absorption differ slightly when swinging weight laterally and angularly, requiring Leg Drive to switch between driving one leg while absorbing with the other, as can be seen in the Side Hip Snap and the Side Hip Root.

An exercise that exemplifies Leg Drive and Shock Absorption is the ***Rock-it Drill.***

Begin in the "Silverback" Ready Position: flat back with crown to coccyx alignment, gripped thumbs down, arms locked, shoulders packed, sitting back, toes gripping.

Perform the Forearm Preswing: Sit up slightly and allow the Clubbells to rock back by turning your thumbs and elbow pits outwards, away from your body. Work to keep the barrel head of the Clubbells swinging parallel to the ground as you rock them back and forth by rotating your arms.

Execute the Body Piston: The piston-action of the hips folds and absorbs down and releases upwards as you reach and extend the Clubbells forwards and backwards. Fold chest to thigh as you dip your bottom down as far back as possible, projecting the Clubbells backwards. Sit deeply backwards into an imaginary chair as you project the Clubbells forwards.

ROCK-IT DRILL

Clubbell® Training Mechanics

Contributed by Carol Britton and Will Chung

CLUBBELL® BASIC POSITIONS

The Basic Positions are the starting and ending points in Clubbell® exercise:

1. Floor Park
2. Ready Position
3. Shoulder Park
   a. Chest Park
4. Arm Stop
5. Order Position
   a. Side Order Position
6. Guard Position
7. Flag Position
   a. Side Flag Position
8. Torch Position
9. Back Position

There are additional variations on these positions which include *Leverage Holds*. These will not be described as Basic Positions because they are less structurally-oriented and more tension performance-oriented than the positions listed above.

Finally, there are a couple other movements that are actually exercises in and of themselves. However, they are also important techniques in the event that you must bail out of a failed movement:

1. *Parry Cast*
2. *Reverse Parry Cast*

Please practice these exercises first. They can be found in the Exercise Selection section below.

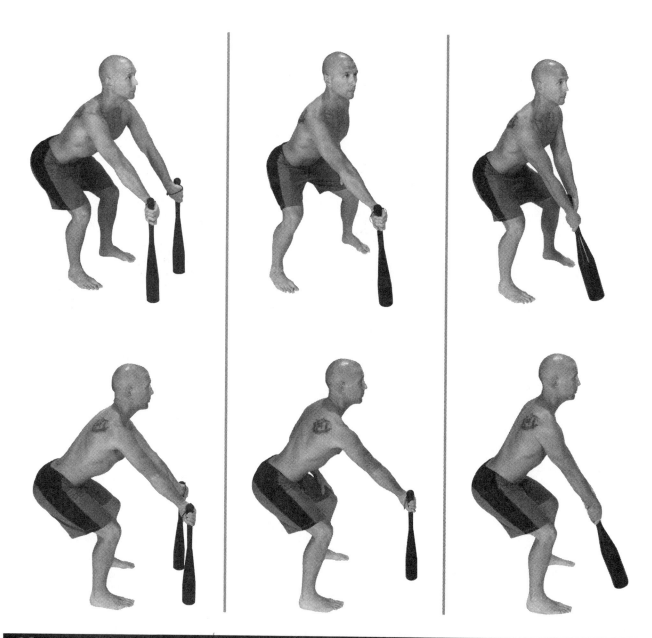

FLOOR PARK

In the park position the Clubbell® sits bottom (barrel head) down just outside your shoulder frame. Floor Park is the ONLY parked position that is not a skill. It is a START position because you have not yet touched the Clubbells. If you are concluding an exercise you move the Clubbell® to Floor Park to complete that exercise, because Floor Park is also an END position.

The park position for a 5-lb Clubbell® or Mini-Clubbell®, or any Clubbell® on an uneven surface, is to lay it down flat.

Avoid jerking the Clubbells to Floor Park position. Move smoothly and deliberately. Always measure the distance between the bottom of the Clubbells and the surface of the floor or ground, taking into account surface contour as well. Remember the length of the Clubbells, and be sure to adequately accommodate their length when parking them on the floor.

READY POSITION — THE SILVERBACK

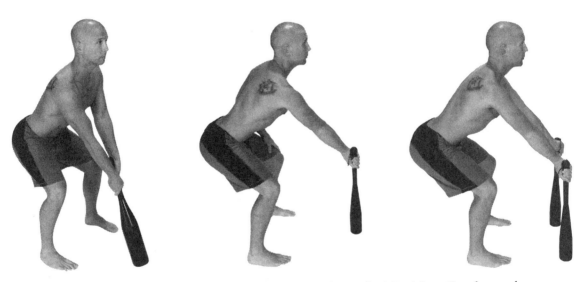

Assume this position after you engage the Clubbells in the Parked Position. Bend your knees to change your level. Keep your back straight and your eyes forward. Bend at the hips, not at the spine. Push your weight back on your heels as you push back with your bottom. Make your lower legs perpendicular to the ground. Your hands are inside the safety straps. Confirm your grip on the Clubbells. Two variations exist: Clubbells in Floor Park or in Hang Position (just off the ground).

SHOULDER PARK

This is the prime catch point for presses, ill-timed casts, or an off-balanced Order Position. Be sure to land the Clubbells as high on your shoulder as you can without hitting your ears, neck, head, or bony surfaces (like your AC joint). Use a knee dip to absorb most of the impact, and as always ensure that you're Packing your Shoulders and not lifting them out of joint to hold the weight.

Aside from its use as a safety position, Shoulder Park may also be used for positive effect in your training. For example, in a Clean to Shoulder Park you could perform a squat, jerk, press, or simply dip to absorb the impact. You would then use your stored and released rising motion to send the Clubbells into a subsequent Swing. Practice going into Shoulder Park from both front and side movements to ensure that your neck, head, and ears do not become injured.

CHEST PARK

Chest Park is a variation on Shoulder Park, except that the Clubbell® barrel head rests against the soft tissue of your chest. This is not a structurally secure position. Use it, when possible, as a safety option in the event of sudden movement deviations caused by poor form. Slow down (brake) the Clubbells into Chest Park rather than catch them there. As soon as you do, move the Clubbells into a more secure structure, such as Floor Park or Order Position.

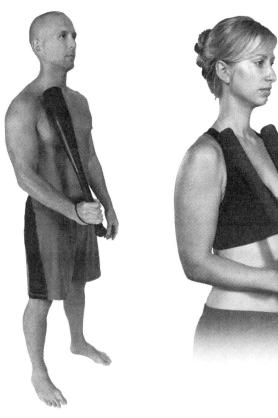

ARM STOP

Hold the Clubbell® in Order Position and yield it across your centerline towards your opposite elbow pit. Catch it in your elbow pit by Shock Absorbing with elbow flexion and hip flexion, as you would catch a football. Do not drop the Clubbell® onto the protruding bones of your elbow or wrist, or even your forearm. As you come out of the absorption, rotate your elbow upwards so that you are balancing the Clubbell® on the thick, soft tissue portion of your forearm.

Remember to absorb with your knees and hips and not with your back. Don't use more force than your arm can withstand!

When on your arm, the Clubbell® sits at approximately a 45° angle to the floor. Your shoulders are down, arms straight and elbows bent in front of you.

Keep your knees bent and your back straight. Keep your shoulders packed; don't shrug. Remember to use the active exhalation of Discipline Breathing when you absorb the Clubbell® into Arm Stop.

ORDER POSITION

Hold the Clubbells bottom-up perpendicular to the floor, parallel with your torso. Keep your elbows pinched inward and bent in front of you using the pec-lat lock of the Shoulder Pack. Hold your hands at approximately the level of your floating ribs. Keep your wrists straight, not bent, to confirm your grip.

Though an isometric hold, Order Position is a dynamic balancing act. Small adjustments in your musculature constantly move the Clubbells, so you must constantly adjust to keep them balanced. Hold Clubbells in Order for between 3–4 seconds, and never longer than 5 seconds.

Do not lock out your knees. Keep your back straight. Keep your shoulders packed; don't shrug. Activate your Core through a deliberate exhalation and core lock-down.

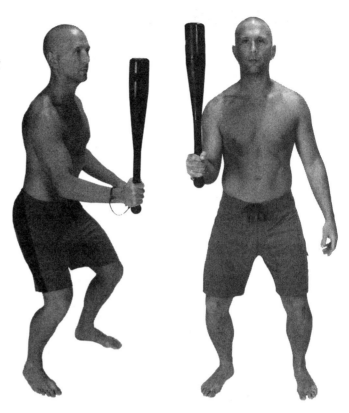

Two-Handed Order Position

Order Position with two hands is relatively the same as it is with one. Keep your shoulders closed and packed and your elbows dug into your ribs so that your entire upper body becomes a single unit under tension. Order position is to be used in conjunction with all frontal swings, cleans, casts, and presses. It is reached when you are holding the Clubbell® directly in line with your centerline.

GUARD POSITION

The Guard Position appears similar to Order but is specialized for two-handed Clubbell® training. Guard position involves keeping the shoulders closed and packed while the elbow of one arm digs into the near hip. The other arm hugs tightly across the front of the body. Both elbows bend at 90° angles in Guard. Given the two sides of the body and the two two-handed grips, there are four possible Guard positions. Identifying them now will save a lot of trouble later in exercise walkthroughs.

- **Right Grip Right Guard** specifically describes holding the Clubbell® with a Right Grip in Guard on the right side of the body.
- **Right Grip Left Guard** identifies holding the Clubbell® with a Right Grip in Guard on the left side of the body.
- **Left Grip Right Guard** refers to holding the Clubbell® with a Left Grip in Guard on the Right side of the body.
- **Left Grip Left Guard** consists of holding the Clubbell® with a Left Grip in Guard on the left side of the body.

FLAG POSITION

Flag Position is an extended Order Position with elbows locked and elbow pits pointed skyward. Pack your shoulders and lock your arms parallel to the ground while maintaining a strong, confirmed grip on the Clubbells.

Flag Position is a dynamic balancing act like Order, but it requires you to totally lock your core to maintain structure, even with the lightest weights at full choke. Flag Position is (and truly all Clubbell® exercise are) not an 'arm' exercise but a whole body experience. As in Order Position, only hold Clubbells in Flag for between 3–4 seconds.

Remember: bend your knees and maintain a straight back. Pack your shoulders tightly and avoid the temptation to shrug them out of position. You'll need very strong core activation to hold them at such a leveraged distance, so deliberately exhale hard and lock down your core.

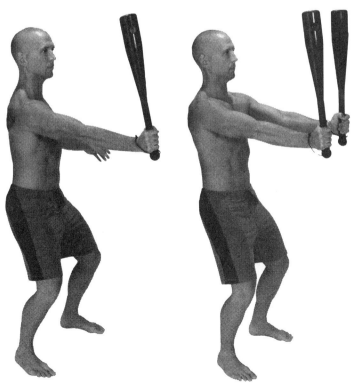

Two-Handed Flag Position

The Two-Handed Flag Position is held in your centerline in either a Right or Left Grip. The Two-Handed Flag Position will require you to focus heavily upon the Complementary Grip as well as the Leverage Grip.

TORCH POSITION

Torch Position involves holding the Clubbells overhead with a confirmed grip, locked out arms, packed shoulders, locked core, with root and legs actively driving into the ground. Initially this will be a highly challenging position, but with practice it will become a "sweet spot" from which you will be able to project your Clubbells through exercises like jerks, presses, snatches, and circles.

An important element of this form requires you to keep your forearms vertical and wrists aligned. If you "lean forward" (a popular technique with the sport of Olympic weightlifting) remember that the tremendous leverage of the Clubbells may send you out of Torch Position. If this happens, use movements such as the Parry Cast or Circles (outward, backward, inward or forward) to bring the Clubbells safely and expediently to Floor Park.

Two-Handed Torch Position

The Two Handed Torch Position requires you to be aware of the Short and Long Arm discussed in Shoulder Pack, as one hand will be gripping higher than the other. You may not be able to lock out the Short Arm elbow initially, but you must still pack the shoulder regardless.

BACK POSITION

One of the more challenging positions involves holding the Clubbells in *Back Position*. In one-handed exercises the upper arms end with the elbows pointing directly towards the sky and the Clubbells hanging in line with the erectors, the long muscles that run along the sides of the spine. The upper arms should rotate the shoulders inward and remain as close to the ears as possible to prevent laterally flaring the elbows. Work to keep the Clubbells from resting on your back, but you may allow them to touch your back. Remember to maintain proper shoulder pack to keep the shoulders safely down in the joint and to prevent the scapula from sliding out.

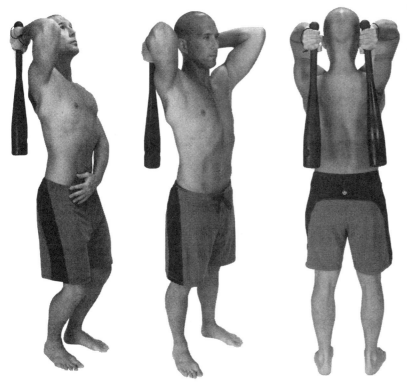

To prevent your spine from arching backwards, ensure that you have appropriate core and root lock while maintaining a crown to coccyx structure. Keep your legs actively driving into the ground.

It is important to mention that, when in Back Position, before one changes forward/backward movement to lateral movement (as in a Shoulder Cast) the elbows do lead and point outwards, as can be seen in the following image.

Two-Handed Back Position

When both hands are attached to one Clubbell®, the elbow flare changes depending upon the direction that the Clubbell® will be swung: if forward, then forward; if lateral, then lateral. However, in general, the side that holds the Clubbell® to the shoulder will have the elbow closest to the ear. The opposite side arm will then flare the elbow to the side (in order to reach across behind the head).

With two-handed exercises, just as we saw with Guard Position, there are four configurations in which you can hold the Clubbell® in Back Position:

- **Right Grip Right Back Position** specifically describes holding the Clubbell® with a Right Grip on the right side of the back.
- **Right Grip Left Back Position** specifically describes holding the Clubbell® with a Right Grip on the left side of the back.
- **Left Grip Right Back Position** specifically describes holding the Clubbell® with a Left Grip on the Right side of the back.
- **Left Grip Left Back Position** specifically describes holding the Clubbell® with a Left Grip on the left side of the back.

CLUBBELL® EXERCISES

The following represent the basics of Clubbell® training. Practice them and develop your skill in the order in which they are presented in this book: first learn and practice the main exercise in each skill family before moving on to the subsequent variations.

The exercises are arranged in related groups:

RHYTHMIC MOVEMENTS:
Swings
Pendulums
Circles
BALLISTIC MOVEMENTS:
Cleans
Jerks
Snatches
GRINDING MOVEMENTS:
Presses
Casts

EQUIPMENT SUBSTITUTES

Some people have substituted lightweight dumbbells for these exercises until they acquired the proper equipment: patented Clubbells. However, the change in grip, profile and center of mass *significantly* alters the exercise nuances. Use only with extreme caution and/or the supervision of a certified CST Instructor.

Although all CST movements were designed for the patented Clubbell®, you may explore the movements with a broom handle, plastic magnum-shaped bottle or even an antique "Indian club" design.

You will **not** receive 100% of the health benefits of CST without using authentic, patented Clubbells.

SWINGS

Think of the goal of a swing as smoothly (without jerkiness) moving the Clubbell® from one side of your body to the other in an arc, with arms locked in order to use the body to move the Clubbell® by rocking (forward and backward) or swaying (right and left).

FRONT SWING

Practice the Front Swing first to refine the best possible swing technique before practicing the other variations.

Approach, strap in, adjust the choke depth, and confirm your grip!

Ready Position: keep your back straight, look ahead, fold at the hip, push back with butt, and keep your weight on your heels and your shins perpendicular to the floor. Keep your shoulders packed. As you begin to stand slightly with still flexed knees and hips, perform a few test Rock-it drill movements to get the feel.

Hip Snap: with your hips exploding through the motion. Contract your abs, legs and butt as tight as possible! Sharply exhale and lock down your core and root; do not consciously inhale. Lock your hips out and grip the ground with your toes. Keep your crown to coccyx alignment.

As you perform the hip snap, allow it to swing your locked arms forward. Swing the Clubbells like weights attached to chains: with no jerking, maintaining constant tension outwards, in a smooth motion. You should feel your balance shift forward onto the balls of your feet. Press back into the ground against this weight shift to stay mid-foot in your balance.

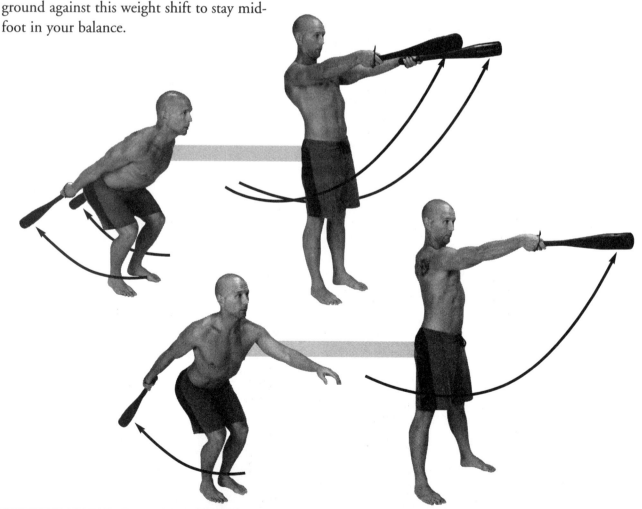

Three levels can be done: hip height, shoulder height, and directly overhead. When overhead, remember to keep your shoulders down. Watch the Clubbells through the entire motion.

Sit and Fold: Keep your core activated and root locked, but allow the air to rush back into your lungs as the Clubbells begin to swing downward on your locked arms and packed shoulders. Push your butt back, folding at the hip.

As the Clubbells swing towards the rear you'll feel your weight shift to your heels. With crown to coccyx spinal alignment, fold as close to chest-to-thigh as comfortable. This will keep your weight on mid-foot. When the Clubbells point directly backward as close to parallel as you can get with the floor, you look "ski-jump" ready to drive your legs into the ground for the next repetition.

Swings

TWO-HANDED FRONT SWING

The two handed Front Swing is the foundation of all forward exercises in two handed training and requires the most practice. The two-handed variant of the Front Swing demands increased attention on Clubbell® floor clearance in the back swing phase.

1. Get into Ready Position. Exhale forcefully as you lock down your core and root. Pack your shoulders and confirm your grip on the Clubbell®.
2. Drive your legs into the ground to begin the motion for hip recruitment. Each of the one-handed Front Swing mechanics still apply.
3. Maintain crown to coccyx spinal alignment as you swing the Clubbell® between your legs. Avoid the temptation to curve your spine to reach farther backward with the Clubbell®. Fold at the hips to allow the Clubbell® to clear the floor.
4. At maximal backward clearance, begin driving your legs to initiate the next repetition.

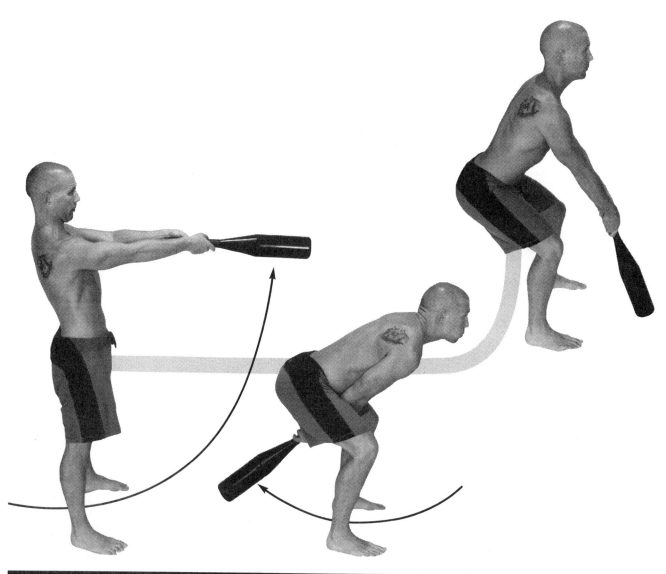

SIDE SWING

As the Front Swing is the foundation of all forward exercises, the Side Swing is the foundation of all lateral exercises.

1. Get into Ready Position to confirm your grip on the Clubbell®. Exhale forcefully as you lock down your core and root. Pack your shoulders and confirm your grip.
2. Exhale and lock down your core as you drive your legs into the ground to begin the motion for hip sway to get the Clubbell® swinging sideways. Explode into a lateral Hip Snap to swing the Clubbell® to increasing heights laterally.
3. Hip Root to allow the fullest range of motion.
4. Maintain crown to coccyx spinal alignment as you swing the Clubbell®, clearing your knees. Avoid the temptation to curve your spine.
5. Hip Sway to absorb and accentuate the backswing. At maximal lateral reach, begin driving your legs (in particular your near, planted leg) to initiate the next repetition.

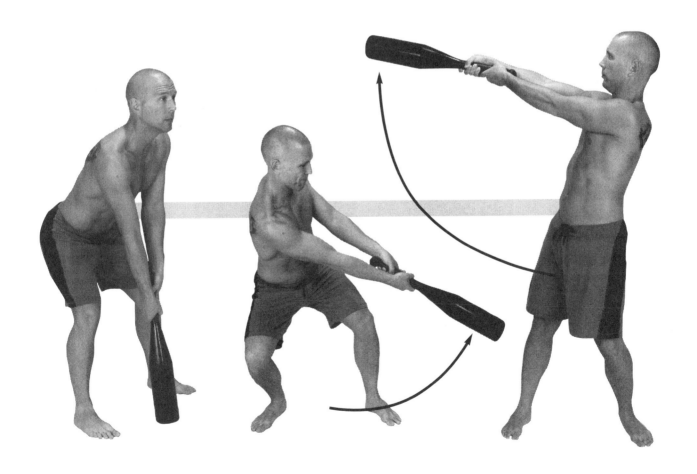

SIDE SEMI CIRCLE SWING

The Side Semi combines two opposite Side Swings. An important caution with these is that, as your grip nears failure, your feet become more and more endangered. As in all exercises, *BE CAREFUL not to let the Clubbell® slip!*

1. Get into Ready Position to confirm your grip on the Clubbell®. Exhale forcefully as you lock down your core and root. Pack your shoulders and confirm your grip.
2. Exhale and lock down your core as you drive your legs into the ground to begin the motion for hip sway, which gets your Clubbell® swinging sideways. Explode into a lateral Hip Snap to swing the Clubbell® to increasing heights laterally. As the downward phase of the swing clears your knees, Hip Sway to absorb and accentuate the motion and then explode into the opposite lateral Hip Snap.
3. Hip Root to allow the fullest range of motion.
4. Maintain crown to coccyx spinal alignment as you swing the Clubbell®, clearing your knees. Avoid the temptation to curve your spine.

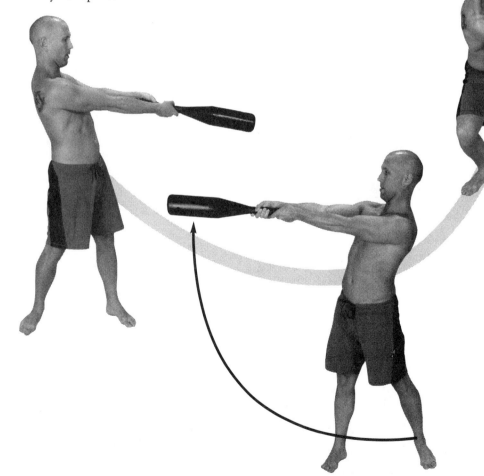

PIROUETTE SWING

The Pirouette Swing involves a basic Front Swing timed with a back step while the Clubbell® swings overhead. The challenge of the Pirouette lies in coordinating the footwork with the moment when the Clubbell® floats weightless. It is a HIGH skill exercise that requires you to have previously mastered the Front Swing to overhead heights.

Line Walking Drill: Before grabbing a Clubbell®, work on the footwork. Draw a line with chalk, lay down masking tape, or draw an imaginary line. Stand on the line with both feet pointed in one direction (i.e. facing south). Lift both arms overhead. Step with one foot backwards and around so that you pivot with your backside, not your front side. Pivot on the inside foot without changing its place. Move your non-pivoting foot behind you onto the tape on the opposite side of your pivoting foot so that you now face the opposite direction (i.e. if you started facing south you should now be facing north, adjusted one shoulder's-width down because of your step). To clarify, if you stand on the line facing forward and you intend to Pirouette to the left, you pivot on your left foot and step behind with your right foot until you place it back on the line and end up facing backwards.

When first practicing the Pirouette do not use a Clubbell®. Practice with a light mallet or even a water bottle. Once you have the timing of the step and swing mastered, begin with a lightweight Clubbell® at full grip choke depth.

Front Swing: Perform a normal Front Swing, sending the Clubbell® to Torch Position overhead. You must be able to send the Clubbell® overhead in the Front Swing before learning the Pirouette!

Pirouette Step: As the Clubbell® floats weightless, step and pivot as in the Line Walking Drill before the Clubbell® begins its downswing. You must step deep enough to ensure that the Clubbell® swings between your legs and not towards one leg or the other.

The path that the Clubbell® actually takes looks like a full circle, if not a spiral, due to the lateral movement of the Pirouette step.

Recovery Swing: Perform the down and backswing as you would in the basic Front Swing to continue on with the next repetition, or park and stop.

Contributed by Jarlo Ilano

PENDULUMS

Think of the purpose of a pendulum as moving the Clubbell® from one side of the body to the other, but unlike basic swings, catching it in a position on either side of the swing.

FRONT PENDULUM

Practice the Front Pendulum first to refine the best possible pendulum technique before practicing the other variations.

The Front Pendulum begins and ends in Order Position. The two critical nuances that distinguish the Front Pendulum from the Front Swing are the projection to arm lock and bouncing out of shock absorption.

Launch: To move from Order Position to the down swing, project the barrel head up and out at a 45° angle until you have full arm lock. Shoulders remain packed as usual. Only once you achieve arm lock should the down swing begin. In this way, when the Clubbell® marries gravity, it swings on a solid structure (arm lock and shoulder pack) and doesn't jerk your joints dangerously.

Swing: Perform the down, back and up swing phases just as you would with the basic Swing. On the upswing use your leg drive, core activation and hip snap to project the Clubbell® up to approximately shoulder height.

Absorb: At shoulder height, contract your elbows down to Order Position and pull the neck of the Clubbell® in line directly behind the barrel head. Shock absorb with your hips and knees while maintaining crown to coccyx spinal alignment. Exhale to do so. Pulse your grip tightly to stop the Clubbell® in Order Position.

Release: As soon as you nail Order Position, release the stored elastic energy of the shock absorption into another launch for the next repetition. It should feel like catching (and absorbing) a medicine ball lobbed at you and then using the loading of the catch to lob it back.

The Big Book of Clubbell Training

Scott Sonnon

Pendulums

119

TWO-HANDED FRONT PENDULUM

The distinguishing characteristics between the one-handed and two-handed Front Pendulum involve the complementary grip store and release and the clearance between the legs on the back swing.

Projecting the Clubbell® out of Order Position requires you to tilt and drive with the upper hand and support and drive with the bottom hand. As soon as you move the Clubbell® outwards enough so that both hands drive, they act in unison as in the Front Swing.

As in the difference between the one- and two-handed variations of the Front Swing, when you grasp the Clubbell® in two hands the clearance between your legs for the backswing diminishes. Work on your timing in the Two-Handed Front Swing before progressing to the Two-Handed Front Pendulum.

Catching the Clubbell® back in Order requires the opposite complementary grip demanded in the launch. After using your leg drive, core activation and hip snap to send the Clubbell® to float weightless at shoulder height, contract your elbows to Order Position. The bottom hand will pull it into place and the top hand acts as a fulcrum to prevent the Clubbell® barrel head from continuing to tip towards you. After you have the timing down you can shock absorb more with the hips and less with your grip to send it into the next repetition.

INSIDE PENDULUM

The major challenge that separates Side Pendulums from the Front Pendulum involves maintaining the arm lock across your centerline and keeping the trajectory of the Clubbell® in the coronal plane so that it does not deviate into the sagittal plane. The range of the Side Pendulum must be kept as perpendicular to the Front Pendulum as possible.

Launch: Beginning in Order Position, cast your Clubbell® up at a 45° angle across your centerline and secure full arm lock before it begins the downswing phase.

Side Swing: Perform the downswing and upswing as you would the Side Swing, ensuring that you clear your knees when you dip your hips and sway.

Snap: Use your leg drive and hip snap to carry the Clubbell® up to shoulder height.

Float: When the Clubbell® floats weightless, contract your elbow to your ribs for Order Position to pull the neck of the Clubbell® directly behind the barrel head.

Catch: As you catch it in Order Position, dip your hips and knees while maintaining crown to coccyx spinal alignment.

Release: Using the stored elastic energy from the shock absorption phase, bounce it into another launch for the next repetition.

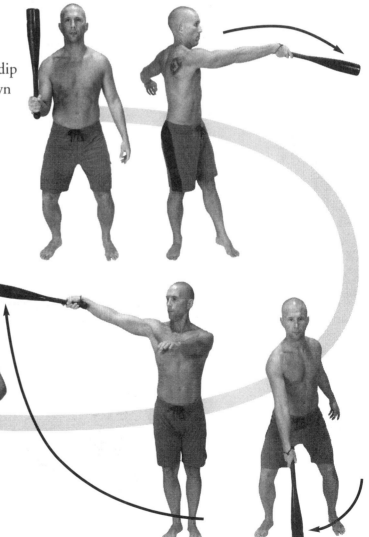

DOUBLE SIDE PENDULUM

The main difference here involves the timing of two independently swinging Clubbells. Ensure that you have arm lock with both Clubbells as close to parallel with the floor as possible when casting to the side and when reeling them back into Order Position.

When shock absorbing, ensure that you clear your knees on the down swing. Use a side hip root to the opposite side of the direction from which you reel in the Clubbells. As soon as you stabilize both Clubbells in Order, move back to normal standing ready position.

TWO-HANDED GUARD INSIDE PENDULUM

The primary difference in this exercise is that the Clubbell® begins in the Guard Position opposite to the direction of the launch and ends in the Guard Position opposite to the upswing. For a Two-Handed Guard Inside Pendulum, always cast the Clubbell® across your centerline and always catch the Clubbell® across your centerline.

Because the Guard Position loads one hip, the leg drive in projecting the Clubbell® up at a 45° angle and out to full arm lock before beginning the downswing feels like it comes from the leg underneath the Guard Position (i.e. left leg for Left Guard).

During the Side Swing phase, remember that attaching two arms to one Clubbell® creates the short arm / long arm phenomenon. You must provide sufficient Hip Sway to clear the floor while maintaining crown to coccyx spinal alignment. The Hip Snap will come from the opposite side of the body (swinging to the left means hip snapping with the right.)

Reeling the Clubbell® across your centerline into Guard requires more skill and time. When developing the skill you can catch the Clubbell® in Order Position and then work on slowly contracting it to Guard. Once you develop the skill of reeling the Clubbell® across your centerline, you will be able to shock absorb effectively enough to feel how to store and release the elastic energy into the next repetition.

OUTSIDE PENDULUM

Moving to the Outside actually requires more skill and strength, as it travels at a distance from your root rather than carrying across it. All nuances from the Inside Pendulum apply.

The Outside Pendulum differs from the Inside in that it does not cast across your centerline for arm lock into the downswing. The Outside Pendulum casts directly to the near side outwards (Right Hand Order Position casts to the Right Side; Left Hand Order Position casts to the Left Side). Remember to cast outward and up at a 45° angle to achieve full arm lock before the downswing begins.

Use the Hip Sway to bring the Clubbell® across and then back up to float weightless before you catch it in Order Position.

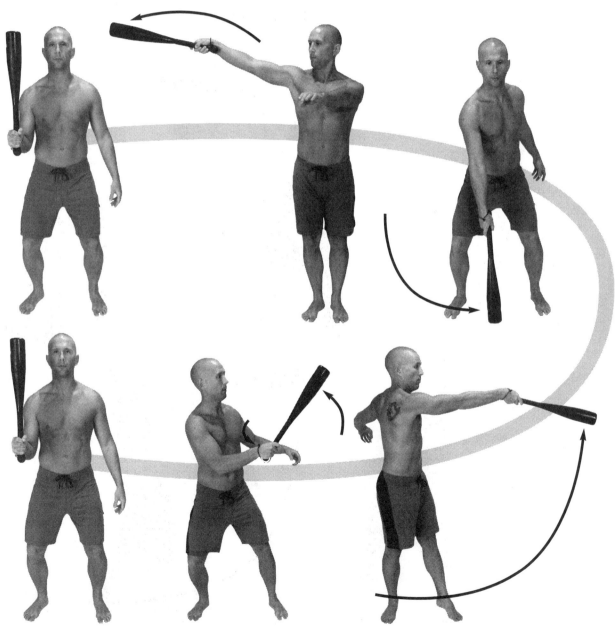

TWO-HANDED GUARD OUTSIDE PENDULUM

The difference between the Two-Handed Guard Outside Pendulum and the Two-Handed Guard Inside Pendulum is that you cast in the direction of the Guard Position rather than away from it. For example, from Right Guard you would cast outside to the right.

You may find it more challenging to achieve arm lock with the short arm. Focus on leg drive to cast out and up at a 45° angle to get full arm lock before the downswing begins. The same holds true for the catch. Focus on hip snap to get the Clubbell® high enough to float weightless with full arm lock before landing it in the near Guard Position. Catch the Clubbell® on the same side as the upswing. For example, when swinging to the left, catch in Left Guard.

To keep your directions correct, remember that in the Two-Handed Guard Outside Pendulum you do not cast the Clubbell® across your centerline.

LUNGE-STEP PENDULUM

Once you become proficient with the basic Pendulums, you may add in footwork. Adding footwork requires a high level of skill.

Back Swing: Begin with a basic Front Swing to send the Clubbell® deep into backswing.

Hip Snap: As you drive your legs into the ground, hip snap with a sharp exhalation, sending the Clubbell® with locked arms and packed shoulders into the upswing phase.

Lunge Step: As the Clubbell® begins to float weightless, take a deep step forward with one foot.

Rotate: Simultaneously, use the forward motion to drive the neck of the Clubbell® under the barrel head.

Catch and Absorb: Catch the Clubbell® in Order Position by shock absorbing into the lunge. Don't allow your knee to touch the ground. Your top thigh should be parallel to the ground and your knee should not move past your planted foot (in other words, your lower leg should be perpendicular to the ground). Point both hips forward in one line.

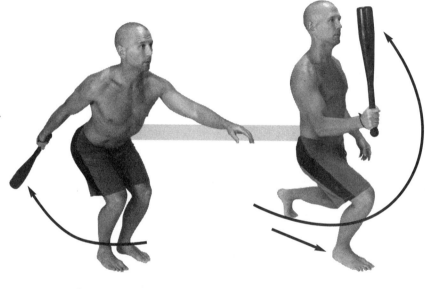

Release: Bounce out of the elastic catch of the shock absorbing Order Position by launching the Clubbell® forward as you would a basic Front Pendulum: lock the arms before the Clubbell® begins the downswing.

Drive and Step: Simultaneously drive off the front leg to recover your back leg to standing position.

Swing and Catch: Fold again at the hips and perform a Front Pendulum, ending in Order Position. You may park from there or begin the backswing again for your next repetition of the lunge step pendulum.

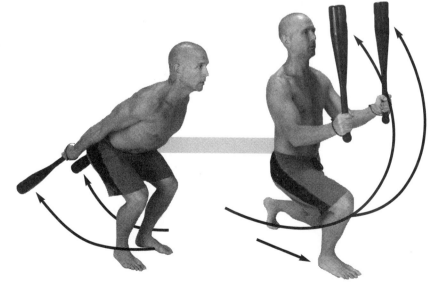

TWO-HANDED GUARD LUNGE-STEP PENDULUM

The challenge of the Two-Handed Guard Lunge-Step Pendulum involves catching the Clubbell® split-legged. Because two arms attach to the Clubbell® in this variation, you must lock down your core completely to stabilize the Clubbell® in Order Position.

Furthermore, because the Clubbell® swings between the legs rather than to the outside of the legs, timing becomes more challenging. For proper timing, ensure that you sufficiently drive and snap the Clubbell® so that it floats weightless before stepping and rotating the Clubbell® into Order Position.

Guard Lunge-Step Drill: A helpful preliminary exercise would be to begin by holding your Clubbell® in Guard Position and stepping deeply into a forward lunge to experience the elastic loading of the planted leg. Practice your sharp exhalation on the shock absorption to feel your core lock down with the hip root. Release that loading by driving your forward, planted leg into the ground to return to standing. Repeat on the opposite leg. Stand. Switch to the opposite Guard Position and repeat on the opposite side with either leg.

Front Pendulum + Guard Lunge-Step: The next intermediary step would be to perform an Two-Handed Guard Front Pendulum followed immediately by the above basic exercise of stepping while holding the Clubbell® in Guard Position. Return to standing and switch to the opposite Guard Position. Perform the opposite Two-Handed Front Guard Pendulum, stopping in Guard Position, and perform the Guard Lunge-Step again with the other leg stepping forward.

SIDE-STEP PENDULUM

The Side-Step is to the Side Pendulum what the Lunge-Step is to the Front Pendulum. As in the Lunge-Step Pendulum, the challenge of the Side-Step involves coordinating the footwork while stabilizing the Clubbell® in a grounded root.

Side-Step Pendulum variations:
1. Cast Inside and Side-Step Inside: Practice this variation first to refine the best possible pendulum technique before training the other variations.
2. Cast Inside and Side-Step Outside
3. Cast Outside and Side-Step Inside
4. Cast Outside and Side-Step Outside

Key performance goals:
- Achieve arm lock before beginning the downswing.
- Step as the Clubbell® begins to float weightless.
- Use the movement to rotate the neck under the barrel head.
- Catch in Order Position by rooting on the planting leg.

TWO-HANDED GUARD SIDE-STEP PENDULUM

As in the one-handed variation, the Side-Step with two hands attached to one Clubbell® concentrates on loading one leg.

Guard Side-Step Drill: A helpful preliminary exercise would be to begin by holding your Clubbell® in Guard Position and stepping deeply and directly to one side to experience the elastic loading of the planted leg. Practice your sharp exhalation on the shock absorption to feel your core lock down with the hip root. Release that loading by driving your leg into the ground to return to standing. Switch to the opposite Guard Position and repeat on the opposite side.

Inside Pendulum + Guard Side-Step: The next intermediary step would be to perform a Two-Handed Guard Inside Pendulum followed immediately by the above basic exercise of stepping while holding the Clubbell® in Guard Position. Return to standing and switch to the opposite Guard Position. Perform the opposite Two-Handed Inside Guard Pendulum, stopping in Guard Position, and perform the Guard Side-Step again in the new direction.

As in the basic Side-Step Pendulum, there are several variations to the Two-Handed Guard Side-Step Pendulum. Practice this variation first to refine the best possible pendulum technique before training the other variations.

1. Begin in Guard Position.
2. Cast the Clubbell® Inside (across your centerline to the opposite side of your body) and up at a 45° angle to achieve arm lock before the downswing.
3. Side Semi Swing the Clubbell® across your body on the downswing using the Hip Sway.
4. Use the Side Hip Snap to bring the Clubbell® weightless before stepping away from the direction from which you reel in the Clubbell® to the opposite Guard Position (i.e. if you began with Left Guard, Side-Step to the right and conclude in Right Guard). You must concentrate on a long reel, since you not only need to bring the Clubbell® across your centerline but also to marry the distance of the Side-Step with the action of reeling it across.
5. Use your sharp exhalation to hip root and absorb when you catch the Clubbell® in the Guard Position over the planted leg.

You can either park directly or return to standing to hold in Guard Position (as in the Guard Side-Step Drill). Once proficient with this you can work on developing massive leg drive off your planted leg to cast the Clubbell® far across your centerline up at a 45° angle. When you achieve full arm lock before the downswing, allow the leg drive off your planted leg to carry you back to standing. Perform the Side Semi Swing using the Hip Sway and Hip Snap to move immediately into the opposite Two-Handed Guard Side-Step Pendulum.

CIRCLES

Think of the purpose of a circle as moving the Clubbell® at full arm lock overhead around one complete, unbroken plane to end in the original position.

FRONT CIRCLE

Practice the Front Circle first to refine the best possible circle technique before practicing the other variations.

The Front Circle begins and ends in Torch Position, with shoulder pack and full arm lock.

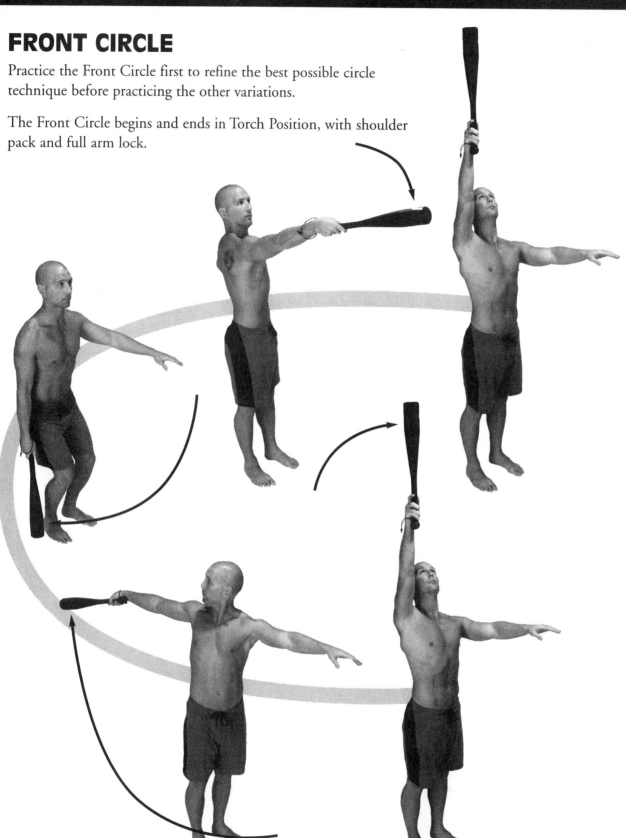

Front ¾ Circle Drill: A preliminary exercise would be to begin in Torch Position overhead and continue with a basic Front Swing, absorbing it in the "ski-jump" position rather than carrying it all the way around.

Back ¾ Circle Drill: The next preliminary exercise would be to choose a light enough weight and a deep enough grip choke depth so that the intensity is mild (RPE3<). Using the Front Swing, swing the Clubbell® forward to hip height. Then, using leg drive and hip snap, let the backswing carry behind and up to Torch Position overhead. You may rotate your torso to the degree that you cannot remain comfortable due to thoracic and / or shoulder inflexibility.

Launch: To perform the full movement, begin in Torch Position and slightly push the Clubbell® forward until it begins the downswing.

Absorb: Slightly dip the knees and hips before the Clubbell® swings down perpendicular to the ground. You will use this loading to carry the Clubbell® up out of the backswing to Torch Position.

Drive: Releasing the absorption, drive your legs into the ground with an exhalation to activate the core. Send the Clubbell® from the backswing up to Torch Position while keeping your shoulders packed. Maintain crown to coccyx spinal alignment, but you may slightly turn the torso until you regain full range of motion in your thorax and shoulders. Work to prevent the Clubbell® from changing its vertical path due to inflexibility, as changing this path will cause you difficulty in securing the lock in Torch.

Lock: Slightly dip with your knees and hips with another exhalation to lock down your core in Torch Position.

If you cannot secure a lock in Torch and the Clubbell® begins to move to one side or the other, you may:

1. Contract your elbows to Order Position to carefully catch it.
2. Perform a Side Semi with a Hip Sway to slow it to park.
3. With control, rotate the neck up and barrel head down to go straight to Floor Park.

If you miss Torch Position due to forward momentum, continue on with the following step:

Park: You may park from Torch, complete a Front ¾ Drill to slow to a park, or you may continue again for your next repetition.

BACK CIRCLE

The primary difference between the Front and Back Circles involves the initial shoulder resistance to moving from Torch Position backwards.

Launch: as you launch by slightly pushing the Clubbell® backwards, work to minimize how much you rotate your torso to accommodate thoracic and shoulder inflexibility. Do not cause pain (RPD <3).

Absorb: Slightly dip the knees and hips before the Clubbell® swings down perpendicular to the ground. You will use this loading to carry the Clubbell® out of the upswing to Torch Position, as in a basic Front Swing to overhead.

Drive: As per Front Swing, drive your legs into the ground with a hip snap and core activating exhalation to create the upswing phase of the exercise.

Lock: Slightly dip with your knees and hips with another exhalation to lock down your core in Torch Position. If you miss the lock, perform any of the parking techniques described in the Front Circle.

Park: You may park from Torch, complete a Front ? Drill to slow to a park, or you may continue again for your next repetition.

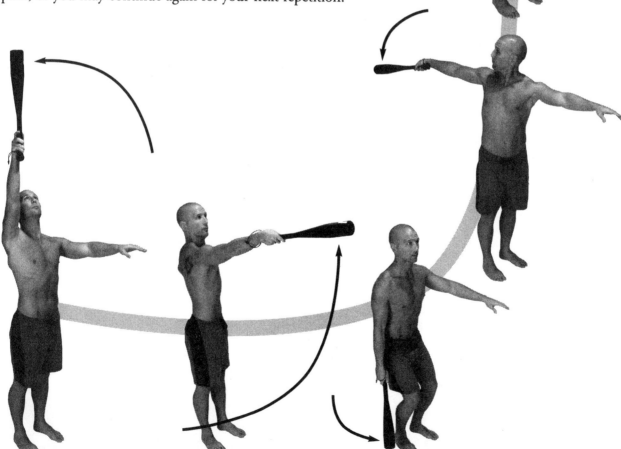

INSIDE CIRCLE

The major challenge that separates Side Circles from the Front and Back Circles involves maintaining the arm lock across your centerline, and ensuring that the trajectory of the Clubbell® travels in the coronal plane and avoids deviating into the sagittal plane. In other words, the Side Circle must be kept as perpendicular to the Front Circle as possible.

Launch: as you launch by slightly pushing the Clubbell® to the inside (across your centerline), allow your torso to slightly turn towards the motion. Try to minimize how much turning you do so that the movement doesn't become a Front Circle.

Absorb: Slightly dip the knees and hips before the Clubbell® swings down perpendicular to the ground. You will use this loading to carry the Clubbell® out of the upswing to Torch Position, as in a basic Front Swing to overhead.

Drive: As per Side Swing, use hip sway to drive your near leg into the ground with minimal hip snap. Try to not turn your hips into the movement, rather keep them facing forward. Exhale as you would with the Side Semi Circle to create the upswing on the outside of your body.

Lock: Slightly dip with your knees and hips with another exhalation to lock down your core in Torch Position. If you miss the lock, perform any of the parking techniques described in the Front Circle.

Park: You may park from Torch, complete a Side Semi to slow to a park, or you may continue again for your next repetition.

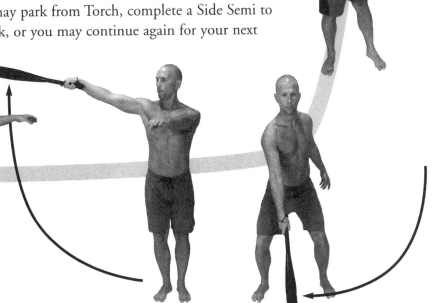

OUTSIDE CIRCLE

The challenge of the Outside Circle involves driving from the near foot to keep frame on the downswing.

Begin in Torch Position and launch to the outside. Drive the leg under the direction of the downswing to avoid being pulled off balance.

Minimize the torso twist on the upswing so that the movement does not become a Back Circle.

Perform all nuances the same as you would for the other circles: Launch, Absorb, Drive, Lock, Park.

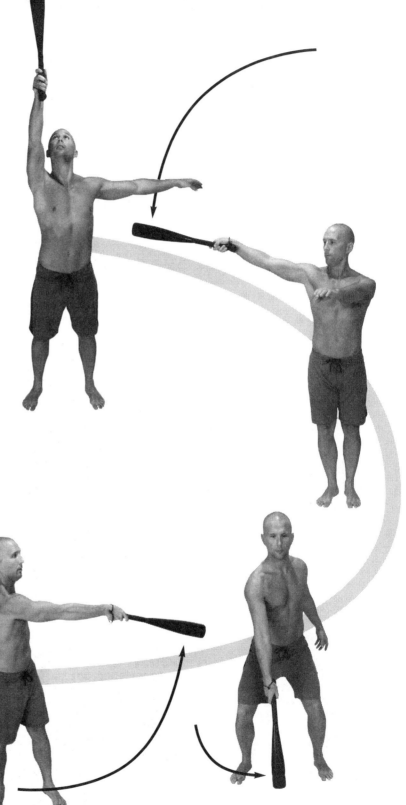

TWO-HANDED SIDE CIRCLE

The type of grip determines which circle you perform. For example, holding the Clubbell® with a Right Grip with the upswing on your left side executes an Inside Circle. Perform an Outside Circle by holding the Clubbell® with a Right Grip and execute the upswing on your right side.

With the two-handed circle, begin by reminding yourself of the Side Semi to prime your hip sway and hip snap. Swing with control to as close to Torch Position as you can. Lock it in Torch, if possible.

If the Clubbell® drifts through Torch Position, just allow it to arc with control into the downswing on the opposite side of the circle. On the downswing, ensure that you load an effective hip root facing the Clubbell®. Pivot to allow the Clubbell® to swing by your centerline to the other side. Use your Hip Sway to accelerate it, and your Hip Snap to send it all the way to the top. Lock it down in Torch Position again before your next repetition.

Park directly with a Side Swing and Hip Sway, or perform another repetition.

ALTERNATING CIRCLES: FRONT STROKE AND BACKSTROKE

Alternating a Circle involves keeping one Clubbell® in Torch Position while performing a Front Circle (Front Stroke) or a Back Circle (Backstroke) with the other Clubbell®.

The key performance goal of either involves keeping the shoulder pack of both shoulders.

CLEANS

Think of a clean as having the purpose of ripping the Clubbell® off the floor as explosively as possible and bringing it to a position around torso height.

FRONT CLEAN TO ORDER POSITION

Practice the Front Clean to Order first to refine the best possible clean technique before practicing the other variations.

Approach, strap in, adjust the choke depth, and confirm your grip!

Ready Position: keep your back straight, look ahead, bend at the waist and not the back, push back with your butt, and keep your weight on your heels and your shins perpendicular to the floor. Keep your shoulders packed.

There are two variations of Clean techniques that you can perform: the swing clean, which begins with a slight back swing on the Clubbells; and the power clean, which begins from a dead hang (with no pre-swing). This description addresses the power clean.

Pull and Rotate: with your hips exploding through the motion. Contract your abs, quads and glutes as tightly as possible to drive into the ground with your feet. Sharply exhale as you lock down your core and root; do not consciously inhale. Rip the Clubbells off the ground directly upwards until they reach approximately belly height. Simultaneously begin to rotate the neck and knob underneath the barrel head of the Clubbell®.

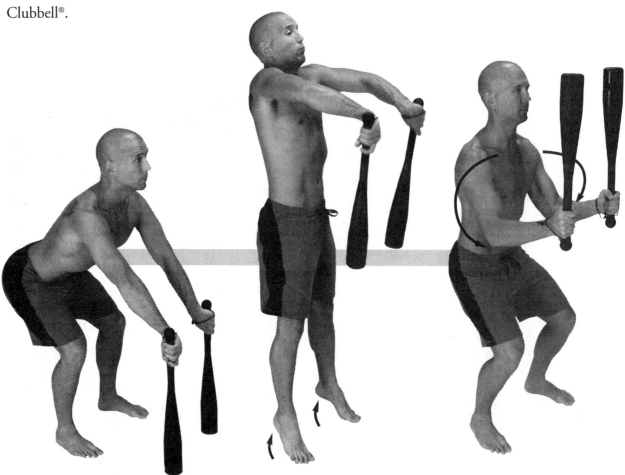

Shock Absorb: "Catch" the Clubbell® in Order Position by confirming your grip tightly to stop all deviations in movement, and absorb the weight downwards by elastically dipping with your knees and hips. Maintain crown to coccyx spinal alignment, perpendicular to the floor. Keep your elbows bent, tight and close to your ribs. Maintain locked forward wrists as though you were going to punch a heavy bag (don't flex or extend your wrist whatsoever!). The Clubbell® should come to a complete stop.

Order Position: Hold this position for no longer than 5 seconds at any one time.

Rotate and Park: To park your Clubbells on the floor, push the Clubbells upwards slightly and begin to rotate the barrel heads towards the ground. The return to Park Position should be smooth. Don't allow the weight to jerk your elbows locked.

TWO-HANDED FRONT CLEAN TO ORDER POSITION

The main between the Two-Handed Front Clean as opposed to the One-Handed Front Clean involves pulling the neck of the Clubbell® up the centerline of the body while not pulling more strongly with the right or left arms. This is actually quite challenging because the coordination needed between right and left grips taxes your handedness.

Practice with a light weight so that you can find the "floating" point where you will rotate the Clubbell® when it is momentarily weightless.

FRONT CLEAN TO SHOULDER PARK

Until you've mastered both the Swing and the Clean to Order Position do not toy with the Clean to Shoulder Park, because of the inherent risk of not catching the Clubbells on the proper soft tissue portion of your trapezium muscles. You will require more explosiveness than in the Clean to Order, as you must pull the Clubbell® much higher to catch it in Shoulder Park.

Brake: To practice, begin by Cleaning to Order Position one Clubbell®, as controlling two independently acting Clubbells is very challenging to the novice. Slowly brake the Clubbell® into Shoulder Park. Keep your other hand ready to assist.

You should feel no discomfort, nor should the barrel head be resting on any bone. Be sure to allow adequate clearance for your ears!

Pop: Extend your hips and knees to carefully launch the Clubbell® off your shoulder, taking great care to give ample room for your ear. Always keep your shoulders packed. Don't try to shrug the Clubbell® off. Pop it off with your knees and hips.

Next, begin by performing a slow Swing to Order Position. Catch the Clubbell® in Order and then slowly brake it into Shoulder Park. This should teach you to exert more control before moving on to the explosion of the Clean to Shoulder Park.

Absorb: You'll need to absorb even more with your knees and hips than in Order Position, since your arms are no longer acting as braking agents once in Shoulder Park. You want to exhale a second time as you absorb into Shoulder Park (the first exhale being on the explosive clean out of floor park).

Pop and Park the Clubbell® as in the basic Clean to Order, continue a basic Swing to slowly stop, or continue with another Swing to Shoulder Park.

TWO-HANDED FRONT CLEAN TO SHOULDER PARK

As in the one-handed variant, you will require more explosiveness in this exercise than in the Two-Handed Clean to Order because you must pull the Clubbell® much higher to catch it in Shoulder Park.

The primary difference between the Two-Handed Front Clean and the one-handed variant involves the braking method of parking the Clubbell® on your shoulder. Once your pull brings the Clubbell® parallel to the ground, use the Complementary Grip. The top hand acts as a fulcrum (pushing away from you) against which the bottom hand pulls (towards you) in order to decelerate the weight until it gently catches on the shoulder.

You also need to be aware that you are moving the Clubbell® from your centerline between your legs in Floor Park to off-centerline on your shoulder. The far arm (the arm opposite shoulder on which you intend to catch the Clubbell®) must provide sufficient room to clear your head and ear, but not so much clearance that it sends the Clubbell® off soft tissue and onto bone. This requires practice, so focus on moving first from two-handed Order Position to Shoulder Park and back.

Popping the two handed Shoulder Parked Clubbell® off your shoulder must be driven by the hips and legs, as in the one-handed variant. Don't shrug the shoulder out of joint. However, because you're returning to centerline from off-centerline, pop the Clubbell® directly forward and use your arms to direct the Clubbell® to centerline only once you have cleared your head and ear.

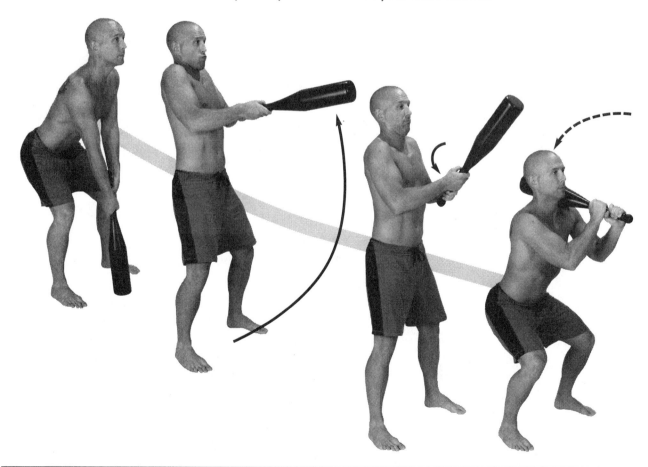

FRONT CLEAN TO FLAG POSITION

The challenge of the Clean to Flag Position is in changing the Pull phase of Clean to Order from a vertical to a slightly angled trajectory. The goal is to "catch" the Clubbell® with elbows locked, elbow pits pointing towards the sky, and shoulders packed.

Generally, you need to "punch" the neck of the Clubbell® into full horizontal arm lock. This requires a deeper exhalation coming off of the initial exhalation of the pull phase of the Clean.

Remember that, despite your arms being fully locked, you must dip your knees underneath the snap out to Flag in order to absorb the shock of the catch in position.

To move to park, begin by bringing your elbows slightly towards Order Position to rotate the Clubbell® barrel head towards floor park.

TWO-HANDED FRONT CLEAN TO FLAG POSITION

The difference between the Two-Handed Front Clean to Flag Position and the one-handed version involves the "punching" action using the Complementary Grip. After your pull and rotate, both hands will be punching out to Flag Position.

The "punching" movement is similar to that used in the one-handed variant. However, just before you are about to 'stick' the Clubbell® in position, the Complementary Grip begins. The top hand's grip acts as a fulcrum (pushing away from you) while the bottom hand's grip pulls towards you to stabilize the weight into place. When practiced, this becomes a very smooth 'pulse' at the end of the movement where both hands simultaneously grip the Clubbell®, causing opposite but complementary forces to stop the Clubbell® in position.

FRONT CLEAN TO BACK POSITION

It is best to begin by practicing moving from Order Position to Back Position before moving directly to the Clean to Back. Keep the elbow from flaring and push the neck in line with the barrel head. Co-contract your biceps and triceps while keeping a crushing grip on the neck of the Clubbell®. Allow ample room to clear your head and ear. Place the barrel head into position in line with the spine by the same side as the shoulder that you cleared. The Clubbell® should not rest against the back, though it may touch. The elbow should point skywards at the end, with the inside of the elbow as close to the ear as possible and not flaring outwards.

After mastering this, work on moving from Front Clean to Order and then placing the Clubbell® in Back Position as above. This will involve an extra step bouncing out of Order, but it will give you a better idea of the movement needed to catch the Clubbell® in Back Position. Once you feel proficient in the above you may move to the Front Clean to Back Position.

Use the Reverse Parry Cast to bring the Clubbell® down out of Back Position to Floor Park.

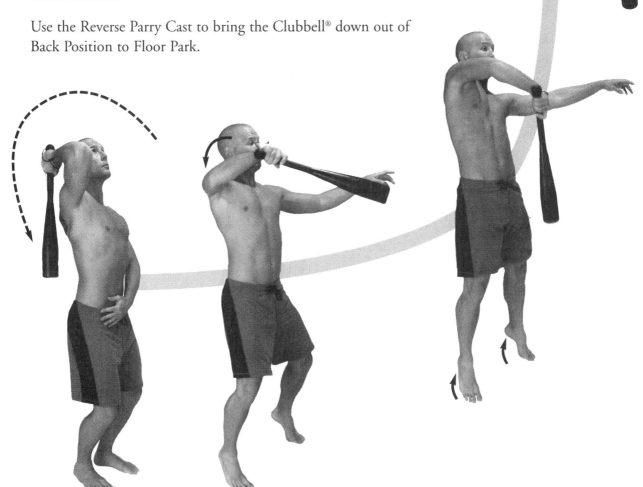

TWO-HANDED FRONT CLEAN TO BACK POSITION

The two handed variation of the Front Clean to Back Position requires practice in moving from Right Guard to Right Back Position and Left Guard to Left Back Position. The far arm (i.e. the left arm in right guard) threads over the head, forearm parallel to the ground. The near arm performs the move to Back Position exactly as in the one-handed variation.

The challenge of the two-handed variant involves the timing of maneuvering the far arm into proper position while the Clubbell® is weightless immediately following the explosive pull phase of the exercise. Practice the Front Clean to Guard combined with slowly moving into Back Position before practicing the full Front Clean to Back Position.

Catch the Clubbell® in Back Position with a shock absorption knee dip. Next, slowly move around the head using the Two-Handed Reverse Parry Cast to return the Clubbell® to Floor Park.

SIDE CLEAN TO GUARD POSITION

Begin practicing the Side Clean to Guard by catching a Side Swing in Guard Position. Remember to keep your shoulders packed, and activate your core by exhaling on the upswing and exhaling again on the shock absorption into Guard Position.

This lateral equivalent of the Clean to Order requires lateral explosiveness from the hip. Additionally, the Clean to Order differs in that the Side Clean and Swing are caught in the Guard of the opposite side from which they were cleaned. For example, if you Side Clean the Clubbell® to the right side, you catch the it in Left Guard.

The key to this exercise lies in how you reel in the Clubbell®. As you pull and pop the weight around, dip underneath as you rotate the neck beneath the barrel head. Simultaneously, pull the Clubbell® across your body to the opposite Guard Position.

Driving your legs into the ground during a Side Clean presents the coordination challenge of pushing first off the back leg (the leg opposite to the direction from which you clean the Clubbell®). Then, as you complete the pull phase and begin to rotate the neck under the barrel head and reel the Clubbell® towards Guard, press off your near leg (the same side leg as the direction of your clean). Finally, shift your weight back to the first leg beneath the Clubbell® as you absorb it in Guard.

As in the basic Front Clean to Order, you can project the barrel head outwards as you rotate the Clubbell® smoothly to Floor Park. You can also project the Clubbell® up at a 45° angle across your body in the original direction until you achieve arm lock, and then use a Side Swing and then a Hip Sway to absorb the exercise to a stop.

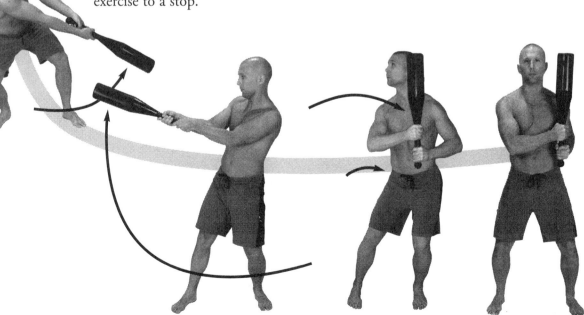

SIDE CLEAN TO SHOULDER PARK

This exercise involves Side Cleaning the Clubbell® and then catching it in Shoulder Park on the same side from which you cleaned it. This exercise differs from the Side Clean to Guard in that the rotation is much faster, since you catch the Clubbell® on the near shoulder rather than reeling it across your body to the opposite Guard. The faster rotation will require a more explosive pull. It will also demand a more evenly distributed leg drive in the pull and evenly distributed shock absorption with the knee dip.

You must observe much more care when catching the Clubbell® on your shoulder from the side than from the Front Clean to Shoulder Park due to the changed angle of the barrel head. In the Front Clean the Clubbell® lands at a perpendicular angle to your trapezium muscle, but in the Side Clean it lands at an approximately 45° angle. Be careful not to hit your head or ear, and be sure to land the Clubbell® solely upon soft tissue. As always, your default breath is to exhale on the pull and to exhale again on the shock absorption as you dip and catch.

When popping the Clubbell® off the shoulder using leg drive, remember to not shrug your shoulder and to keep your shoulders packed.

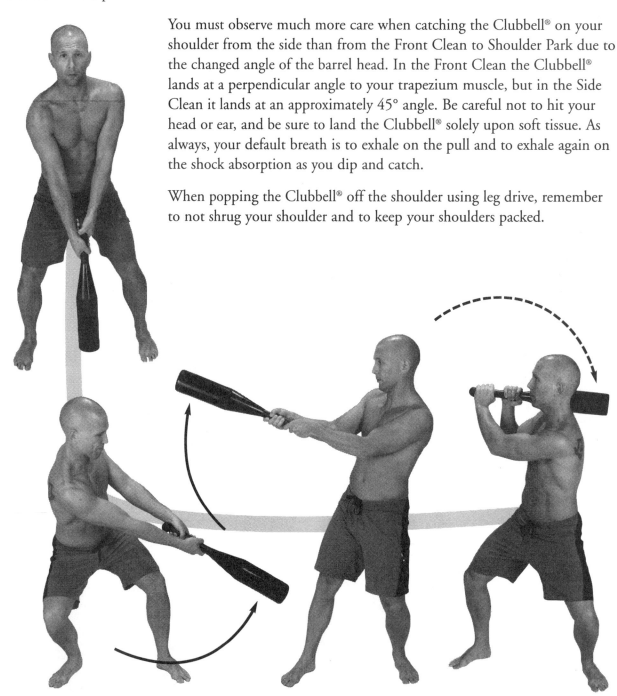

SIDE CLEAN TO BACK POSITION

The Side Clean to Back Position involves a Hip Sway to start the movement, followed by a sharp exhalation and pull to laterally rip the Clubbell® off the ground. Exhale on the exploding lateral Hip Snap. As the Clubbell® becomes weightless, dip under it with your knees as you push the neck around the barrel head. Instead of catching it in Shoulder Park, reel the Clubbell® in a larger arc so that you slowly catch it while shock absorbing in Back Position with another exhale.

As a preliminary, you should master the Side Clean to Guard Position and then practice slowly moving the Clubbell® into Back Position. Be aware of your head and ear as you thread your far forearm (the arm opposite the shoulder in which you're moving to Back Position) over your head with sufficient clearance.

Use the reverse Parry Cast to move the Clubbell® around and down to Floor Park.

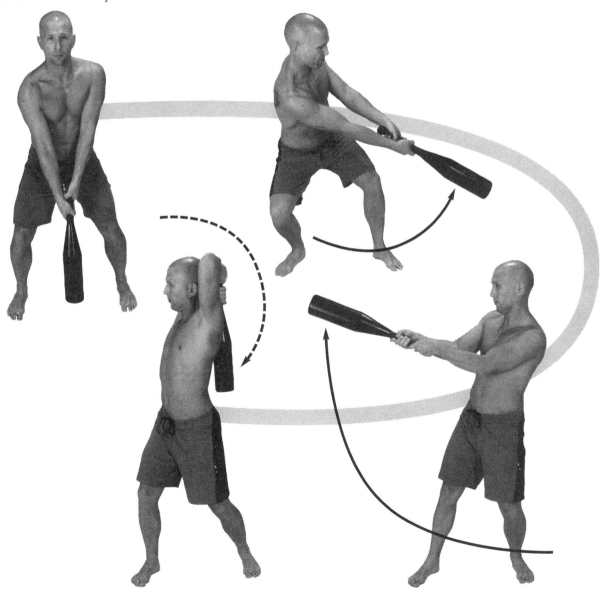

SIDE CLEAN TO SIDE FLAG

The difference between the Side Clean to Side Flag, or "Muscle Out", Position and the Side Clean to Guard Position involves the tight circular rotation of the floating Clubbell® and the 'punch' of the Clubbell® into the Side Flag Position.

Execute the Side Clean while exhaling sharply with the explosive lateral Hip Snap. As you dip beneath the weightless Clubbell®, start to punch both grips outwards to horizontal elbow lockout. You must sharply exhale as you Hip Root to shock absorb.

Use a Side Swing to recover, or contract your arms and move to Floor Park with a Hip Sway to clear your feet and knees.

JERKS

Think of a jerk as having the purpose of driving the Clubbell® off a position around torso height to a position locked out overhead, not by pressing but by dipping under the weight.

FRONT TORCH JERK

Practice the Torch Position variant of the Front Jerk first to refine the best possible jerk technique before practicing the other variations.

Order and Dip: The Bottom-Up Front Jerk is the standard form for Clubbell® training. The exercise starts and ends in Order Position. The movement begins by dipping the hips and knees from Order Position with a sharp exhale and locking your core.

Drive: Drive your legs into the ground as one solid coiled spring with your entire body to send the Clubbell® upward to Torch Position. Keep your shoulders packed and avoid trying to shrug the Clubbell® higher. Use your legs, and exhale while keeping perfect crown to coccyx spinal alignment.

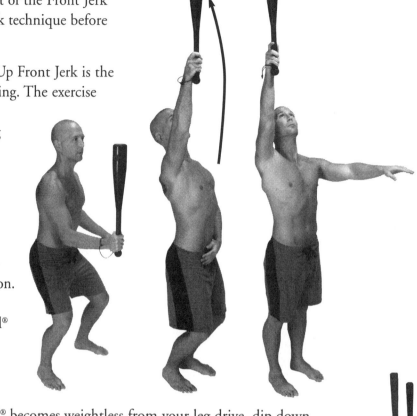

Dip and Lock: As the Clubbell® becomes weightless from your leg drive, dip down again underneath the Clubbell® to get arm lock. Get a solid arm lock so that your arm is completely straight. While in Torch Position, come out of your dip to a standing position with control.

Park: You can shock absorb the Clubbell® back into Order Position with a knee and hip dip, and then rotate the barrel head around to Floor Park. After practicing that skill you can begin to move through without stopping in Order Position to go directly from Torch to Floor Park.

TWO-HANDED FRONT TORCH JERK

The primary difference between the one-handed and two-handed Bottom-Up Front Jerk involves the long and short arm coordination.

All of the one-handed nuances apply, except that on the short arm you may have difficulty locking the arm. This requires practice of the leg drive and the second dip (while the Clubbell® floats weightless). Focus on pressing the elbow pits upward to face the sky, with elbow points facing downward (rather than let them face in towards each other, elbow points outward). This is a very challenging nuance that requires you to focus on a grip choke depth and Clubbell® weight appropriate for you to accomplish the movement. Keep going down in weight and up in choke depth until you can lock the short arm as well as the long arm.

FRONT JERK

The less technical Front Jerk requires greater attention to the Leverage Grip, since the exercise's climax is an overhead leverage hold of approximately 45°.

Perform the Jerk as you would a Front Torch Jerk, but as the Clubbell® floats weightless punch your arm lock out with your elbow pit upward. Accompany this with a second forceful exhalation (after the exhalation of the Jerk's Leg Drive) to fully lock down your core.

The Leverage Grip will be taxed heavily in the crease of the thumb and forefinger, so tightly curl your fingers around into your hand while squeezing from the pinky first to evenly distribute the Clubbell® in your grasp.

Jerking one Clubbell®, you project towards your centerline while slightly rotating your torso towards the lifting arm. You can also perform a strict jerk, which projects straight out from Order Position. To perform the double Clubbell® Front Jerk you must develop a strict jerk, since both Clubbells must project directly upwards from Order Position.

Be careful when parking the Clubbell®. To ensure safety, work on pulling the neck under the barrel head as you drop the height from 45° to having your forearms parallel with the ground in Order Position. Then park from Order as usual. As you become more proficient you can tip the barrel head inwards, circling the neck around outwards to move immediately to floor park. This latter movement takes practice and naturally develops out of the former.

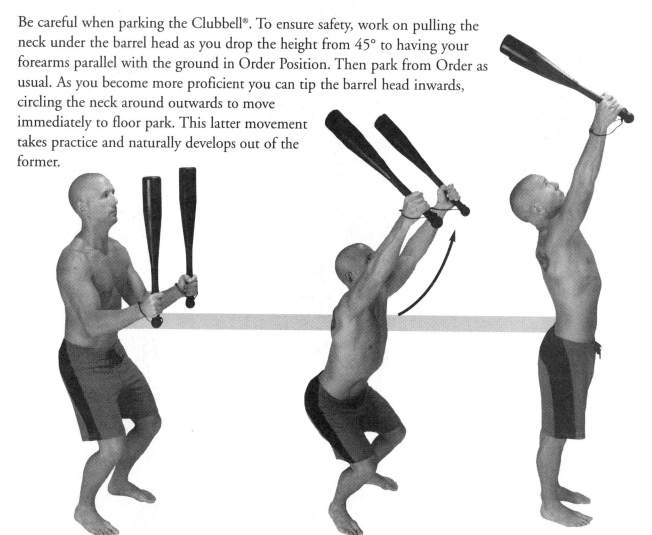

TWO-HANDED FRONT JERK

The Two-Handed Front Jerk requires the use of the complementary grip: force is produced upwards from the bottom grip and stabilized by the top grip. When locking the Clubbell® in place overhead, the top grip acts as the fulcrum and the bottom grip pulls against it to equal out the leverage hold. Ensure that you have full elbow lockout.

The Leg Drive and Hip Dip differ in the two-handed variant in that the Clubbell® now moves towards your centerline. You'll find this easier from a coordination standpoint but more challenging in terms of force production. Dip deep under to get arm lock and drive!

SHOULDER PARK FRONT JERK

The Shoulder Park Front Jerk can act as a building block to the full Front Jerk. However, the mechanics of jerking from the Shoulder Park differ from those of jerking from Order Position.

Take care to sufficiently clear your ear and head. When jerking one Clubbell®, project it up into your centerline while slightly rotating your torso towards the lifting arm. Use special caution here, since you must move from your shoulder to your centerline. You must first clear your head and ear before moving the Clubbell® inwards.

You can also perform a strict jerk, which projects straight out from Shoulder Position. A strict jerk is similar to a Front Jerk in that both Clubbells must project directly upwards from Shoulder Park. Develop your single Clubbell® strict jerk from Shoulder Park first.

TWO-HANDED SHOULDER PARK FRONT JERK

The primary difference in the two-handed variant of the Shoulder Park Front Jerk involves the initial load of the Clubbell®. Since it rests on one shoulder with two arms attached to it, the near arm (the same arm as the shoulder that the Clubbell® is parked upon) provides the primary force and the far arm acts mainly as a guide and stabilizer.

Additionally, the near leg (the leg beneath the shoulder upon which the Clubbell® rests) carries the load. Avoid the temptation to press the Clubbell® off of Shoulder Park while driving with the same side leg. Dip under with both legs and attain arm lock overhead at your centerline, then drive with both legs evenly.

FRONT CLEAN + JERK

For this combination routine, develop the following rhythm: Sit and Load, Drive and Pull, Float and Catch, Drive and Dip, Lock and Clench, Rise then Park.

To discipline the breath in this exercise, sharply exhale on the pull, the catch, the drive and the lock. The inhalation will happen on its own. In such a high skill and high tension exercise you should remain approximately 80% exhaled and locked after the pull. In other words, allow an approximately 20% ("short and sharp") inhale during the float and dip to keep your core locked down tightly.

Perform the Clean as you would normally to Order Position. Be elastic in your catch in Order Position so that you can absorb it in your hips to give you immediate leg drive. Once sufficiently driving, dip under when you have the Clubbell® weightless and get arm lock. Stand while maintaining shoulder pack, arm lock and core activation.

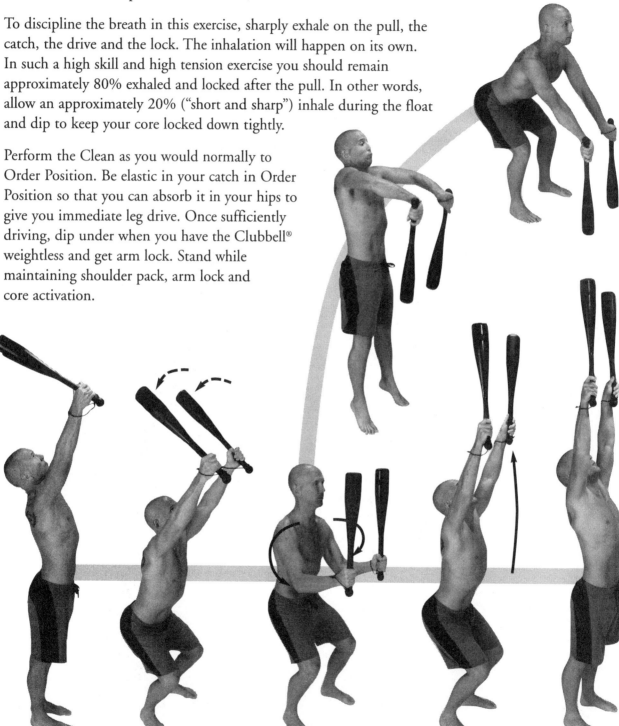

Leverage Tip finish

Torch finish

SIDE TORCH JERK

The Bottom-Up Side Jerk begins in Guard Position. Keep your shoulders packed throughout the entire motion. Avoid lifting your shoulders to your ears.

Rotate your torso to the side, allowing your planted foot to pivot slightly if you must. Dip deeply to the same side of the body as the Guard Position. Exhale and lock your core, then drive your legs powerfully into the ground to project the Clubbell® across your body.

Dip underneath as the Clubbell® becomes weightless and hip root in the opposite direction of the Jerk. Lock your arms with the Clubbell® in Torch position.

You can slowly yield the Clubbell® back into Guard position and stand in Guard Position before performing another repetition. You can also park the Clubbell® carefully directly from Torch.

Develop the following rhythm: Dip, Drive, Float, Root and Lock.

SIDE JERK

The Side Jerk is to the Bottom-Up Side Jerk as the Front Jerk is to the Bottom-Up Front Jerk. Where the Front Jerk begins in Order Position, the Side Jerk begins in Guard Position with a Hip Root, and both conclude with an approximately 45° Leverage Hold.

As in the Side Torch Jerk, rotate your torso to the side allowing your planted foot to pivot slightly if you must. Dip deeply to the same side of the body as the Guard Position. Exhale and lock your core, then drive your legs powerfully into the ground to project the Clubbell® across your body. More force will be transmitted through the hand on the same side as the rooted leg. The opposite hand guides and stabilizes the Clubbell®.

Dip underneath as the Clubbell® becomes weightless and hip root in the opposite direction of the Jerk. Lock your arms with the Clubbell® in an overhead leverage hold using the complementary grip to secure it in place.

Slowly grind back down to Guard Position and rise back up to standing before the next repetition, or park with a Side Swing and Hip Sway. Once you are proficient enough to avoid jerking the joints out you could also go immediately to Floor Park.

SHOULDER PARK SIDE JERK

The Shoulder Park Side Jerk holds the same cautions as the Shoulder Park Front Jerk: safely clear your head and ear before moving the Clubbell® to your center line.

As in the previous two Side Jerks, rotate your torso to the side allowing your planted foot to pivot slightly if you must. Dip deeply to the same side of the body as the Shoulder Park. As in the Two-Handed Shoulder Park Front Jerk, the near arm (the same arm that the Clubbell® is shoulder-parked upon) performs the primary force production and the far arm acts primarily as a guide and stabilizer.

Additionally, the near leg (the leg beneath the shoulder upon which the Clubbell® rests) carries the load. Avoid the temptation to press the Clubbell® off the Shoulder Park by driving with the same-side leg.

Exhale and lock your core, then drive your legs powerfully into the ground to project the Clubbell® across your body. Dip under with both legs and attain arm lock in the leverage hold overhead at your centerline.

Choose to slowly grind the Clubbell® back to Shoulder Park and rise before the next repetition, or use a Side Swing and Hip Sway to bring it to Floor Park. Once proficiency has been gained, you could also simply move straight to Floor Park.

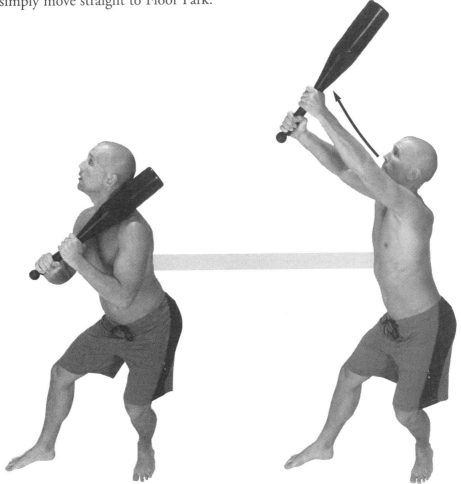

SIDE CLEAN + JERK

Develop the following rhythm in this short but high-skill combination routine: Sway and Pull, Float and Catch, Drive and Dip, Root and Lock, Rise then Park.

As in the Front Clean and Jerk, to discipline the breath in this exercise you must sharply exhale on the sway and pull, on the catch, on the drive and on the lock. The inhalation happens on its own. With such a high skill and high tension exercise you should remain approximately 80% exhaled and locked after the pull. In other words, allow an approximately 20% ("short and sharp") inhale during the float and dip to keep your core locked down tightly.

Perform the Side Clean as you would normally to Guard Position. Be elastic in your catch in Guard Position so that you can absorb it in your rooted hip to give you immediate leg drive upwards. Once sufficiently driving, dip under when you have the Clubbell® weightless and get arm lock.

Unlike the Front Clean and Jerk you do not stand to finish but instead remain rooted and locked, parking immediately afterwards. You could grind the Clubbell® back to Guard and then park, perform a Side Swing and Hip Sway to park it, or park the Clubbell® directly to the floor.

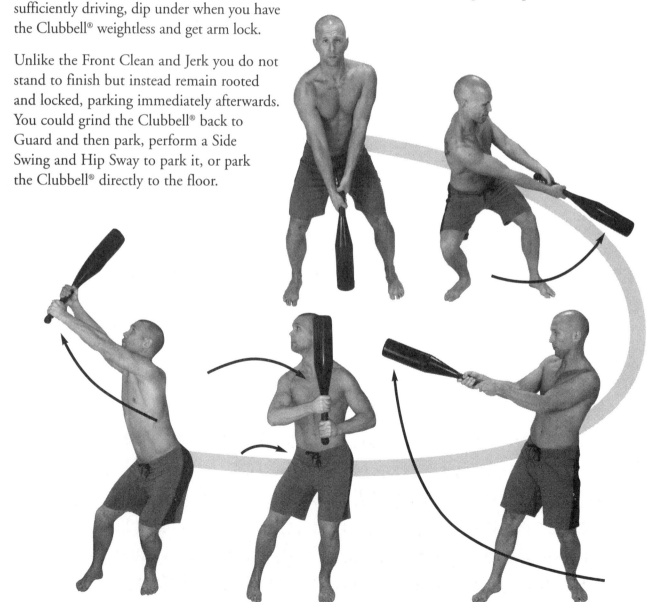

SNATCHES

Although not actually accurate from a biomechanical standpoint, think of a snatch as a seamless combination of the clean and jerk without any pause. Think of the goal of a snatch as ripping the Clubbell® off the ground and locking it overhead as quickly as possible by dipping underneath it to get your arms locked, rather than by pressing it upwards once at torso height.

FRONT TORCH SNATCH

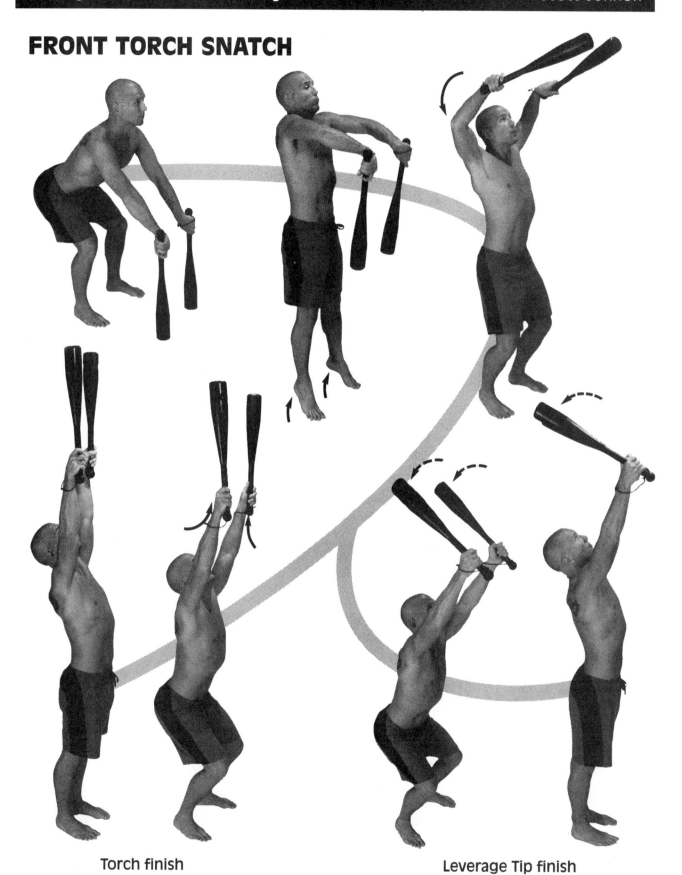

Torch finish　　　　　　　　　　　Leverage Tip finish

Snatches

Practice the Torch Position variant of the Front Snatch first to refine the best possible snatch technique before training the other variations.

Approach, strap in, adjust the choke depth, and confirm your grip!

Ready Position: keep your back straight, look ahead, bend at the waist and not the back, push back with your butt and keep your weight on your heels and your shins perpendicular to floor. Keep your shoulders packed.

There are two variations of Snatch techniques that you can perform: the swing snatch, which begins with a slight back swing on the Clubbells; and the power snatch, which begins from a dead hang (with no pre-swing). This description addresses the power snatch.

Pull and Rotate: with your hips exploding through the motion. Contract your abs, quads and glutes as tightly as possible to drive into the ground with your feet. Sharply exhale and lock down your core and root. Do not consciously inhale. Rip the Clubbells directly upwards until approximately belly height. Simultaneously begin to rotate the neck and knob underneath the barrel head of the Clubbell®.

Dip and Squat: Simultaneous to your pull, as the Clubbell® becomes weightless, dip down in a flat foot squat to get your thighs parallel to the ground (but not so far that your tailbone begins to curl under towards your heels).

Shock Absorb: "Catch" the Clubbell® overhead in Torch Position by confirming your grip tightly to stop all deviation in movement and absorb the weight downwards by elastically dipping with your knees and hips. You should still be maintaining crown to coccyx spinal alignment, perpendicular to floor. The Clubbell® should come to a complete stop.

Rise: While maintaining arm lock (with elbow pits pointed upward and towards your ears) as well as shoulder pack, use your leg drive and hip snap to come to a standing position.

Rotate and Park: To park your Clubbells on the floor, push the barrel heads upwards slightly and begin to rotate the barrel heads towards the ground. The return to Park Position should be smooth. Don't allow the weight to jerk your elbows locked. As a safety precaution you can also slowly grind the Clubbell® down into Order or Guard Position and then park, or you can perform a Front Swing to slow it down into Floor Park.

Develop the following rhythm for this high-skill exercise: Load, Drive and Pull; Float, Squat and Catch; Lock, Drive and Stand; then Park.

TWO-HANDED FRONT TORCH SNATCH

The primary difference between the one-handed and two-handed Bottom-Up Front Snatch involves the long and short arm coordination.

All of the one-handed nuances apply, except that on the short arm you may have difficulty locking the arm. This requires practice of the leg drive and second dip (while the Clubbell® floats weightless). Focus on pressing your elbow pits upward to face the sky with elbow points facing downward (rather than letting them face inward towards each other, elbow points outward). This is a very challenging nuance that requires you to focus on a grip choke depth and Clubbell® weight appropriate for you to accomplish the motion. Keep going down in weight and up in choke depth until you can lock the short arm as well as the long arm.

FRONT SNATCH

The less technical Front Snatch requires greater attention to the Leverage Grip, since the exercise culminates in an overhead leverage hold of approximately 45°.

Perform the Front Snatch as you would a Torch version, but as the Clubbell® floats weightless punch your armlock out with your elbow pit upward. Accompany this with a second forceful exhalation (after the exhalation of the Snatch's Leg Drive) to fully lock down your core.

The Leverage Grip will heavily tax the crease of the thumb and fore-finger, so curl your fingers around into your hand squeezing tightly from the pinky first to evenly distribute the Clubbell® in your grasp.

When snatching one Clubbell®, pull it from ready position between your legs (at your centerline) while slightly rotating your torso towards the lifting arm. To perform the double Clubbell® Front Snatch, pull both Clubbells from directly in front of your knees, if not slightly farther apart at shoulder's width.

Next, slowly grind to Order or swing to park. As you become more proficient you can tip the barrel head inwards, circling the neck around outwards to move immediately to Floor Park.

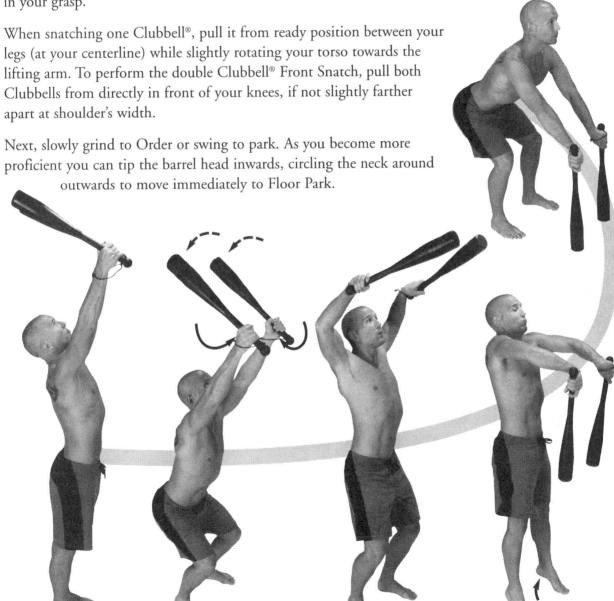

TWO-HANDED FRONT SNATCH

The main difference in the Two-Handed Front Snatch, as opposed to the one-handed variant, involves pulling the neck of the Clubbell® up the center line of the body, being sure not to pull more strongly with the right or left arms. This is actually quite challenging, as coordinating forces between the right and left grips taxes your handedness.

Practice with a light weight in a split grip so that you can find the "floating" point where you can rotate the Clubbell® when it is momentarily weightless. Start with a weight with which you can achieve full arm lock, even on the short arm!

Focus your attention on sticking the Clubbell® in Torch position with perfect arm lock by squeezing your complementary grip equally.

SIDE TORCH SNATCH

Begin practicing the Side Snatch by catching a Side Swing in Torch Position. Doing so will get you acquainted with how to address deviations in overhead movement, how to protect yourself, and how to effectively catch the Clubbell® overhead. Remember to keep your shoulders packed and to activate your core by exhaling on the upswing.

Sway and Load: This lateral equivalent of the Front Snatch requires lateral explosiveness from the hip. Begin with a Hip Sway to load your body. You will need this additional loading because, due to the lateral mechanics, you cannot dip under as deeply as you can in the Front Snatch to get the arm lock overhead.

Drive and Snap: Drive your loaded leg into the ground and snap your hip to begin to rip the Clubbell® off the Hip Sway.

Rotate: Begin rotating the neck under the barrel head as the Clubbell® floats at approximately shoulder height.

Dip, Root and Lock: Dip down in a Hip Root to catch the Clubbell® overhead in Torch Position with full arm lock and shoulder pack.

Park: Park with a Side Swing, take it directly to Floor Park, or grind down to Guard or Order Position before parking.

SIDE SNATCH

All of the nuances of the Side Torch Snatch apply, except that the distance traveled is not as great because the Clubbell® must not be caught overhead in Torch Position. Like the Side Jerk, the Side Snatch concludes with an approximately 45° Leverage Hold.

After the Leg Drive and Hip Snap off of the Hip Sway, rotate the Clubbell® in a tighter circle to punch your arms to lockout with a leverage hold.

The Hip Root can feel more challenging on this one because the leverage hold causes the complementary grip to rely heavily upon the absorbing hip and leg for shock absorption.

Remember to exhale and lock down the core on the pull and on the catch.

PRESSES

Think of a press as having the purpose of driving the Clubbell® off a position from an unlocked arm position to a locked arm position, not by jerking (dipping under the weight) but by grinding it up or out smoothly.

TORCH PRESS

Practice the Torch Press first to refine the best possible press technique before practicing the other variations.

Confirm and Activate: Begin with the Clubbell® in Order Position. Tightly confirm your grip around the neck of the Clubbell® with a sharp exhalation. Ensure crown to coccyx spinal alignment and lock down your core.

Drive: Drive your elbow underneath the neck of the Clubbell®. Push your body away from the Clubbell® to maintain proper shoulder pack. Drive your legs into the ground, lock your core, and root completely with a hard exhalation.

Lock: Establish arm lock at an angle greater than 45°, where the Clubbell® is locked in a Torch Position. In arm lock, your elbow pits should be pointing behind you. Keep tight shoulder pack and avoid shrugging.

Keep proper crown to coccyx spinal alignment! You may perform the single Clubbell® Torch Press with a slight turn of the torso, or strictly pressing with no twist. Develop the strict press to perform the double Clubbell® Torch Press.

Lower: Lower the Torch Hold in a slow and controlled manner until the Clubbell® once again rests in Order.

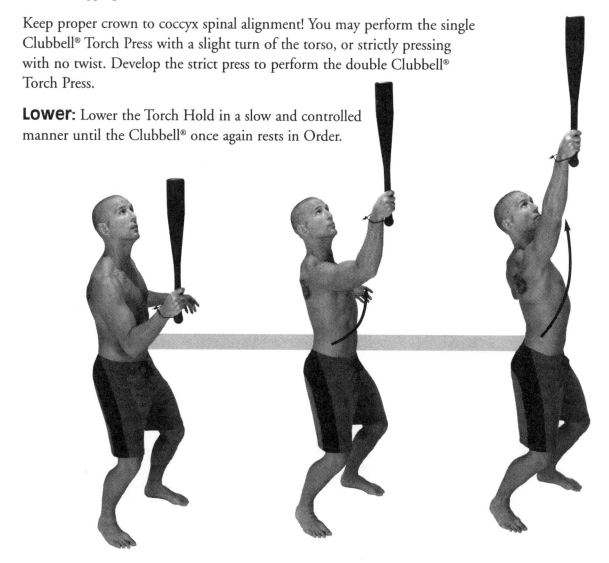

TWO-HANDED TORCH PRESS

The challenge of the two-handed variation of the Torch Press involves securing proper arm lock with the short arm. Proper arm lock involves elbow pits pointing to the rear, elbow points pointing to the front.

Decrease weight and grip choke depth until you can perform the two-handed variation with proper arm lock. Train proper arm lock to gain 100% of the benefit of this exercise and to prevent future counter-productive performance impediments, as well as potential soft tissue strain.

Your will need to exhale sharply to activate and lock your core and root in the two-handed variation. You must avoid shrugging, and keep proper shoulder pack.

FRONT PRESS

Although it appears less technical, the challenge of the Front Press involves performing the leverage grip while driving the Clubbell® in an arc upwards.

Confirm and Activate: Begin with the Clubbell® in Order Position. Tightly confirm your grip around the neck of the Clubbell® with a sharp exhalation. Ensure crown to coccyx spinal alignment and lock down your core.

Drive: Drive your elbow underneath the neck of the Clubbell®. Slightly rotate the neck of the Clubbell® underneath the barrel head so that you achieve arm lock at an angle of greater than 45° upwards. As you press squeeze the neck tightly, especially with the pinky finger side of the hand where the Clubbell® threatens to rip out of your grasp. Tighten your pointer finger and the thumb side of your hand to ensure a more effective leverage hold.

Lock: In arm lock your elbow pits point upwards! Keep tight shoulder pack and avoid shrugging.

Keep proper crown to coccyx spinal alignment! However, as in the one-handed Torch Press, you may perform the Clubbell® Front Press with a slight turn of the torso, or you may do it strictly pressing with no twist. Develop the strict press to perform the double Clubbell® Front Press.

Lower: Lower the Torch Hold in a slow and controlled manner until the Clubbell® once again rests in Order.

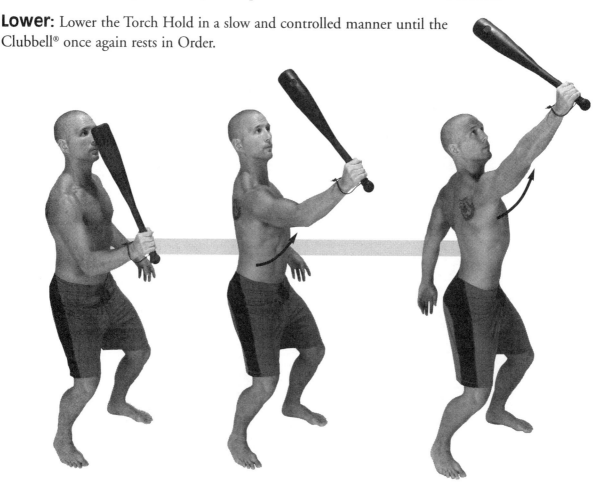

TWO-HANDED FRONT PRESS

The primary difference between the two-handed Torch Press and two-handed Front Press involves the complementary and leverage grips. All of the nuances of the Torch Press apply to the Front Press except your grip confirmation, as this press takes you into a disadvantageous leverage position.

As you press upwards the long arm drives in a longer arc than the short arm to rotate the neck underneath the barrel head of the Clubbell®.

The short arm acts as both a forward press and as a fulcrum around which the long arm levers the Clubbell® into position.

Ensure that you keep straight wrist alignment on this grind. Maintain shoulder pack, and avoid shrugging at all costs.

FLAG PRESS

The challenge of the Flag press that differentiates it from the Torch and Front Presses involves the lack of support in pressing to Flag Position.

The drive to Flag requires you to fully activate your core and lock your root. Shoulder pack and activate your chest and back simultaneously as if you were trying to brace a door against someone trying to push it from the other side.

For a double Clubbell® Flag Press, flex your chest as you come to arm lock.

The most difficult portion of the Flag Press involves rotating the elbow pits up towards the sky.

To return to Order Position perform a grinding, slow pull to bring the Clubbell® back into place.

TWO-HANDED FLAG PRESS

The difficulty in the two-handed variant of the Flag Press involves the short arm rotation in arm lock to bring the elbow pit upwards. You must ensure proper arm lock to gain 100% of the benefit of this exercise and to prevent future counter-productive performance impediments, as well as potential soft tissue strain.

Decrease weight and grip choke depth until you can perform the two-handed variation with proper arm lock. You must keep proper wrist alignment (no flexion or extension) as you press the Clubbell® forward. This will involve minor sliding of your grip as you extend.

You will need to exhale very sharply to activate and lock your core and root in the two-handed variation. You must avoid shrugging, and keep proper shoulder pack.

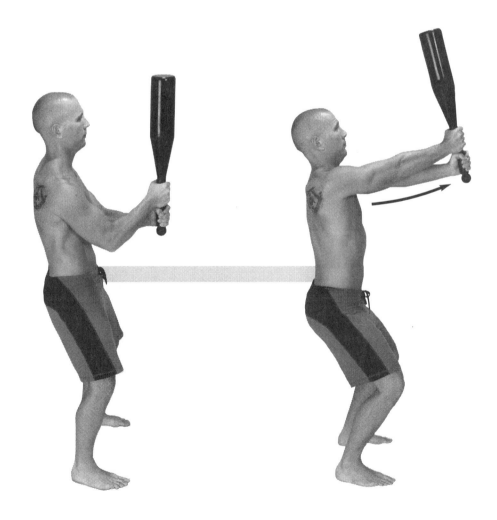

SIDE TORCH PRESS

The Side Torch Press requires careful timing when coordinating the overhead press with the side hip root.

Confirm and Activate: Begin with the Clubbell® in Guard Position. Tightly confirm your grip around the neck of the Clubbell® with a sharp exhalation. Ensure crown to coccyx spinal alignment and lock down your core.

Drive: Drive your elbow underneath the neck of the Clubbell®. Pack your shoulders tightly as you press the Clubbell® up and across your centerline and simultaneously rotate your torso in the direction of the press.

Root: Hip root deep to the opposite side of the original Guard Position simultaneous to your drive. As you root, feel the support from your rooted hip and planted leg come under the Clubbell® to press your body away from the Clubbell® by pushing down on the Earth.

Lock: Lock your arms in Torch Position (higher than 45° to the ground). Your elbow pits must point upwards to receive 100% of the benefit of this exercise and to prevent the development of performance impediments or potential injuries. Keep tight shoulder pack and avoid shrugging.

Lower: Lower the Torch Hold in a slow and controlled manner until the Clubbell® once again rests in Guard.

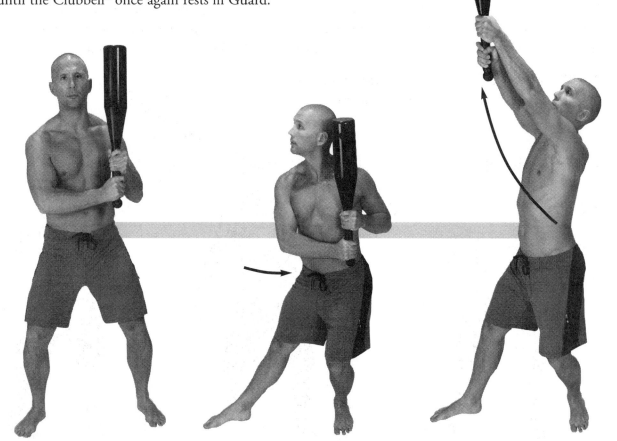

SIDE PRESS

The Side Press is to the Side Torch Press as the Front Press is to the Front Torch Press. The difference between the Side Press and the Side Torch Press involves performing the leverage grip while driving the Clubbell® in an arc upwards, from Guard Position, across your centerline with a deep hip root. To do this you will need the skill that you learned in the Front Press: the complementary and leverage grips to press into a disadvantageous position.

Confirm and Activate: Begin with the Clubbell® in Guard Position. Tightly confirm your grip around the neck of the Clubbell® with a sharp exhalation. Ensure crown to coccyx spinal alignment and lock down your core.

Drive: Drive your elbow underneath the neck of the Clubbell®. Pack your shoulders tightly as you press the Clubbell® up and across your centerline, at the same time rotating your torso in the direction of the press. As you press upwards the long arm drives in a longer arc than the short arm to rotate the neck underneath the barrel head of the Clubbell®. The short arm acts as both a forward press and as a fulcrum around which the long arm levers the Clubbell® into position

Root: Hip root deep to the opposite side of the original Guard Position simultaneous to your drive. As you root, feel the support from your rooted hip and planted leg come under the Clubbell® to press your body away from the Clubbell® by pushing down on the Earth.

Lock: Lock your arms in a Leverage Hold (higher than 45° to the ground). Your elbow pits must point upwards to receive 100% of the benefit of this exercise and to prevent the development of performance impediments or potential injuries. Keep tight shoulder pack and avoid shrugging.

Lower: Lower the Torch Hold in a slow and controlled manner until the Clubbell® once again rests in Guard.

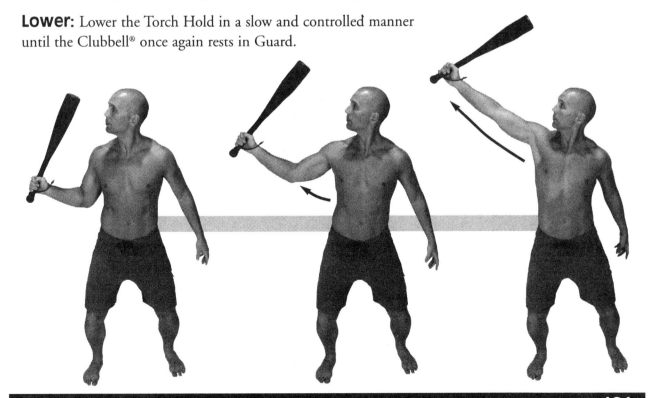

SIDE FLAG PRESS

The challenge of the Flag press that differentiates it from the Side Torch and Side Front Presses involves the lack of support in pressing to Side Flag Position.

Hip root deeply to one side, because the drive to Flag requires you to fully activate your core and lock your root. Shoulder pack and activate your chest and back simultaneously as though you were trying to brace a door.

Drive across your centerline from the top hand of the Guard as you rotate and hip root deeply. The bottom hand of the grip will pull the Clubbell® until you can get it behind the neck and begin pressing with it as well towards full arm lock.

The most difficult portion of the Flag Press involves rotating the elbow pits up towards the sky. You must rotate the elbow pits skyward to receive 100% of the health benefits of this exercise and to prevent performance impediments and potential soft tissue injuries.

To return to Guard Position perform a grinding, slow pull to bring the Clubbell® back into place as you rotate out of hip root to standing.

CLEAN AND PRESS

As in the Clean and Jerks, you may perform combination routines with the above list of Presses once you've master them individually. Here is the formula to plug into numerous permutations of Clean and Presses:

1. Front or Side Clean
2. Clean to Order Position, Guard Position or Shoulder Park
3. Perform a Torch, Front or Flag Press

Never sacrifice the basic form of each Clean and each Press. To receive 100% of the benefit of combination routines you must ensure that you maintain proper form in each constituent part of the combination routine.

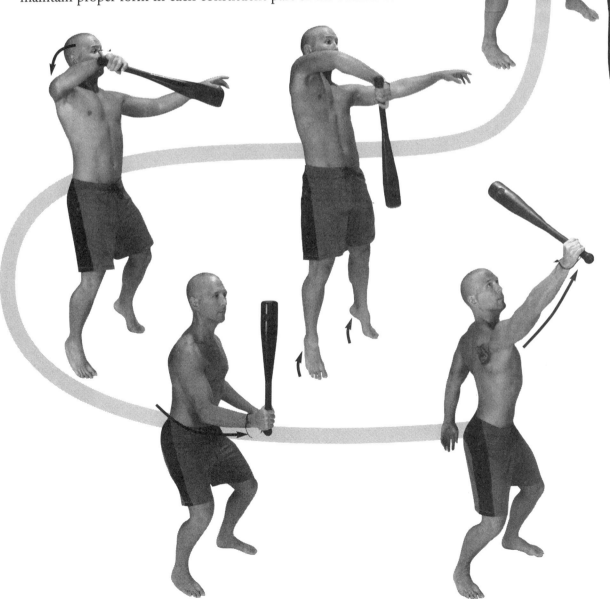

Photographer: Wesley Buckingham • Contributed by D. Cody Fielding

CASTS

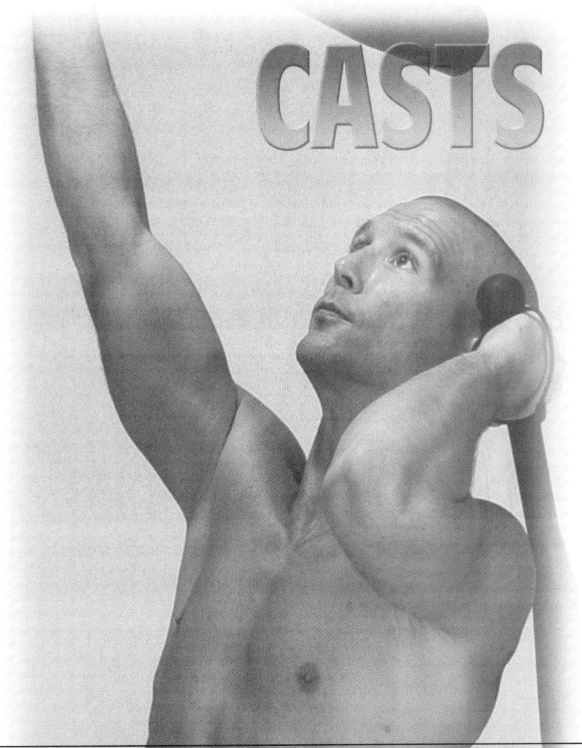

Think of a cast as having the purpose of holding the Clubbell® at approximately torso height and slinging it from bottom-up to bottom-down (or bottom-down to bottom-up) position.

WRIST CAST

This is the basis of all casting exercises. Practice the Wrist Cast to refine the best possible casting technique before practicing the other variations.

1. Begin in Order Position.
2. Lift your elbow to the side so that your forearm rests parallel with the ground and your upper arm points outwards from your torso.
3. Slowly tilt your wrist so that you drift the barrel head of the Clubbell® towards the upper arm of the hand that is holding the Clubbell®.
4. Use the Leverage Grip to slow down the descent of the barrel head so that it gently touches your upper arm.
5. Again relying upon the Leverage Grip, tilt your wrist back down and slowly cast the barrel head back up to Order Position. Avoid moving your elbow and avoid shrugging your shoulders. Keep proper shoulder pack and spinal alignment. Use a sharp exhalation to lock down your core, and get a firm root on the ground.

You must work to keep your entire palm squeezed tightly against the Clubbell® in order to receive 100% of the health benefits of this exercise and to prevent performance impediments or potential soft tissue injuries.

TWO HANDED WRIST CAST — THE CROWBAR

The difference between the one- and two-handed variations involves the coupling of the complementary grip with the leverage grip.

1. Begin with the Clubbell® in Guard position.
2. Lift your elbow to the side so that the forearm of the top grip rests parallel with the ground and your upper arm points outwards from your torso.
3. Separate your hands laterally so that the head of the Clubbell® lowers to rest on the upper arm of the hand in the top position of the grip.
4. Slowly press your top hand toward your bottom hand while you push with the bottom hand towards the top hand to cast the Clubbell® back into Guard Position.

You must work to keep both palms squeezed tightly against the Clubbell® in order to receive 100% of the health benefits of this exercise and to prevent performance impediments or potential soft tissue injuries.

ARM CAST

After the Wrist Cast, the Arm Cast forms the foundation of the total movement of the arm when casting. Practice the Arm Cast to refine the best possible casting technique before practicing the other variations.

The Arm cast begins in Back Position and moves over the shoulder to Order Position. However, once understood, the movement between Order to Back and returning to Order also includes a storage and release of elastic energy that gives you access to 100% of the health benefits of this exercise.

Place: Begin by practicing moving from Order to Back Position. Ensure that you have proper crown to coccyx spinal alignment and shoulder pack. Drive your elbow behind the knob, and drive the neck in line behind the center of mass. Exhale as your move into Back Position. Place — do not swing — the barrel head into Back Position.

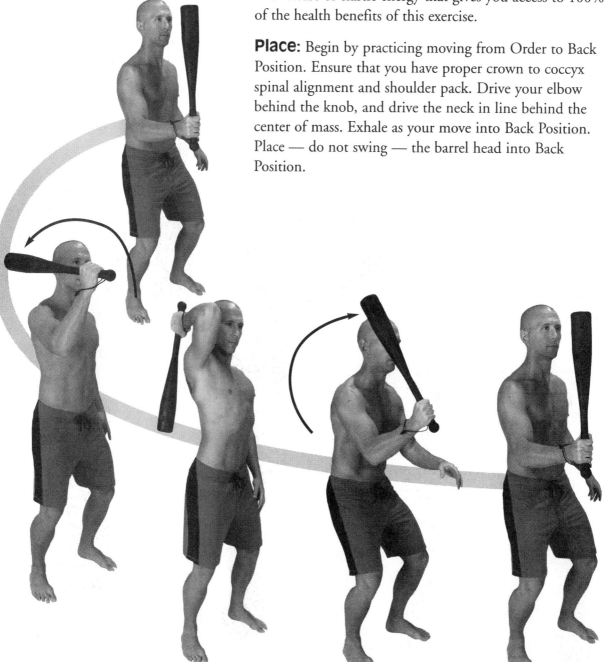

Pass the Clubbell® by your ear (not over your head.) Place it into position without hitting your back (though it may touch your back). Keep your elbow and upper arm pointed directly towards the sky. Avoid letting your elbow rotate your arm to the side.

Absorb: Popping out of Back Position takes practice as you learn to store and release the elastic energy of the position. Shock absorb as the Clubbell® moves into Back Position by dipping your knees without bending forward or backward.

Cast: With a strong exhalation, contract your core, glutes and quads, grip the ground with your toes, and tighten your legs. As you do so, pull your elbow up and around to pull the neck of the Clubbell® in line with the center of mass. Pass the Clubbell® by your ear. Avoid swinging it over your head.

Stick: Continue to pull the neck in front of the barrel head like a horse leading a cart. Bring your elbow to your ribs and stick the knob in Order Position. When performed properly there will be no deviation in the Clubbell®.

ALTERNATING ARM CAST — DRUMMING CAST

Alternating Arm Casts with two Clubbells requires mastery of the basics to avoid compromising form for economy of motion. When "drumming" two Clubbells, you must maintain strict form. Do not allow your elbows to flare outwards and do not allow your torso to twist into the equal and opposite swinging motion.

There are two variations:

Beginner: perform an Arm Cast with the right arm (Back Position, Order Position, Back Position), then perform an Arm Cast with the left arm.

Advanced: begin with one Clubbell® in Order Position and the other in Back Position. Simultaneously switch their position so that they pass the ears in opposite directions at the same time.

TWO-HANDED ARM CAST — THE GAMA CAST

The primary distinction between the one- and two-handed variations of the Arm Cast involves threading the head around the far arm connected to the Clubbell®. Avoid crossing your face. The forearm lifts parallel to the ground like a face shield on a Medieval knight's helmet. The second distinction involves the elbow flare in two-handed work.

Place: Begin with the Clubbell® in Order Position. Confirm your grip tightly into the handle with a strong exhalation. Keep proper crown to coccyx spinal alignment and lock down your core.

Choose one shoulder for the movement. Because you will move off of your centerline and over one shoulder, be sure to provide sufficient clearance for your head and ear such that you don't need to lean away. Drive your elbow behind the knob of the near arm (i.e. the right arm if traveling over right shoulder) and drive the neck behind the barrel head. Exhale as your move into Back Position. Place — do not swing — the barrel head into Back Position.

Pass the Clubbell® by your ear (not over your head). As you do so, thread your far forearm over your head (i.e. the left arm if traveling over your right shoulder). Place it into position without hitting your back, though it may touch your back. Your elbows will flare out to the sides, unlike the one-handed variation. Keep your chin level and your chest lifted, and keep your back straight but not arched.

Absorb: Popping out of Back Position takes practice as you learn to store and release the elastic energy of the position. Shock absorb as the Clubbell® moves into Back Position by dipping your knees without bending forward or backward.

Cast: With a strong exhalation, contract your core, glutes and quads, grip the ground with your toes, and tighten your legs. As you do so, pull your elbow up and around to pull the neck of the Clubbell® in line with the center of mass. Simultaneously unthread your far arm. Pass the Clubbell® by your ear. Avoid swinging it over your head.

Stick: Continue to pull the neck in front of the barrel head. Bring your elbows to your ribs and stick the knob of the Clubbell® in Order Position.

TWO-HANDED ARM CAST CIRCULAR PIVOT

The Two-Handed Arm Cast can be made cyclical by changing the direction and location of the Back and Order Positions:

Back Position Pivot

Perform an Arm Cast from Order Position to the right shoulder Back Position. Adjust your reach to place the Clubbell® in the left shoulder Back Position. Perform an Arm Cast to Order Position. Reverse Directions.

Order Position Pivot

Perform an Arm Cast from right shoulder Back Position to Order Position. Perform an Arm Cast from Order Position to left shoulder Back Position. Reverse directions.

Circular Pivot

Perform an Arm Cast from right shoulder Back Position to Order Position. Perform an Arm Cast to left shoulder Back Position. Adjust your arms to place the Clubbell® in right shoulder Back Position. Perform an Arm Cast to Order Position. Continue or reverse directions.

TWO-HANDED ARM CAST TO FLAG POSITION — THE BARBARIAN

The distinction of this variation is that it requires the arm casting power to move from Back Position directly out into a fully arm locked Flag Position. The tremendous power generation required for this demands that you first master the basic Arm Cast.

An intermediate exercise that you could perform would be to execute an Arm Cast (to Order Position) followed by a Front Press to Flag Position.

The key to this powerful movement lies in the breath and in driving the elbow pits upwards while the Clubbell® passes over the shoulder. Sometimes this can be felt as a contraction of the triceps, but it involves full bodily coordination and synergy.

SHOULDER CAST

The challenge of the Shoulder Cast involves grinding the Clubbell® outside and away from the core and guiding it with alignment to return to Back Position.

Flare: Place the Clubbell® in Back Position. Exhale and lock your core and root. Keep your shoulders packed throughout the movement, and maintain crown to coccyx spinal alignment. Flare your elbow in the direction that you intend to cast your Clubbell®. Look in the same direction and keep looking there throughout the exercise.

Release: With a strong exhalation, pull your elbow down while flexing your lat as though you were performing a pull-up. Pull the neck in line with the barrel head of the Clubbell®. Pay attention to the fact that you are moving the Clubbell® in a slightly angled trajectory from behind your back to directly at your side. Confirm your grip tightly to stabilize. Do not allow your wrist and forearm to rotate your elbow backwards.

Stick: Place your elbow tight against your ribs with your elbow pointed downward. Flexing your lat will prevent you from bringing your elbows to touch your ribs, but work to do so nonetheless.

Return: Drive the neck under the barrel head and your elbow under your grip to move the Clubbell® out of this laterally held Order Position. Pay attention to the return trajectory of the barrel head. Because you must be looking in that direction for the exercise, you will be able to watch to ensure that the barrel head does not come towards your head but travels properly into Back Position.

Place: As your elbow lifts higher flex your entire arm, shoulder and back to slow down the Clubbell®. The slower that you return to Back Position, the more effectively you'll be able to place the Clubbell® in Back Position with no deviation.

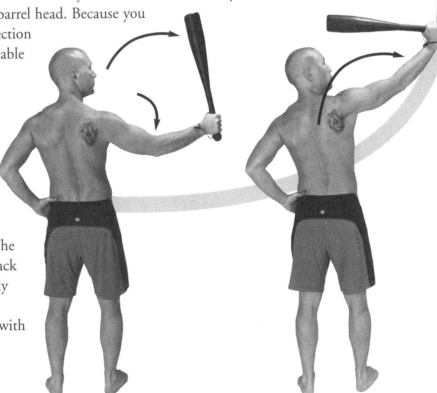

TWO-HANDED SHOULDER CAST

The difference between the Two-Handed Arm Cast and the Two-Handed Shoulder Cast is that the latter begins and ends in Guard Position, rather than in Order Position like the Arm Cast.

As in the Arm Cast version you must thread and unthread your head with the far arm. The near arm elbow stays tight next to your head as your drive the elbow completely skyward.

The Clubbell® rotates on a much tighter arc in this exercise, since it travels over the same shoulder of the Guard Position from which it was launched. As a result, you must use both the complementary and leverage grips to prevent the sudden acceleration as the barrel head passes over your shoulder by your ear.

Work to stick the barrel head into Back Position. Use the stored elastic energy to bounce out of Back Position with a strong exhalation, proper crown to coccyx spinal alignment, and no forward or backward bending.

As in all the casts, keep your knees and hips slightly bent to allow for additional shock absorption and to help you with leg drive, even when just stabilizing the weight by rooting it to the ground.

SHOULDER CAST TO SIDE FLAG POSITION — THE MUSCLE OUT

The difference between this exercise and the basic Shoulder Cast involves the Hip Root to the side with the torso twist. You simultaneously perform the lateral version of an Arm Cast to Flag Position.

Place: Move to Guard Position and immediately thread your head to move into Back Position, as in the basic Two-Handed Shoulder Cast (with the near arm elbow tight next to the head – elbow not flaring).

Root: Rotate and perform a deep hip root to the opposite side of the direction in which you intend to cast. As you root, feel the support from your rooted hip and planted leg come under the Clubbell® to press your body away from the Clubbell® by pushing down on the Earth.

Cast: Perform a sharp exhalation to lock down your core for the pull. Allow no spinal bending, forward or backward. Pull your near arm elbow around and down to your ribs to rip the Clubbell® out of back position, pulling it in line neck before barrel head. The arc will be longer moving directly to Flag Position, so use your core activation to pull harder to avoid form deterioration.

Lock: Drive your elbow pits skyward by flexing your triceps and lifting your chest. Keep proper crown to coccyx spinal alignment and avoid any backward spinal bending. You must ensure proper arm lock to gain 100% of the benefit of this exercise and to prevent future counter-productive performance impediments and potential soft tissue strain. You may feel a natural inhalation when you lift your chest and crown to finalize the Flag Position. You must avoid shrugging, and keep proper shoulder pack.

Decrease weight and grip choke depth until you can perform the exercise with proper arm lock. You must keep proper wrist alignment (no flexion or extension) as you press the Clubbell® forward. This will involve minor sliding of your grip as you extend.

DOUBLE SHOULDER CAST — THE CRUCIFIX

The primary challenge of the Double Shoulder Cast involves the timing of casting the two barrel heads in opposite directions without clanging them together.

To maintain proper separation of the two Clubbells on the cast out of Back Position, perfect the skill of pulling the neck upwards in line with the barrel heads as though you were pulling an arrow out of a quiver on your back. Avoid "wristing" the Clubbells directly out to the side, or one of two things may happen:

1. The Clubbells bang together and change their trajectory: a potential shoulder health danger.
2. The barrel heads of the Clubbells flare backwards, out of line with the neck: a potential wrist and elbow danger as the barrel head of the Clubbells backwardly rotate while you attempt to cast them to Side Flag Position.

Keep your shoulders packed, lift your heart, and flex your latisimus muscles as though you were holding two horses pulling in opposite directions. Rotate your elbow pits skyward and flex your triceps. Maintain proper wrist alignment.

Contract your elbows to your sides and park.

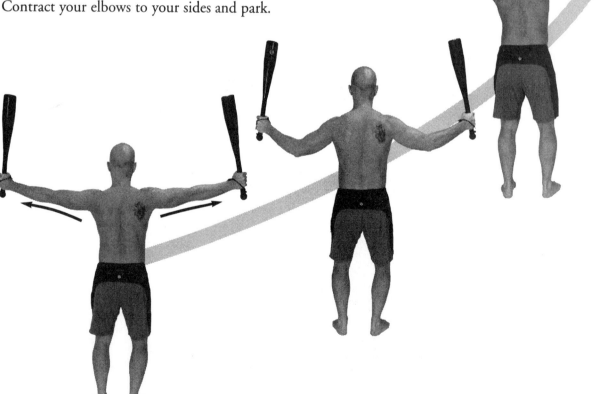

ALTERNATING SHOULDER CAST — THE KODO CAST

An intermediate exercise to build your Double Shoulder Cast is the Alternating Shoulder Cast, also known as the Kodo Cast. With two Clubbells in Back Position, Shoulder Cast one to Side Flag Position. Return it to Back Position. Cast the other Clubbell® to Side Flag Position. Return it to Back Position. Repeat.

HEAD CAST

The Head Cast differs from the Shoulder and Arm Cast by traveling from Back Position directly overhead to Torch Position or to Leverage Hold.

Place: As with the Arm and Shoulder Cast, ensure that you have proper crown to coccyx spinal alignment and shoulder pack. Drive your elbow behind the knob, and drive the neck in line behind the center of mass. Exhale as your move into Back Position. Place — do not swing — the barrel head into Back Position.

Absorb: Popping out of Back Position takes practice as you learn to store and release the elastic energy of the position. Shock absorb as the Clubbell® moves into Back Position by dipping the knees without bending forward or backward. Avoid leaning and rocking at all costs. Focus on a very strong exhalation to launch out of Back Position.

Launch: With a very strong exhalation contract your core, glutes and quads, grip the ground with your toes, and tighten your legs. Flex your triceps and latisimus muscles. Avoid shrugging. Keep your shoulders packed.

Grip the Clubbell® tightly. Pull the neck upward as you rotate it underneath the barrel head. Feel the Leverage Grip take over as the Clubbell® rotates parallel to the ground. Begin to tilt your wrist to head towards Torch Position lockdown.

Stick: Lock down the neck in Torch Position with the barrel head center of mass directly over the top of your grip. Your grip should feel like you are hanging by your hands on two ropes. When performed properly, there will be no deviation in the Clubbell®.

Return: Tip the barrel head slightly backwards and slowly grind the Clubbells to return to Back Position for your next repetition or to park from there.

SHOULDER CAST LEVERAGE HOLD VARIATION

This variation differs from the strict Head Cast in that it does not travel all the way to Torch Position, but stops in a Leverage Hold: barrel head pointing backwards approximately parallel with the ground. Although it requires less explosiveness from the core, the Leverage Hold demands greater grip and arm-intensive work.

ALTERNATING HEAD CAST — THE SEE-SAW

The Alternating Head Cast is the upward projecting complement to the forward projecting Alternating Arm Cast.

Alternating Head Casts with two Clubbells requires mastery of the basics to avoid compromising form for economy of motion. When "see-sawing" two Clubbells you must maintain strict form. Do not allow your elbows to flare outwards. Keep them tight next to your ears. Do not allow your torso to twist into the equal and opposite swinging motion.

There are two variations:

1. **Beginner:** perform a Head Cast with the right arm (Back Position, Torch Position, Back Position), then perform a Head Cast with the left arm.
2. **Advanced:** begin with one Clubbell® in Torch Position and the other in Back Position. Simultaneously switch their positions so that they pass the ears in opposite directions at the same time.

TWO-HANDED HEAD CAST

The primary distinction between the one- and two-handed variations of the Head Cast relates to the coordination of the Complementary Grip with the upward explosion of the Clubbell®.

Avoid the temptation to move the Clubbell® along the length of your spine. Keep it in Back Position on either the right or left side to avoid casting the knob into the back of your head when you begin the upward movement of the exercise.

Place: Begin with the Clubbell® in Back Position. Confirm your grip tightly into the handle with a strong exhalation. Keep proper crown to coccyx spinal alignment and lock down your core.

Absorb: Popping out of Back Position takes practice as you learn to store and release the elastic energy of the position. Shock absorb as the Clubbell® moves into Back Position by dipping your knees without bending forward or backward.

Launch: With a tremendously strong exhalation contract your core, glutes and quads, grip the ground with your toes, and tighten your legs. At the same time, pull your elbows upwards and begin to rotate the Clubbell® neck under the barrel head. Use your bottom hand (closest to the knob) to pull down as you pry upwards with your top hand (closest to the barrel head).

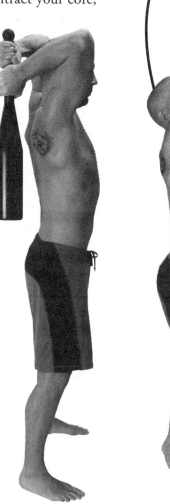

Stick: Lead from your core activation as you cast the Clubbell® upward in front of your face until your arms lock at an angle greater than 45° with the Clubbell® stuck in Torch Position. Point your elbow pits directly behind you. Press your body away from the Clubbell® as a way of keeping your shoulders packed throughout the movement.

Return: Tip the barrel head slightly backwards and slowly grind the Clubbells to return to Back Position for your next repetition or to park from there.

SHIELD CAST

The Shield Cast requires prior mastery of the Arm, Shoulder and Head Casts, since it could be considered an amalgam of the essential elements of all three.

The unique challenge of the Shield Cast involves sticking the Clubbell® in the far side Back Position, and swinging the barrel head in a short arc to the near side Back Position to propel it back to Order.

Use all of the basic nuances present in all casts: shoulder pack, wrist alignment, core activation, spinal alignment, hip recruitment, and leg drive.

Arc: Begin in Order Position. With an exhalation, drive the neck in line with the barrel head of the Clubbell® in front of your face and over your far shoulder. The Clubbell® should not cast over your head. Simultaneously, thread your arm in a manner similar to the action of the far arm in a Two-Handed Arm Cast.

Stick: When you stick the barrel head in the far side Back Position your forearm should be approximately parallel to the ground behind your head.

Swing and Cover: Do not hold the far side Back Position. With a tightly confirmed grip, swing your elbow from flaring to tucked close towards your ear, as in the action of covering your head against an incoming blow to the side of your head. Due to your grip, this elbow and shoulder motion will cause the barrel head of the Clubbell® to swing rapidly towards the near side Back Position.

The momentum will carry the Clubbell® barrel head beyond your near side back position so that the neck points at a slight angle towards your centerline and the barrel head points outwards away from your centerline.

Return Arc: You will feel the Clubbell® reach the zenith of the outward flare of the barrel head center of mass, where if you did nothing it would begin the return swing to your near side Back Position perpendicular to the ground. Pull when the Clubbell® floats at that zenith. With a strong exhalation and no spinal rocking, rip the neck of the Clubbell® in line with the angle of the outwardly swung barrel head. Pull the Clubbell® in an arc over your shoulder towards Order Position in front of you.

Stick and Move: Land in a modified Order Position held in your centerline. Slightly shift the Order Position to its proper place to your near side.

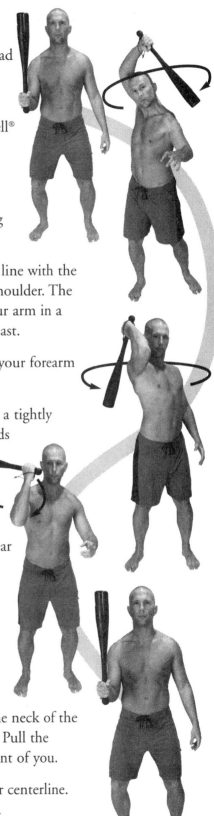

TWO-HANDED SHIELD CAST

The challenge of the two handed variation lies in the timing of the barrel head swing in Back Position and the long arc from Guard Position to far side Back Position. The long arcing move from one Guard Position around in the Shield Cast to the opposite Guard Position distinguishes the Two-Handed Shield Cast from the Two-Handed Arm Cast Circular Pivot Variation (which moves from Order to one Back Position to the other and returns to Order again).

Arc and Stick: Begin in Guard Position. Use the far arm (which will have the grip closest to the barrel head) to control the rotation and lift and the near arm (with the grip closest to the knob) to drive under the Clubbell®. Properly thread your near arm (if beginning in Right Guard, then thread your right arm over your head) to stick the barrel head in far side Back Position.

Swing and Cover: When the Clubbell® moves from far side to near side Back Position, use the far arm (which will have the grip closest to the barrel head) in complementary grip to help drive the center of mass. The near arm counters against that drive to achieve the alignment into the angle ready to be ripped over your shoulder. When in position, the near arm of the shoulder that you intend to bring the Clubbell® over will be in the tight cover position learned in the one-handed variation.

Return Arc and Stick: When you will feel the Clubbell® reach the zenith of the outward flare of the barrel head center of mass, pull when the Clubbell® floats. With a strong exhalation and no spinal rocking, rip the neck of the Clubbell® in line with the angle of the outwardly swung barrel head. The near arm (gripping closer towards the barrel head) of the shoulder that you are pulling over will be the primary force, and the far arm (gripping closer to the knob) will be directing the pull in an arc over your shoulder towards the opposite Guard Position, where you began. Land in the original Guard Position.

PARRY CAST

The Parry Cast could be considered the pinnacle of basic Clubbell® exercise, for it travels through all three planes (front/back, right/left, top/bottom). The Parry Cast, once mastered, also acts as a movement "safety valve" for when you fail to perform an exercise correctly. The Parry Cast (and its mirror twin the Reverse Parry Cast) may be used to move an improperly performed exercise to Floor Park. However, in order to be able to carry out this bailing maneuver you must practice and refine your Parry Cast.

Stand: Begin in Ready Position with the Clubbell® parked on the floor between the width of your shoulders. Maintain proper crown to coccyx spinal alignment, and exhale to lock your core. As you drive with your legs to a standing position, lift the Clubbell® with your elbow pointed upwards pulling the neck in line with the barrel head.

Revolve: Keeping the Clubbell® hanging perpendicular to the ground and thread your head (as in the Shield Cast) as you extend your forearm towards your far shoulder. Reach beyond your shoulder and revolve the Clubbell® around your shoulder to far side Back Position. Continue until you arrive at near side Back Position.

From near side Back Position, bring your elbow across to your centerline while counter-rotating your gripping hand around your nearside shoulder with the Clubbell® still hanging perpendicular to the ground.

The revolution ends with your elbow tucked into your centerline approximately below the level of your ribcage. Your thumb has rotated up and over to face downwards. Your forearm faces directly forwards, with the Clubbell® hanging perpendicular to the ground.

Unwind: Extend the elbow pit until you achieve arm lock. Continue to rotate your entire arm until your thumb points downward. End in the original Ready Position in Floor Park.

PARRY CAST (SIDE VIEW)

REVERSE PARRY CAST

Because the Reverse Parry Cast involves the same movement performed in the opposite direction as the standard Parry Cast, it distinguishes itself with the "winding" initiation of the exercise out of Ready Position.

Winding: Begin in Ready Position with the Clubbell® parked on the floor between the width of your shoulders. Maintain proper crown to coccyx spinal alignment, and exhale to lock your core. As you drive with your legs to a standing position, rotate the Clubbell® as you rotate your elbow to a level approximately below your rib cage. The Clubbell® should hang perpendicular to the ground.

Revolve: Continue the winding action by cutting your elbow upwards while revolving the perpendicularly hanging Clubbell® around your near shoulder. Pass from near side to far side Back Position with the Clubbell® remaining perpendicular throughout the movement.

Extend your elbow and reach behind your head as you revolve the Clubbell® around your far shoulder. Unthread your arm over your head.

Place: Holding the Clubbell® leading from the elbow, replace it to Floor Park as you begin to sit back into Ready Position.

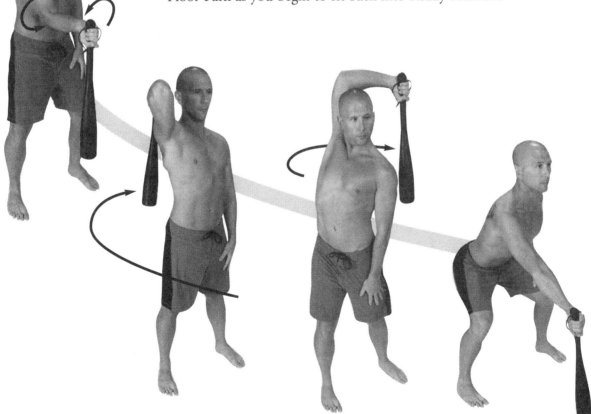

REVERSE PARRY CAST (SIDE VIEW)

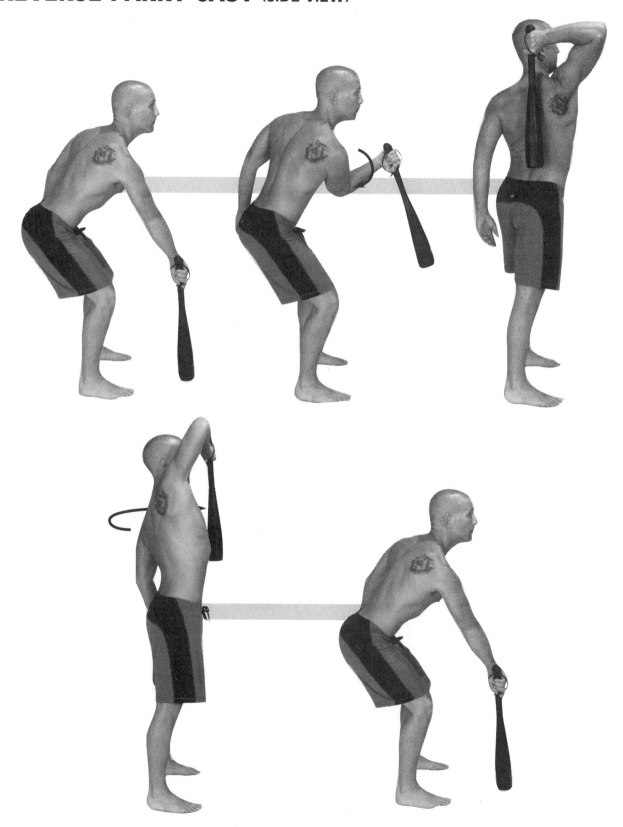

TWO-HANDED PARRY CAST

The Two-Handed Parry Cast differs from the one-handed variant in that one arm performs the standard Parry Cast and the other arm simultaneously performs the Reverse Parry Cast.

Because the Clubbell® hangs perpendicular throughout the entire movement, you should feel no complementary grip work. Both grips act together in pulling along the line of the neck to barrel head.

The challenge comes from the simultaneous action of standard and Reverse Parry Casts: the range of motion demand of each arm becomes greater than if the movements were completed separately, because both arms are attached to one Clubbell®. Master the one-handed variation in both directions (standard and reverse) in order to accommodate the mobility demands of the two-handed variation.

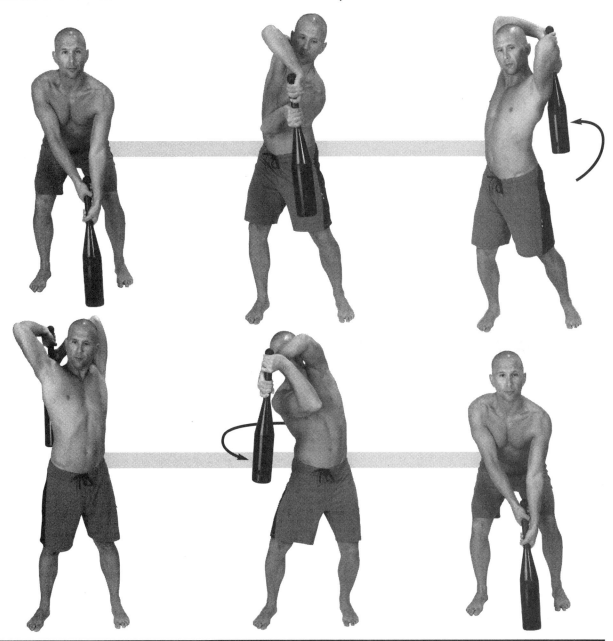

TWO-HANDED PARRY CAST (REVERSE)

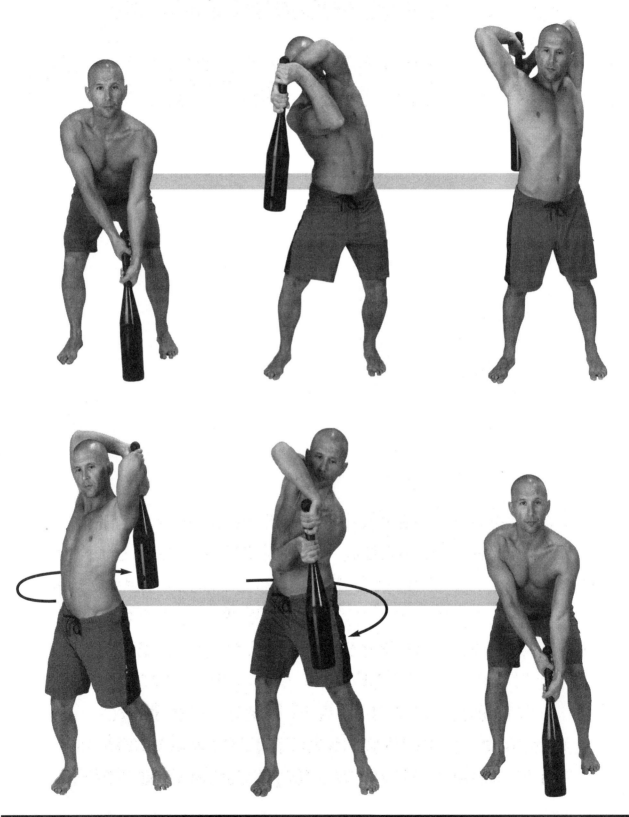

CLUBBELL® SUPERIORITY

If the Clubbell® wasn't a superior piece of equipment I wouldn't have invented it. If CST didn't create a superior training effect it wouldn't be so successful for the complete spectrum of people, from elite athletes to the average Joe and Jane. If the Clubbell® didn't convey such superior benefits, people wouldn't have been gushing consistently (for years) with reports of transformed health, enhanced performance in their sports and vocations, and an endless stream of injury rehabilitation stories.

Of course there is not one right way to train, but there are certainly correct ways to train. To achieve the greatest results, each piece of equipment and each training protocol should offer the athlete superior characteristics.

I find it prudent to give my official position on the evolution of the Clubbell® and on how it became the optimal, and the only sensible, equipment for use in CST

I will never endorse plate-loaded versions of equipment because I did a few years of experimenting, not just with plate-loading prototypes but with quite a few "adjustable" apparati as well (I have described these in various articles). I found plate-loading equipment to be HIGHLY dangerous for CST, for obvious reasons. I could never in good conscience endorse such equipment for CST.

The differences between a "plate-loading" device and the Clubbell® have to do with safety, functionality, durability, and results-producing characteristics.

CONSTANT CENTER OF MASS

Let me state this simply right off the start. Constant Center of Mass (COM) does not necessarily mean fixed weight. Plate-loading and shot-loading do not necessarily mean adjustable.

Anyone who has done any type of grip/forearm exercise knows that plate increments (2.5-lbs) are too great of a leap for CST. There's just no feasible way to elicit progress in CST using Olympic plates. Years of trial and error taught me this.

Further, the unpredictable "sloshing" effect of shot-loaded (or penny-loaded) devices is horribly dangerous to joint integrity when absorbing and retranslating force at extreme ranges of motion. This also applies to the danger of plate adjustment in motion.

Anyone who would call the Clubbell® "non-adjustable" has never practiced CST. If they knew anything about an authentic Clubbell®, they would know that the grip length was specifically designed to make the implement **micro-loading adjustable.** The closer that the grip moves to the knob, the more distant it is from the Center of Mass (COM). And the more displaced the COM, the greater the challenge.

Your grip on the Clubbell® can be moved even millimeters at a time to ensure the Incremental Progression that allows for constant development. This prevents the plateaus that can result from the dramatic leap of adding another plate. It took me years of design tweaking to create the final evolution of CST — the Clubbell®. It's simply eons beyond any of the contraptions that I tried in the past, including: telescopic extension bells, plate stacked pins, sand loaded balls, et cetera.

The bottom line is this: a strength training implement is only truly adjustable if you can increase the load incremental to your progress. If the addition of another plate is too great a jump, then that implement is categorically **not adjustable.** In other words, plate-loadable does not mean adjustable.

I had to create a new design that could continue to be incrementally progressive. I threw all of my plate-loading designs into the junk pile, classed categorically as incapable of accomplishing the task functionally and safely. My friends and clients saw some of my many contraptions, and they can attest to the inherent dangers that plate stack pins cause in CST.

It was during one of my consulting sessions with an engineer that the benefits of sledgehammer training dawned on me. With sledges, as you continue to pound a tire, your hands slip farther and farther away from the hammer head. The farther your grip is from the COM, the greater the challenge. When I worked a new swing, or when I worked on new terrain, or in different weather, or partially submerged in water, I choked up on the handle to learn the new skill. I realized that this variable grip depth afforded me precisely the graduated development that I needed to make it consistently and safely to the next level.

Over the years this design nuance inspired the long handle (and as a result the variable-distance COM) of the authentic Clubbell®. This special neck allows anyone at anytime to increase the load by even the most miniscule of increments. The long handle design of a secure COM in the Clubbell® is the only truly adjustable-weight CST implement.

DANGERS OF THE SHIFTING CENTER OF MASS IN PLATE AND SHOT LOADED TOOLS

When I first began to create CST I built quite a few prototypes with which to experiment. I was guided by a rule of thumb in firearms development: the more moving parts that there are in a piece of equipment, the greater the possibility for error and product failure.

Swinging weight in 3 dimensions, as only CST does, brings with it unique considerations. If the implement's COM shifts due to its plate-loading or shot-loading nature, then the trajectory of the motion changes. One of several things then happens: you must let go, duck and cover; your body's stretch reflex kicks in, causing micro-tears when trying to absorb and retranslate force (which it cannot do in the extreme ROM of CST); the weight carries outside of a joint's ROM, creating injuries (plate-loading devices sidelined me for months with a shoulder injury); and/or you try to change the movement to somehow catch the implement as it follows its new trajectory (dangerous acrobatics). I found none of these options to be fun, obviously.

Anyone that's ever even bench pressed — the most one-dimensional exercise that you can do, because it involves only one half of one plane — knows that plates clang, move, push collars, and change the COM of the press. No one enjoys it when that happens, and it happens with even the world's most "secure" collars. Imagine swinging plates and collars over and around your head in circles and other patterns. Doesn't sound fun, does it? It's an exercise in stupidity (and yes, stupidity is how I learned not to do it).

Lifting a water-filled keg overhead to stabilize deviating weight is a great exercise. However, you do NOT want to be required to stabilize an unpredictable Center of Mass when carrying weight in the extreme ranges of motion of your shoulder. It's just plain unsafe, and it's why a plate-loading implement could never be used for CST.

DANGERS OF THE CONTOUR OF PLATE-LOADED TOOLS

Anyone who has swung a stack of plates around their body knows that the diameter of the plates makes it impossible to maneuver safely through the exercise without dangerous impact to the body. As with everything else, I learned this the hard way.

Obviously, if an exercise such as an Arm Cast requires that the implement be moved from Back Position into Order Position, the implement must be perpendicular to the ground in Back Position to keep the arm in its normal range of motion. Due to the diameter of plates, when you swing a stack of plates behind your head your grip will carry beyond the normal ROM of the shoulder, resulting in injury — not to mention the bruises (if not bone breaks) that you'll receive when the stack hits your back. I feel very fortunate that none of my injuries, caused by experimenting with these design types, were permanent.

This is why years of experimentation and research evolved the smooth profile of the coated Clubbell® — the only true "club" for exercising ("bell").

PROTECTIVE COATING OF THE CLUBBELL®

I never intended for all of "this" — I was just creating a piece of equipment for myself. I had no problem investing enormous funds in research and development. It was a fun labor of love, creating the safest and most functional apparatus possible for CST.

Since I trained out of the sanctuary of my mountain home, I required some protection for the surfaces of my house and my gym. Bare steel caused so many cosmetic and even structural damages to my home (and my car) that I realized something needed to be changed or added.

When I reluctantly lent my equipment to friends, it reinforced this need. Most of my clients train out of their homes and in professional studios. You need a special place for parking a stack of plates, iron cast or steel lathed devices. The Clubbell® can be placed and taken anywhere, and is protective of property due to its thick polyurethane coating.

DANGERS OF CAST AND LATHED DESIGNS

After several prototypes broke from falling over on the knob, I consulted with several engineers who apprised me of the failings of "cast" single piece units. In single piece units the weakest point of the structure is where the handle meets the knob. After investing far too much money in replacing these designs and in trying to increase material density, we realized that we needed to have a knob that was a screw type attachment to the neck.

KNOB DESIGN

I quickly discovered that small balls have ZERO functional value. The "gum-drop" handle of old time 'bowling pin' designs never went over 10–15-lbs without gaining ball size. Because I created a long neck for the micro-loading adjustable nature of the Clubbell®, the Center of Mass was distant. Small balls were insufficient to stop the implement from sliding out of even the smallest of hands, not to mention larger hands that wouldn't even feel it slipping through their grasp. Couple that with some of the polished-handle madness of early designs, and I had a recipe for disaster. And that's just the outward projection of CST.

After years of research and study we settled on a specialized knob for the Clubbell®. We chose this large knob because it was sufficiently large to create a grip purchase that would prevent the implement from sliding out of the hand if gripped correctly. Further, the knob was chosen because its special composition allowed a large purchase without adverse weight increase – in other words, without shifting the constant COM towards the grip.

DANGERS OF COLLAR FAILURE IN PLATE LOADED TOOLS

What would stop a plate-stack from pushing the weight down through the grip (obviously it's actually the Earth pulling it down)? Some miniscule ribbing? Iranian *meels* incorporated dramatic changes in diameter, but that precludes the ability to make the implement adjustable through changes in grip depth.

Anyone who has done any of the overhead exercises of CST understands the importance of having a safe and substantial device exterior profile to prevent injury. Polished-handled implements slid right up to the plates when holding it in Torch Position overhead, and the same thing happened with any type of Snatch shock absorption – that's if I was able to keep it from flying upward into the sky when I snatched it, due to tiny 'gumdrop' knob designs.

I finally decided upon the magnum-shaped design of the Clubbell® because the rapidly expanding diameter prevented the grip from moving higher. Couple that with the specialized "CRINKLE COATING" grip texture and you can see why the design of the Clubbell® is the best imaginable.

MORE COLLAR DANGERS

Folks, this should be right in front of everyone's eyes. Unfortunately it was directly in front of mine — because collars failed. Collars were designed for keeping plates from adjusting outward. Collars were not designed to keep plates from falling downward onto your head. Unfortunately I found out the hard way.

Imagine holding a stack of plates overhead. Now imagine that the only thing between you and those plates is a collar. This sealed it for me. One cannot safely produce a collared device for moving weight in 3 dimensions — in other words for CST. Further, since friends and clients had started asking to borrow my equipment, care and consideration for their safety was my highest priority. I couldn't in good conscience offer them any sort of plate-loading collared device.

We finalized on the **constant Center of Mass** (an internally weighted device) of the Clubbell® to guarantee that product failure from collars could never happen.

CHOOSING METAL OVER WOOD

- **Grip security** impacts the user in this type of training. Wood absorbs hand oils and sanding makes the surface smooth. As such, wooden implements do not allow for alterations of grip depth. Wooden bowling pins are fine when doing ultra-light weight movements, but when moving real weight with torque the poor design of wooden grips become an exercise in lethal projectiles.

- **Density:** Can you imagine how large a wooden 25-lb, not to mention a wooden 45-lb version, of the Clubbell® would have to be? The lathed wooden variants that I created early in the evolution of the Clubbell® were impossibly oversized in order to meet the weights needed for functional strength training.

- **Consistent Center of Mass:** Having a consistent Center of Mass (COM) is related to the density issue. Because of the nature of wood grain it's impossible to establish consistency in the constant center of mass from one implement to the next. The danger in this results from having expectations of a COM from one user to the next and from one arm to the next.

- **Durability** is the other obvious factor. The wooden prototypes that I created over the years (as well as the old "Indian Club" antiques that I procured from auctions) remained subject to material inconsistencies. Wood has grain. Any drop, topple or clank caused the grain to create splits in the wood, especially at the neck, where wooden variants are most fragile.

- **Cost:** Combine the cost of producing such large wooden implements with the rate of breakage due to the inherent flaws of wood grain, and you have an unacceptably high cost burden that would have to be carried by the consumer.

These were also the reasons why metal lathing and casting produced inferior prototypes.

People can create whatever Frankenstein invention they wish. I didn't create my "Cadillac" for anyone else but myself initially, and later for my close trainees. Only much later, after protracted, convincing argument, did I consent to make my design commercially available so that everyone could benefit from it. My goal was always to create the MOST FUNCTIONAL, DURABLE, ADAPTABLE, SAFE, and RESULTS PRODUCING device possible for CST.

We accomplished that in the Clubbell®, which is why RMAX.tv Productions will always be the original, the leader, and the best source of CST.

Early in my journey of creating the Clubbell® I experimented with many more designs than those mentioned above. Each of these resulted in product failure, personal injury and/or property injury — EXCEPT FOR THE FINAL EVOLUTION of the Clubbell®.

I had no interest in making my "Cadillac" commercial. I wanted the safest, most durable, most functional and most results-producing implement that I could create for CST, because that's how I trained. When people began to insist that I make it available to the public my desire for safety increased. I would NEVER risk the safety of the public with a design that I had not thoroughly evaluated and personally experimented with on myself.

One company actually did try to "borrow" the Clubbell® name to market their own version of our Clubbell® equipment. Their response to our initial polite "cease and desist" letter (regarding their infringing use of our Registered Trademark (Reg. No. 2,727,333) and Patented (Patent No. D492373) Clubbell® was unapologetic and belligerent. They left us with no choice but to immediately engage our lawyers to prosecute the infringement of our trademark.

I would like to express my gratitude to Nikolay Travkin and our attorneys for their swift and effective work in resolving this matter. In particular, we at RMAX.tv Productions would like to express our deepest thanks to Jorge Colon, Esq. Jorge is a certified CST instructor and legal advisor to myself, Nikolay Travkin and to RMAX.tv Productions, as well as former Corporate and Trademark counsel to one of the largest publishing companies in the U.S., American Media Inc., and Weider Publications, LLC.

These minor diversions aside, I'm pleased that CST and the Clubbell® have become so wide-spread and popular that other designs for CST are coming out of the woodwork. We can only hope that these people have actually invested the time to understand CST and to experiment extensively with their designs before mass producing them and shipping them off to market.

As you know, personal profit was not my reason for designing the Clubbell®. The Clubbell® is the natural evolution of my desire and my efforts to create the safest, most functional, durable, adaptable and results-producing piece of equipment possible for CST. Keep the vision alive — and be careful out there.

NOTES

FREQUENTLY ASKED QUESTIONS

WHAT ARE THE ADVANTAGES OF USING CLUBBELLS FOR CST?

Clubbells are the ONLY Combat and Sport Specific Equipment for Circular Strength Training®: Only Clubbells were specifically researched, engineered and designed to target the rotary and angular/diagonal muscles, to target the grip, wrist and forearm strength, and to target enhancing shoulder synergy. They are the only tools created specifically for use in Sophisticated Training as a conservative injury prevention and rehabilitation tool, as well as for use in sports-specific performance enhancement.

Displaced Center of Gravity: With dumbbells the weight can be supported by your skeletal structure, as though it were sitting on top of a column. Further, with dumbbells your grip is located directly upon the center of gravity, which remains constant throughout the exercise through the entire range of motion. This results in a more gross action, power without coordination. The Unique Balance Scheme of Clubbells forces athletes to use proper technique and to concentrate on sophisticated skills during the movement. The Displaced Center of Gravity forces you to keep the weight inside of its proper groove throughout the entire lift. At times, having the weight pull away from you is desirable. For example, many people do not have the shoulder flexibility to do overhead squats. The Clubbell® will pull your arm into the proper position and keep it there.

Leverage Lifting Principle: The unique benefits of leverage challenge include a superior training effect. Decreased leverage of the Displaced Center of Gravity translates force more effectively to develop superior grip strength, as well as lower arm, upper arm and shoulder synergy, stabilization and dynamic flexibility. Additionally, Clubbells have a *Thick, Crinkle Coated Neck* and a uniquely engineered *Knob* to provide a specialized purchase for the grip in order to facilitate increased inertia and poundage — giving a better grip workout than any other piece of equipment. NO other apparatus translates this amount of leveraged force!

Pendulum Swinging Principle: With Clubbells your grip is at the end of an extension attached to the weighted center of gravity. As you go through the range of motion the weight moves in relation to the fixed point of your grip in much the same way that a pendulum swings from a fixed point. The leverage and the force constantly change position, along with the strength of the pull throughout the range of motion, creating resistance and stressing your muscles from varying angles. This produces a totally different dynamic effect in the exercise which is impossible to obtain with any other piece of equipment. This Pendulum Swinging Principle, which has been used for centuries and has been lost to modern training, has been reborn through Clubbells — a patented breakthrough in training.

Micro-Loading Adjustable Grip: Clubbells are a means of *Incremental Resistance Progression*. The special design of the handle allows minor increases in weight, *never overloading your muscles but always challenging them.* Micro-Loading Adjustable Grip is a special design function that uniquely promotes constant progress and strength gains. No other piece of equipment has this versatility!

Specialized Knob: This specialized attachment is both threaded and bonded with Lock-Tight. The Specialized Knob design allows for grip purchase in order to assist in leverage lifting, protects the user from releasing the Clubbell® equipment through slippage, and acts as a gripping surface for certain lighter-weight exercises.

Rubberized Coating: Clubbells are made from <u>steel</u> with a <u>Black Urethane Rubber-coating</u> cast around the weight mass and a portion of the handle to protect floor surfaces.

WHAT ARE THE DIFFERENCES BETWEEN TRADITIONAL ANTIQUE CLUBS AND MODERN CLUBBELLS?

The difference is about 200 years, plus hundreds of thousands of dollars of technology, research, testing, experimentation and experience. Clubbells were designed specifically to be the physical manifestation of CST. No expense was spared to produce this innovation. The difference between old designs and the modern engineering design of the Clubbell® is analogous to the difference between a Model-T and a Cadillac.

Can an individual create or find a cheaper alternative to Clubbells? Of course they can. RMAX.tv Productions did not intend to provide the cheapest equipment, but rather the best, safest and most durable equipment to fit the needs of the gym, field, home or suitcase.

WHICH SPORTS HAVE BEEN IMPROVED BY THE USE OF CLUBBELLS?

All of them. Further, people with a wide range of occupations and enthusiasts of all recreational activities have benefited from Clubbell® training, including: computer technicians, beauticians, masons, postal workers, massage therapists, clerks, janitors, physicians, as well as police officers, fire fighters, and soldiers. Here are a few specific examples of what Clubbell® training will bring to individual sports:

WRESTLING: Increase clinch dominance, strengthen wrist control, and increase static strength for sprawls, jams and shucks.

BOXING: Enhance wrist stability in striking, increase early power generation and arm endurance.

MARTIAL ARTS: Strengthen strikes, clinch work, and the application of holds, as well as prevent loss by submission.

POWER-LIFTING: Add tonnage to your maximum deadlift and bench from increased bar grip strength.

ICE and FIELD HOCKEY: Strengthen stick stability and agility. Achieve stronger, more accurate shots, and prevent shoulder injury.

RUGBY and FOOTBALL: Increase ball handling, blocking and tackling skills which rely on coordinated arm force generation.

GOLF: Strengthen fingers to remove handedness bias and strengthen wrist snap to increase distance, accuracy and consistency.

RACQUETBALL and TENNIS: Improve racket control and strengthen wrist action for all strokes.

ROCK CLIMBING and RAPPELLING: Develop and maintain hand, wrist and forearm strength and endurance.

BASEBALL: Develop stronger grip and wrist snap for increased accuracy and velocity in ball throwing. Increase bat control and swing speed and power.

MOTOCROSS and BMX: Diminish arm-pump to enhance bar control and endurance.

BASKETBALL: Shoot, dribble and pass with a higher level of consistency and accuracy.

Clubbell® training has been successfully applied to these sports as well: swimming, kayaking, gymnastics, bowling, javelin throwing, volleyball, Olympic lifting, shot put, fencing, windsurfing, water skiing, bodybuilding, jet skiing, and any sport using the arms.

WITH WHICH CLUBBELL® WEIGHT SHOULD I BEGIN?

Seek your physician's approval before beginning any type of strenuous resistance exercise. Physically fit adult **males** can get started with this **book**, the **Clubbell® Training for Circular Strength DVD**, and a pair of **10-lb Clubbells**. Physically fit adult **females** can start with this **book**, the **DVD**, and a pair of **5-lb Clubbells**. These weight selections are challenging at first, but people generally adapt over the first two weeks, and some are even ready for a heavier Clubbell® within the first month or two of training.

Men with thorough strength training experience and above average strength have begun with a pair of 15-lb Clubbells. Women with such experience and strength have begun with a pair of 10-lb Clubbells. Competitive male power-lifters, Olympic style lifters, and experienced Iron Game athletes have begun with a pair of 20-lb Clubbells. We do not recommend starting with anything larger than 20-lb Clubbells regardless of background, as you will always have a use for lighter Clubbells in your training.

WHICH SHOULD I PURCHASE NEXT?

The usual guideline for **adult men** is to build your home gym such that you own at least one pair of any weight for practicing Sophisticated combination routines, and at least one each of the 10, 15, and 20-lb Clubbells. After that you could start over from the bottom and work to acquire your second pair, and then purchase the 5 and 25-lb Clubbells to complete your gym. Clubbell® pairs add variety, challenge and significant gains to your programs. You can and should begin with a pair of Clubbells. Different weights help you progress in strength and fitness.

For most adult women the purchasing guidelines are the same, but one division lighter. Begin with one pair of 5-lb Clubbells, and then collect one each of the 10 and 15-lb Clubbells. You can then work towards completing pairs of both.

The exception to this general guideline is the person who is focused more on coordination, agility, and strength-endurance than on explosive/ballistic strength. It is perfectly possible for a male tennis player, baseball player, or wrestler to do all of their training with a pair of 15-lb Clubbells and to never use a larger size. It's equally fine to stop with a pair of 20-lb Clubbells, though the physiological and psychological benefits of incrementally increasing heavier weight should not be underestimated. Some people prefer to own the heaviest Clubbells that they can manage, even if only for low repetition work.

WHAT ABOUT THE 45-LB CLUBBELLS?

Do not be fooled by the "light-weight" sound of 45-lb Clubbells. They are Steel Sadists, the Iron Monsters of <u>*CST*</u>! Consider these a goal, the horizon of your strength. He who swings these with form and ease is one of *the strongest of all men!*

SHOULD I PURCHASE THE ENTIRE CLUBBELL® PRO GYM IMMEDIATELY?

No one will use all of the weights immediately, so in that regard you need only ever begin with one particular weight of Clubbell®. However, these questions only comprise a **general guideline.** There is no way to compare Clubbells with dumbbell, barbell, and kettlebell weights, since Clubbells involve not linear strength but circular. Therefore, without a personal trainer present, you must guess which weight you can handle.   The advantage of purchasing a **Clubbell® Total Gym** or **Clubbell® PRO Gym** is the ability to personally <u>**discover which weight you need**</u>. Plus, you can <u>**work incrementally**</u> through each weight division as soon as your strength and fitness skyrocket. You will also <u>**save a considerable amount of money**</u> in both cost and shipping by outfitting your home with a complete Clubbell® gym.

SAFETY GUIDELINES

Consult your physician before beginning any physical training program and before using any new physical training equipment. To use Clubbells, minors (under the age of 18) must be supervised by an adult.

Read and understand all instructions for exercises using Clubbells before attempting the exercises.

Inappropriate use of Clubbells can cause property damage, personal or other injury. Consult a certified Clubbell® trainer for proper use of Clubbells, and study official Clubbell® materials to refine your technique.

Do not use Clubbells near unaware children, animals, or breakable, fragile property.

Only use Clubbells after wiping hands and equipment with a dry cloth to remove wetness or oiliness.

Use Clubbells only on a flat, firm, dry surface. Adverse weather conditions (including sunlight, rain, snow, and ice) will adversely affect equipment temperature and grip security. Establish a clear training environment, consisting of your arms length + the Clubbell® length + a safety zone in 360°.

Inappropriate use of Clubbells can lead to equipment malfunction and destruction. Do not throw Clubbells. Do not hit anything with Clubbells. Do not drop Clubbells.

When not in use, carefully place your Clubbells in appropriate racks or on the floor in parked position. Do not expose them to direct sunlight or to a heat source for prolonged periods of time.

Do not use Clubbells with only the strap (not gripping the Clubbells). The safety strap only aids the user in the event of accidental slippage until your grip develops.

Never use Clubbells for longer than your ability to safely and securely hold them in your grip. Never spin Clubbells so that straps are twisted.

Many clients enquire about rehabilitating shoulder injuries. Only your physician's care, your physical therapist's care, and your own informed, common sense decisions should be applied when rehabilitating your shoulders. No one can offer you training guidance without knowing your situation and without interfacing directly with your attending physician or physical therapist. You cannot get this from a book alone. That being said, the following general guidelines will assist you:

Get permission from your physician and/or physical therapist for any movement in any exercise before you begin.

"Prime" your shoulders with the limited ROM exercises prescribed by your physical therapist and included in such resources as Intu-Flow.

Limit exercises to those at the ceiling or within the Safety Zone. If you hold your arms directly out in front of you, anything below that is safe. Avoid elbow over head movements with weight.

Avoid all extreme range of motion grinding exercises.

PERFECT YOUR TECHNIQUE optimally with qualified supervision to critique what you will miss.

Practice in front of a mirror without Clubbells. Use a broom handle or hammer. Then close your eyes and concentrate on the sensation of the exercise.

If you feel pain, stop. See your physical therapist and/or physician, and describe the sensation, location, and activity that caused you pain.

Develop your skills at full choke (farthest away from the knob of the Clubbells).

Never go to failure in training, and don't even train "on the nerve" (close to failure).

If possible "grease the groove" by training single sets distributed throughout the day, and distribute your sets throughout the week instead of compressing them into fewer days.

KEEP YOUR SHOULDERS DOWN in every exercise. Lifting or shrugging your shoulders translates force to the soft tissues.

Keep control and do not go to extreme ranges of motion. Let your ROM develop incrementally.

Rest and ice after every session.

Supplement your diet with essential fatty acids and glucosamine to maintain joint health and lubrication.

Make sure that you do not accidentally overtrain by forgetting to factor in other "normal" activities, especially if your occupation involves physical labor.

Focus on fun, variety and safety.

Contributed by Jarlo Ilano

SAMPLE PROGRAMS

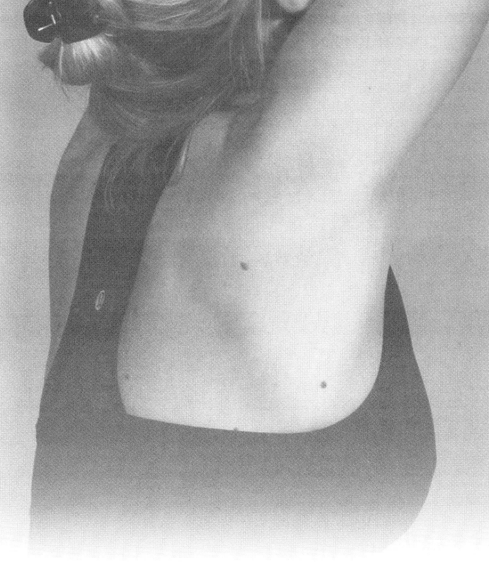

BASIC TYPES OF WORK

Volume: increased duration, distance or repeated effort equal more work.

Intensity: increased load, speed of performance, variation of rest intervals, and decreased leverage in load handling equal more work.

Density: increased frequency of performance and compression of rest periods equals more work.

Complexity: increased coordination demand equal more work.

Variety: change in the physical skills selected requires more work.

You must know how to use these types of resistance work as a tool to make gains.
Work results in adaptation.

LONGEVITY PROGRAM GUIDANCE

- Choke up (away from the knob towards the head) or decrease weight until your Rate of Technique is 8 or higher and your Breath is at minimum at the level of "Discipline" (active exhalation on effort, passive inhalation on the relaxation phase of the movement).
- In general, train 2–3X/week if you have a heavy work schedule (whether labor or other training), and increase to 3–5/week if you are cycling through with low intensity in other aspects of your training or if you use Clubbells for GPP as well as SPP.
- Complete your Clubbell® circuit in 30 minutes or less, but vary the length of your workout from one session to the next. For example, train for 30 minutes on one day, 40 the next, 30 minutes on the following day, and 20 the day after that.
- Vary the intensity of your workout. For example, schedule one day for high intensity work, the next for low intensity work, and the following for medium intensity work.
- Be flexible with your set scheme but target 5 to 15 sets/exercise/day, varying the number of sets from one workout to the next.
- Do multiple sets per day rather than one set of large repetitions. Do one or more sets every day of the week rather than do all of your sets in one day.
- Vary the difficulty of your sets from one to the next.
- Alternate the difficulty of exercises, and alternate the reps accordingly. For example, alternate 2–4 reps with hard exercises and 10–12 reps with easier exercises.
- Learn as many exercises as you wish. It is when you learn a new exercise that you will see the greatest amount of improvement. Your nervous system remains excited and responds with enormous energy levels to new exercises. Once you adapt to an exercise you respond with lesser intensity and energy over time. As you repeat the exercise you come to require greater and greater degrees of mental toughness and variation in your training protocol.

- Do not be overly concerned about the order of your exercises but do them in circuit fashion, working from most technically demanding to least. Increase the length of each rest period in direct proportion to the difficulty of each exercise.
- To develop the skill of an exercise, move slowly and smoothly. To coordinate a skill after developing it, pause every 15° (hold for 3–4 seconds and continue) through the motion where you find it possible to do so at your grip-strength level.
- To improve your form, work on your non-dominant arm.
- Never go to failure. If you experience tremors during an exercise, you have exceeded your workout threshold. Park your Clubbells immediately.
- When focusing upon strength, you can: increase to heavier Clubbells, decrease your leverage (grip closer to the ball), compress the rest period time, or perform more sets.
- In general, when devising training protocols for your Clubbell® workouts, dedicate 60–70% to concentric, 10–15% to eccentric, 10–15% to isometric, and 5–10% to isokinetic (or same-speed motion) conditioning over the course of your annual training cycle.
- In general with regard to rest periods, when training for strength rest longer (approximately 4–5 minutes), for cardio-endurance rest for shorter periods (10–60 seconds), and for muscular endurance set your rest periods somewhere in the middle (1–2 minutes).
- Do any exercise for any rep scheme 1 to 100, but leave all sets of more than 10 reps for end of your workout.
- Incorporate changes into your program every 3 to 4 weeks. These changes in protocol, set, rep, and resistance give the nervous system time to regenerate and to prepare for higher performance levels. In general, change your program whenever progress plateaus.
- If you perform a Joint Mobility Program such as Intu-Flow each morning you'll be more than adequately prepared for the day. Perform a compensatory movement session at least once per week with Prasara yoga to unwind.
- To learn a new skill practice it for 5 sets of 5 reps, spreading the sets throughout the day, for 3 to 5 weeks.
- Be certain to increase your hydration.

Contributed by Carol Britton and Will Chung

BASIC STRENGTH CONDITIONING

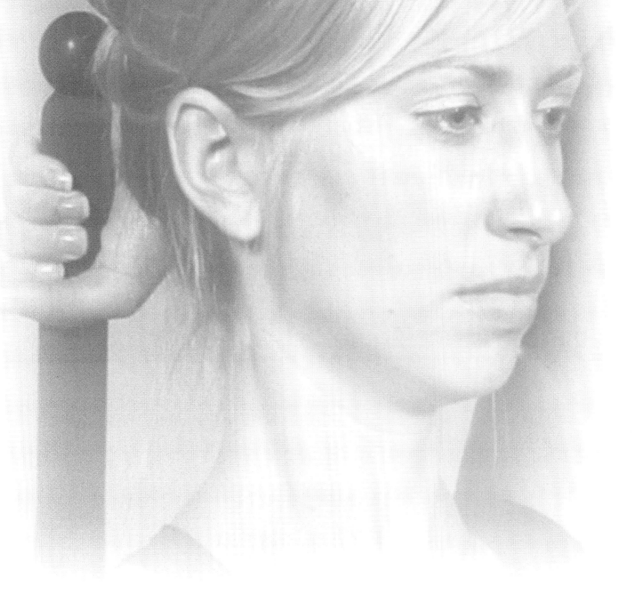

DENSE STRENGTH (inspired by Tsatsouline, _Power to the People_)

This program will improve strength and muscular density without gaining bulk.

Select 1 to 3 compound exercises that will work the entire body. Select exercises based on the criteria that you could perform each for at least 7–10 reps in one set. Perform 2 sets of 3–5 reps with each exercise 2–5 days / week.

Begin with each exercise at full choke (with your grip farthest from the knob and closest to the barrel head of the Clubbell®). Perform one set of 3–5 reps followed by a rest period of 3 minutes. Next, choke down 10% towards the knob and perform another set of 3–5 reps (90% of the original leverage challenge). Continue to choke down towards the knob in small increments until you cannot complete at least 3 reps on the first set.

At that point, start a new cycle. You may increase your "grip choke depth" within a cycle in a linear, step, wave, or any other ladder. Never work to failure.

SWING POWER (inspired by Charles Staley's "Escalating Density" training)

This program focuses on pure power gains. Select 1 to 3 exercises that you can only perform for 2–4 repetitions at full choke (you're your grip closest to barrel head and farthest from knob). You are going to focus not on total repetitions but on total sets, so begin with a goal for the number of sets that you want to complete (i.e. 10 sets).

Perform sets of 2 reps with a one-minute break between exercises. Once you can complete all ten sets with a Rating of Technique of 8 or higher at full choke, progress on to 10 sets of 3 repetitions, and then 10 sets of 4 repetitions. Once you can complete all ten sets of 4 reps, decrease the choke by 25% (¼ of the way down the grip towards the knob; in other words, 75% of the previous cycle's grip choke depth) and then begin again at sets of 2 reps.

NEURAL STRENGTH (inspired by Tsatsouline's "Grease the Groove" training)

This program focuses on nervous system adaptation (pre-synaptic facilitation) and strength endurance. You may modify it for strength gains by using less choke depth, greater weights and lower repetitions.

Select 1 or 2 unrelated exercises. Practice them in single sets throughout the day. Perform approximately half the reps that you are capable of completing for each set. For example, if you can perform only 10 reps, then perform sets of 5 throughout the day.

You may start with only one or two sets, and gradually increase the number of sets as you neurologically adapt. Work up to many sets throughout the day separated by long periods of rest.

To test your new strength gains, rest for 2 to 3 days and then perform one 'maximum' set (completing as many reps as you can do). Taking the gain from that result, halve that number in your subsequent cycle to calculate how many reps to perform.

CLUB MASS (inspired by Tsatsouline's "Bear" training)

This is a superb program for muscle mass gains.

Select 2 to 3 compound exercises. Perform each exercise 2 to 4 times per week.

Perform one set of 5 repetitions at full choke (with your grip closest to the barrel head and farthest from the knob) using a weight with which you would be unable to perform 7–8 repetitions. Next, reduce your choke depth by 90% of that weight and perform another set of 5 after a 1 minute rest period. Reduce your choke depth by another 10% (80% of the original 'full choke') and perform as many sets of 5 as you can while maintaining proper form (Rating of Technique of 8 or higher).

Take as little as 30 second and no more than 90 second rest periods, and never take a set to failure. You may choose to use a split schedule. Do not train every day.

POWER PLANT (Doug Szolek, Anabolic Bruiser Conditioning)

For explosiveness, practice the basic anabolic ballistics: cleans, jerks, and snatches. Train three days per week, alternating the performance emphasis so that each of the three exercises receives primary attention on one day. For the emphasized exercise of the day do 5 sets of 2–5 reps. Perform 2 sets of 2–5 reps of the other two exercises.

Choose whichever variation of the three skills you wish to develop. Let your application of the power guide your exercise choice so that you can most appropriately surpass your goals. If you have no immediately definable goals, choose varying types of lifts (side, front, leverage, torch, etc.) to develop well-rounded fitness. Vary the exercise selection in the next power cycle of your annual training.

Sample Power Plant Workout:

Monday:
1. Side Clean to Back Position, 5 sets of 2–5 reps
2. Front Jerk, 2 sets of 2–5 reps
3. Front Torch Snatch, 2 sets of 2–5 reps

Wednesday:
1. Front Jerk, 5 sets of 2–5 reps
2. Front Torch Snatch, 2 sets of 2–5 reps
3. Side Clean to Back Position, 2 sets of 2–5 reps

Friday:
1. Front Torch Snatch, 5 sets of 2–5 reps
2. Side Clean to Back Position 2 sets of 2–5reps
3. Front Jerk, 2 sets of 2–5 reps

FUNCTIONAL HYPERTROPHY (Doug Szolek, Anabolic Bruiser Conditioning)

Functional Hypertrophy is *the development of lean muscle mass that enhances rather than hinders your natural range of motion.* CST Coach Doug Szolek developed the following template for generalized Functional Hypertrophy:

Select the first exercise (or combination routine) based upon its **high skill demand** in order to increase your coordination ("the sophisticated application of strength"). Perform that routine or exercise first in a session so that fatigue will not hinder your Rate of Technique.

Select the second exercise based upon its **whole-body recruitment:** a combination routine or exercise that you can perform with a high enough technique (8 or higher on a scale of 1–10, 10 being the highest) that you can push yourself safely to the extremes of your fitness.

By activating maximum skeletal muscle with heavy weight and extreme ranges of motion you will create a very anabolic internal environment. This results in whole-body growth of lean mass.

Select the final exercise based upon its **high effort demand:** one that you know well enough to grind slowly and smoothly, but that requires constant and consistent strength development.

Perform these 3 exercises for 2–4 sets and 8–12 reps each, depending on frequency of training and recovery time allowed.

Perform these sessions 2 to 4 times per week once a day, and up to 6 times per week if you choose to go with an AM/PM split session 3 days a week. If you perform the full 6 sessions per week, do no do any other training during this cycle. Sandwich an extensive dynamic range of motion practice session (Intu-Flow™ or Warrior Wellness™) between every workout.

To add variety to a 6 session per week training schedule, craft 2 separate workouts with the above template and train them alternately. Perform workout "A" in the AM and workout "B" in the PM, alternating with a "B" workout in the AM and an "A" workout in the PM. By training each workout in both the AM and PM sessions you will erase the possibility of differing daily energy levels affecting one or the other workout exclusively.

Sample Functional Hypertrophy Workout:
1. ABC Mills, 4 sets of 8–12 reps
2. Snatch (any one of the 5+ variants), 4 sets of 8–12 reps
3. Muscle-Out Press, 4 sets of 8–12 reps

LADDER TRAINING

LINEAR (GEOMETRIC) LADDER

This program is a compressed version of Neural Strength that focuses on strength and cardio endurance.

Perform one additional repetition in each set (i.e. 5 repetitions in the first set, 6 repetitions in the second set, 7 repetitions in the third set, etc). Stop two reps short of your maximum or at any time that a repetition drops beneath a Rate of Technique of 8. If you wish to repeat after reaching the top of a ladder, drop back to your beginning number of repetitions and start again.

Rest periods between sets should be 30 seconds to 2 minutes. Perform your ladder every other day. Never go to failure, and never get close to being *"on the nerve"* (near failure).

Here are some more challenging versions of the basic ladder:

WAVE LADDER

Perform an increasing 'wave' of 4 sets, dropping back to set one step higher than where you started. For example, reps/set: 1, 2, 3, 4, 2, 3, 4, 5, 3, 4, 5, 6, 4, 5, 6, 7.

A variation on the Wave Ladder is the Fibonacci Wave Ladder, which involves the following reps/set: 1, 2, 3, 5, 2, 3, 5, 8, 3, 5, 8, 13. You could also experiment with the Inverted Fibonacci Wave Ladder: 13, 8, 5, 3, 8, 5, 3, 2, 5, 3, 2, 1.

COMPETITIVE LADDER

Train with a partner. Continue to perform sets until your partner cannot perform as many repetitions as you can. You can also hold this competition between your right and left arms.

STEP (EXPONENTIAL) LADDER

- 1 clean to order, 1 arm-pit cast, 2 basic arm swings (10 sec rest)
- 2 cleans to order, 2 arm-pit casts, 4 basic arm swings (15 sec rest)
- 3 cleans to order, 3 arm-pit casts, 6 basic arm swings (20 sec rest)
- 4 cleans to order, 4 arm-pit casts, 8 basic arm swings (25 sec rest)
- 5 cleans to order, 5 arm-pit casts, 10 basic arm swings (30 sec rest)
- Continue until you can no longer perform with a Rating of Technique of 8 or higher. Never train to failure. Keep the vomit can nearby.

RATCHET LADDER

Move *two steps forward, and fall one step back* (to 'latch' in development by allowing for slight recovery through diminished effort). The sequence progresses like this: 1, 2, 3, 2, 3, 4, 3, 4, 5. Whenever your technique drops beneath an 8 dial back one rep on the next set.

CHOKING LADDER

Take any exercise that requires a Rating of Perceived Exertion of 6 or higher and perform repetitions in the following scheme: Set 1 – 5 repetitions, Set 2 – 4 repetitions, Set 3 – 3 repetitions, Set 4 – 2 repetitions, Set 5 – 1 repetition. Begin on Set 1 with your grip as high as you can grasp away from the knob and towards the head of the Clubbell®. With each set move your grip closer to the knob to decrease the leverage advantage. Allow yourself 1 minute of rest for each repetition in each set. For example, 5 reps = a 5 minute rest period.

CONTROL PAUSE LADDER

The "Control Pause" is the 'dead' space at the end of the exhale: when you have no more air that you can consciously expel but before you've begun to inhale. Performing your repetitions on the Control Pause gives you an incredibly well-developed, strong and well-defined core.

Begin by exhaling hard and performing one rep on the Control Pause. Park it and relax slightly – just enough to allow air to be sucked back in, but don't actively inhale. Exhale hard twice in a row (with a cumulatively stronger exhale). Do two reps on the Control Pause. Park and relax slightly – just enough to recover. Exhale three times in a row (cumulative) and do three reps. Then four. Then five. If you can make it to 10 repetitions on your first try you should be on top of Mt. Olympus, for you are truly a Fitness God! Another version is to do an *Inverted Control Pause Ladder,* beginning with 10 reps and working down to one.

Photographer: Wesley Buckingham • Contributed by D. Cody Fielding

CENTURY TRAINING

Many people look in horror at the number 100 when they see how many repetitions CST Athletes perform. Here's a powerful formula to accomplish this task.

Influenced by Ethan Reeve, Strength and Conditioning Coach of Wake Forest University, Century Training is an ingenious plan that takes the participant through a **Cascading Training Effect** in each cycle. This doesn't spell an end to *periodized* training, but is rather a *refinement* of it.

It is currently held that, for a holistically developed athlete, it is necessary to periodize training so that they will work a strength only cycle followed (perhaps) by an endurance cycle and then a power cycle and so on until they have trained all of the necessary attributes of their game. Then the periodization begins again.

This method flew in the face of the previous norm of *cocktail* training (a.k.a. cross training), where the athlete would train for many different attributes in one cycle, usually ignorant of the fact that each energy system was competing with the others for limited recovery ability.

Century Training opens the possibility to cascading training effects so that the athlete can train every major energy system in the course of one cycle. That cycle is made up of mini-steps through each of the different types of training.

As you begin at 5–7 repetitions / set you develop your foundation of **strength and power,** from which all other skills are launched. As you progress on through 8–10 repetitions / set you stimulate **functional muscle growth,** which allows your anatomy to catch up to your strength and power. At 11–15 repetitions / set you open the field of muscular endurance. At 15+ reps per set you scratch at the beginnings of **circulo-respiratory ("cardio") endurance.** Beyond this you add the life-changing power of the full 100 rep "Century" and step into the realm of **mental toughness,** one of the most transformative mind-body-spirit experiences that you can achieve through physical culture.

Here's an easy reference to these attributes and their corresponding rep numbers:

Strength and Power	5–7 reps
Hypertrophy (Muscle Growth)	8–10
Muscular Endurance	11–15
Circulo-Respiratory Endurance	13–15+
Mental Toughness	40+

Here are some general guidelines to help you achieve your Century:

- Start with a relatively simple full ROM routine, such as any basic exercise.
- Do this 3 times per week maximum, and only once per week if you're doing heavy singles in your other strength conditioning.
- Never go to failure to avoid extended recovery. If you feel extremely sore, you're going too far.
- Don't exceed 20 minutes per session.
- **Keep perfect FLUID FORM!** If you detect that your form is about to deteriorate, stop at that rep scheme but continue out and finish your total volume. For instance, if you intend to do 12 reps but will fail at 9, then stop at 8 reps in 25 minutes and keep going until you finish your total of 100. Keep dropping reps per set until you finish your 100.
- When you are able to accomplish a step without going to failure, when it becomes easy, it's time to move on to the next step.

The goal in programming the formula is to decrease the sets while increasing the reps so that the total volume is no less than 100 — your goal. You then perform one set every minute until you finish. In other words, the higher the volume of repetitions per set the more work you're doing and the smaller the rest period that you have between sets. This is an ingenious method of incrementally progressive resistance training that also taps your cardio, stamina, power, muscle building and fat burning in a cascading effect.

Here are the steps to the 100 rep "Century":

- 35 sets of 3 repetitions in 35 minutes
- 25 sets of 4 repetitions in 25 minutes
- 20 sets of 5 repetitions in 20 minutes
- 18 sets of 6 repetitions in 17 minutes
- 16 sets of 7 repetitions in 16 minutes
- 15 sets of 8 repetitions in 14 minutes
- 12 sets of 9 repetitions in 12 minutes
- 10 sets of 10 repetitions in 10 minutes
- At this point, for your next session you will be able to do 1 set of 100 repetitions.

Take some time off and celebrate your achievement!

DOUBLE CENTURY TRAINING (formerly known as Double Density Training)

Double Century Training™ (DCT) may give you significant useable muscle growth in the arms, chest, neck, back and core. DCT will improve your stamina, endurance, mass and strength, and can replace all of your cardio AND fat-burning work. DCT is absolutely comprehensive.

DCT refers to performing an AM/PM split of 2 separate Century Training models by strategically placing an Intu-Flow session sandwiched in-between for active recovery. A DCT cycle has no termination date, since it is based upon achieving two 100 rep sets in one day through a density training protocol. Density Training basically means that, as you increase the volume slowly while compressing the rest periods, you trick your nervous system into mega-high volume, resulting in tremendous gains in strength endurance.

DDT uses a proprietary neurological/biochemical phenomenon of ***recovered but not reset*** training frequency. It was originally inspired by one of my courses in Russia with a strength and conditioning coach who took us through training once every 6 hours round the clock for 5-day blocks (we learned to sleep almost on demand).

DDT involves two short-duration work sessions in one work day separated by approximately 12 hours, with one full day of rest in between each work day. This method strikes a balance between neuromuscular rest and neurological recovery, which basically says that if you go over approximately 24 hours you're fully rested. However, at around 12 hours you can be actively recovered though not fully *rested*.

When **recovered but not reset,** your central nervous system still hums with excitement but you have recovered sufficiently from the prior session to work again. This allows you to supercharge a download into your muscle software. It's like temporarily having extra RAM to operate your computer. Basically, the sum total training effect (neurological stimulation) peaks between 8–12 hours, decreasing to reset at 20–24. If you're under approximately a half day when you train again, you impinge upon recovery. This time corridor may vary based upon the individual: some people recover faster, others slower; some reset more easily, some less easily.

You can't push this neurological (and perhaps biochemical) phenomenon more than two sessions sequentially without facing fatigue, muscle ache and exhaustion. But you may pull it off for a 5-week cycle alternating work days with rest days, as I have. Week #5 includes a full rest to reset your nervous system totally. If you ignore this 5th week of rest you'll hit a massive fatigue wall.

I don't suggest this program to anyone doing any other type of strength and conditioning, nor to people with highly physical jobs. My experience in Russia involved us using a similar (but unrefined) approach every 6 hours, but we were professional athletes heavily supervised and monitored, and the course duration was 5 days. We had a 2 ½ day break and then we did the course again with a different exercise selection.

Since the cycle is 4 weeks (of active work) long, you must take proactive measures to release stored tension to ensure that micro-trauma does not accumulate and result in injury. This is why you must perform an **active recovery session** sandwiched between the two work sessions. You can use Intu-Flow™ for this, or you can choose from CST's menu of dynamic mobility courses such as Warrior Wellness™ or Freedom By Degree™.

The intended steps for both the AM/PM split are:

- 20 sets of 5 repetitions in 20 minutes
- 18 sets of 6 repetitions in 18 minutes
- 16 sets of 7 repetitions in 16 minutes
- 15 sets of 8 repetitions in 15 minutes
- 12 sets of 9 repetitions in 12 minutes
- 10 sets of 10 repetitions in 10 minutes
- 8 sets of 12 repetitions reps in 8 minutes
- 7 sets of 14 repetitions reps in 7 minutes (due to the duration of most exercises, by this step you should nearly be at one full minute of movement, which means that you're prepared for the final hurdle)
- 1 set of 100

Train smart and have fun with the incredible fitness gains that may come as a result of this cycle.

Contributed by Carol Britton and Will Chung

PHI CENTURY RATCHET SEQUENCING

This program integrates the following three principles:

1. **Incremental Progression:** to always progress without overtraining fatigue and burnout.

2. **Peak Performance:** so that extreme exertions always happen on the days when you're 'most' genetically primed.

3. **Recovery Training:** proactively programming the ability to recover so that progress continues, injuries do not occur, and MORE energy is gained through training.

This is an incredible, power-packed, time-efficient method to consistently progress with optimal function!

If you're not interested in math or in the beauty of the inner workings of human performance, if you prefer pre-fab, force-fed, follow-along programs, then read no further! This is all about understanding the nature of what it is to be a high-performance human being, and the sheer mystery of what it is to reveal the Divine within you through meticulous dedication to recording and observing your daily personal practice. If you still want to read on, you may now ask...

WHAT IS THIS METHOD COMPOSED OF?

1. Century Training

Let's begin with the Density Cycle:

Step 1: 20 sets of 10 repetitions in 20 minutes

Step 2: 19 sets of 11 repetitions in 19 minutes

Step 3: 17 sets of 12 repetitions in 17 minutes

Step 4: etc...

Final Step — 1 set of 100

The basic premise of Density training is that, as you incrementally compress rest periods by gradually increasing repetition volume and decreasing set volume, the nervous system never becomes overwhelmed and continues to progress without long periods of recovery. This is an excellent form of strength endurance development — the pinnacle of athleticism.

2. Phi Sequencing

Next we look at the 3-day Phi Sequence:

Day 3: Active Recovery

Day 2: Active Recovery

Day 1: Active Recovery

Day 1: Light

Day 2: Moderate

Day 3: Peak

Day 7: Rest or Active Recovery

The basic premise of Phi Sequencing is that there is a "golden ratio" of work to rest: you need three days of rest to feel its benefits before a peak performance. For reference, read the section in this book on Phi Sequencing.

3. Ratchet Ladders

Finally, we include the escalating Ratchet "ladders" of moving two steps forward and falling one step back (to 'latch' in development by providing slight recovery through diminished effort). The sequence progresses like this: 1, 2, 3, 2, 3, 4, 3, 4, 5.

Each Step is a Peak Performance!

Read that again.

The main problem that I have seen with Density Training is that people RUSH to the "final step" of 1 set of 100. As a result, not only do I see serious form deterioration, but people neglect to maximize the results that they could achieve from EACH and EVERY step! To counter this, we need to time every step "up" for a peak day.

Additionally, because the goal of Density Training is to incrementally increase work capacity we continue with the volume progression by decreasing intensity.

To follow this program you will need at LEAST 3 incrementally increasing Clubbell® weights — a light weight, a moderate weight and a heavy weight (for you). Even better to have an entire Total or Pro Gym of every weight!

PHI CENTURY RATCHET SEQUENCING

	Week 1
Day 3:	Intu-Flow™
Day 2:	Intu-Flow™
Day 1:	Prasara™
Day 1:	29 sets of 7 in 29 minutes with light Clubbell® (In other words, Step 3 of the Density Cycle)
Day 2:	34 sets of 6 in 34 minutes with moderate Clubbell® (In other words, Step 2 of the Density Cycle)
Day 3:	40 sets of 5 in 40 minutes with heavy Clubbell® (In other words, Step 1 of the Density Cycle)
Day 7:	Intu-Flow™
	Week 2:
Day 3:	Intu-Flow™
Day 2:	Intu-Flow™
Day 1:	Prasara™
Day 1:	Density Ratchet Step 4 with light Clubbell®
Day 2:	Density Ratchet Step 3 with moderate Clubbell®
Day 3:	Density Ratchet Step 2 with heavy Clubbell®
Day 7:	Intu-Flow™
	Week 3:
Day 3:	Intu-Flow™
Day 2:	Intu-Flow™
Day 1:	Prasara™
Day 1:	Density Ratchet Step 5 with light Clubbell®
Day 2:	Density Ratchet Step 4 with moderate Clubbell®
Day 3:	Density Ratchet Step 3 with heavy Clubbell®
Day 7:	Intu-Flow™
	And so on, week by week, until you reach the final step of the "Century" cycle — 1 set of 100 with the heavy Clubbell®.

You may, of course, drop down an extra weight for the whole or part of the Light or Moderate days as long as you completes the entire volume within the required time compression. Furthermore, you can select whatever weight of Clubbell® is appropriate for you — one for each of the light, moderate and heavy workouts.

YOUTH CLUBBELL® CLASSES

Youth training with resistance equipment was lost over the years because of the myth that it stunts growth and damages growth plates and developmental connective tissue. No substantial research to my knowledge can be found that proves these presumptions.

In the *Spetzshkola,* specialized schools for the gifted athletic super-achievers of the former Soviet Union, athletes began as early as age 6 with a course in General Physical Preparedness that included resistance equipment. In that first year trainers worked with athletes on technical mastery of the clean and snatch. Between the ages of 7 and 10 youth athletes began to focus upon more complex SPP training. The health and performance of adult athletes from the former Soviet Union offers evidence of the sustained success of resistance training for youth athletes. Former Soviet athletes have demonstrated dramatic strength gains with minimal bulking (Yessis, <u>Secrets of Soviet Sports and Fitness Training</u>; Raiport, <u>Red Gold: Peak Performance Techniques of Russian and East German Olympic Victors</u>. Siff, <u>Facts and Fallacies of Fitness</u>).

The American Society of Pediatrics and the American Orthopedic Society for Sports Medicine stated that resistance training can have a positive impact on child development, with the disclaimer that proper program design and scheduling, proper technique, and qualified supervision are necessary. These organizations correctly advise that training youth athletes too hard, too fast, and/or too often leads to injury and performance decline. They further advise that, without direct and qualified supervision, technique declines and injuries occur. Resistance training produces positive results in the health and performance of youth athletes. Poor instruction and poor supervision produce ill effects, as is true with any endeavor, whether youth or adult (J. Hale, *"Youth Athletes and Weight Training"* 2000).

YOUTH ATHLETIC TRAINING GUIDELINES

Goals should be achievable and fun: Youth athletics involves enjoyment, play and skill acquisition. Unrealistic goals focused on heavy win-oriented or achievement-oriented programming results in youth injuries and in general burnout at an early age to athletics. Program design without clearly established and readily achievable goals leads to deterioration of technique and to improper training habits. Without proper, qualified supervision resistance-training equipment becomes hazardous, as does any other piece of equipment in the hands of untrained or poorly training youth.

Master mechanics first: Work from no to little to moderate resistance in order to develop skill. Teach exercises as skills to be practiced and enjoyed rather than coach youth athletes in pushing performance. Set performance goals and reward behavior based upon technical mastery rather than upon increased volume or intensity.

Success not failure: Do not include maximal or supra-maximal efforts: as intensity increases, technique deteriorates. Focus on skills first! Youth athletes should never to train to failure, and never "on the nerve" (close to failure). The only failure in youth athletic training is OVER-training. Youth athletes require and expend energy more rapidly than adults.

Coaches concentrate because youth cannot: Because of the rapid learning curve of youth athletes, their focus may flip from one topic or goal to the next. Proper, qualified supervision monitors the concentration and focus of youth athletes to guarantee proper technique and safe performance.

Flexible programs accommodate diversity: Youth athletes develop at different rates, both mentally and physically. Some youth fatigue more rapidly than others. Proper, qualified supervision attends the diverse range of developmental issues in youth athletics. Be flexible in your program design and implementation to allow youth athletes to develop at their own individual pace.

Get Certified: Attend a CST Certification Seminar to refine your ability to perform, understand and assess proper technique and program design.

Photographer: Wesley Buckingham • Contributed by D. Cody Fielding

INTERNATIONAL CLUBBELL® SPORT

ICS (International Clubbell® Sport) was created in 2003 as "Olympic Clubbell® Sport" by Coach Scott Sonnon, former USA National Sambo Coach and Distinguished Master of Sport in Sambo. Using his intimate knowledge of the Russian national sport of Sambo, coupled with the Russian strength endurance competition of Girevoy Sport (or kettlebell lifting), Scott established a "high bar" for International Clubbell® Sport requirements.

The first National Championships were held in 2005, represented by 5 regional qualifiers: USA Northeast, South, Midwest, Southwest, West and Northwest. Later in 2005 the UK and Japan sought representation in ICS, making it truly an "international' sport.

ICS RULES AND REGULATIONS

In International Clubbell® Sport there are two events: the Swipe (a combination routine involving the basic swing plus an arm cast) and the Mill (a combination routine involving the inward pendulum and a shield cast). Video clips of these events can be watched online at WWW.INTERNATIONALCLUBBELLSPORT.COM.

Athletes have ten minutes to complete as many repetitions as possible with proper form and without their Clubbells touching the platform. Athletes are allotted no less than 30 minutes and no more than a 60 minute recovery period in between events. Athletes are allowed to rest during their lift sets provided that their Clubbells are in Shoulder Park position. Clubbells cannot be parked on the floor to rest during a lift.

Athletes will be required to sign competition registration and participation waivers before competing.

Swipes score 1 point per repetition and Mills score 1 point per repetition of both sides (1 point for both a right and a left Mill completed). The number of Mills completed to the weaker side is registered. For example, if an athlete has completed 17 Mills to one side and 18 to the right side, he receives 17 points plus the points from his Swipes (for example, 25 Swipe repetitions = 25 points). In this example the athlete would score 17 + 25 = 42 points in total.

National Ranking can only be achieved by using 25-lb Clubbells in the Men's Division and 15-lb Clubbells in the Women's Division. Athletes are encouraged to compete using lower-weighted Clubbells (at the Regional Director's discretion), but those Athletes will not receive National ranking in International Clubbell® Sport.

No gloves, weight belts, or lifting chalk of any kind are permitted during lifts.

Athletes may use a rag during competition to dry their hands, provided that their Clubbells are in Shoulder Park position when drying.

Note: The Clubbell® weights shown in the charts below are for national ranking in International Clubbell® Sport. Regional Directors may allow competition with lower-weighted Clubbells. In order to achieve National ranking in ICS, however, you must use the qualifying weight Clubbells.

ICS SWIPE

2005 MEN'S QUALIFICATIONS

Division	25lbs. Clubbells				
Category (weight in pounds))	MS	CMS	I	II	III
105	124	112	106	95	90
114.5	137	123	117	105	100
125.5	151	136	129	116	110
136.5	166	149	142	128	122
149.5	188	169	161	145	138
163.5	200	180	171	154	146
180	220	198	189	170	162
198	243	219	209	188	179
220	266	239	227	204	194
220+	296	266	252	226	214

2005 WOMEN'S QUALIFICATIONS

Division	15lbs. Clubbells				
Category (weight in pounds))	MS	CMS	I	II	III
114.5	242	202	155	129	108
136.5	302	252	194	162	135
163.5+	364	303	233	194	162

ICS RATINGS

MS	Master of Sport, National Champion
CMS	Master of Sport Candidate, Nationally Ranked Athlete
Category I	Advanced Class Athlete
Category II	Intermediate Class Athlete
Category III	Beginner Class Athlete

Contributed by Jarlo Ilano

SPORT-SPECIFIC PROGRAM EXAMPLES

Given the wide diversity of sports I cannot, nor would I want to attempt to, address every nuance of specificity within this book. My book does not intend to give you a fish, but to teach you how to fish on your own. SPP is a problem-solving activity in which the movement skills of your intended sport are used to produce the necessary solutions to performance.

However, here you will find a few successful design samples for popular sports, based upon client feedback. The following exercise selections are presented to help stimulate strength and conditioning coaches into the Circular Strength Training® mindset.

BASKETBALL TEAMS

3X/week for transitional pre-season conditioning cycle.

Begin with a pre-cycle where you hone the following basic exercises: Scissors Jumps (with bodyweight), Swings, Head Cast, Arm-pit Casts, and Snatches to Jerks to Presses. Do not continue unless athletes have mastered the basic skills.

Session 1: With Clubbells held firmly in Shoulder Park position, execute 10 alternative scissors jumps (5 with the right leg forward, 5 with the left leg forward). On the fourth landing perform a Jerk to Torch Position. That is one repetition. Complete 15 sets of 1 in 15 minutes. In between sets execute one lay-up.

Session 2: Explosively bring Clubbells to Torch Position when extending out of a squat to standing. That is one repetition. Complete 15 sets of 8 in 20 minutes. In between sets execute one jump shot.

Session 3: Perform Swings immediately to Back Position to Head Cast with shooting arm. Complete 20 sets of 5 in 20 minutes. With the remainder of time in between sets, execute one free-throw shot.

BASEBALL SWINGING

5–6X/week during pre-season, 1–2X/week during competitive period

Athletes must master the basic skills of the Parry Cast, Hammer Throw, and Arm-pit Cast before continuing. This program concentrates on strike power.

Begin by performing 5 slow and steady repetitions of the Parry Cast (counter-clockwise). Follow this by explosive two-handed Hammer Throws for 5 repetitions. Take 5 swings at bat. This is one set. Continue for 5 sets, subtracting one rep each set down to one Parry Cast, one Hammer Throw, and one bat swing. Allow 60 second rest periods between sets.

BASEBALL PITCHING
5–6X/week during pre-season, 1–2X/week during competitive period

Athletes must first master the basic skills of the Shield Cast and Arm-pit Cast. This program concentrates on throwing power.

Beginning in Order Position with the throwing arm, perform 2 slow and steady repetitions of the Shield Cast. Immediately afterwards, perform 1 repetition of the Shield Cast, changing at Back Position to an Arm-pit Cast. When in Back Position, tighten the entire musculature and death-grip the Clubbell® to EXPLODE forward with the Arm-Pit Cast. Do not stop the Arm-pit Cast. Let it your explosion accelerate and follow through into a basic arm Swing. Never train to interrupt the follow-through (such as stopping the Arm-pit Cast in Order Position).

Complete a total of 4–5 sets, stopping well short of fatigue or failure. This program stimulates neurological development, primarily. Make the rest periods 2 to 5 minutes. In between sets perform an initial pitch at maximum speed, and afterwards 3 to 5 throws for technique at medium speed. This is one set.

FOOTBALL QUARTERBACKS
2X/week during competitive period for enhanced neurology

Athletes must master the basic skills of the Cleans, Parry Cast and Arm-pit Cast before continuing.

Session 1: Parry Cast to Back Position, and use maximal tension to explode through an Arm-pit Cast (explosive cast with throwing arm) into a basic arm Swing (this is the "Bullwhip" Combination Routine). Complete 30 sets of 2, followed by a lateral 10-yard sprint and a long, slow pass with a football. Complete the total work in 30 minutes.

Session 2: Comlpete Clean and Casts at 20 sets of 3 reps with one 10 yard sprint diagonally and a short and quick pass with the football. Complete total work in 20 minutes.

Alternatively, use the Baseball throwing program above.

SOCCER GOALIES
2X/week for pre-season conditioning cycle

Begin with a pre-cycle to hone the following basic exercises: Forward, Inward and Outward Pendulums, lunges and jump switches. Do not continue unless athletes have mastered the basic skills.

Session 1: Begin in Order Position. Perform a double Clubbell® Forward Pendulum with a lunge, catching Clubbells in Order Position. Hold for 4 seconds. Explosively return and alternate legs to perform the lunge on the other leg. Complete 30 sets of 6 repetitions (3/leg). The total work should be completed within a 30-minute time limit.

Session 2: Begin in Order Position with two Clubbells. Perform a Forward Pendulum to a lunge. In the lunge, do a jump switch to the opposite lunge while holding the Clubbells in Order Position. Return and alternate legs. Complete 30 sets of 4 repetitions (2/leg), within a 30-minute time limit.

Session 3: Perform alternating Inward/Outward Pendulums with Side steps for 30 sets of 6 repetitions (3/leg), in a 30-minute time limit.

TENNIS PLAYERS
2X/week during competitive season to augment serving power

Begin with a pre-cycle honing of the following basic exercises: Snatch to Torch Position, Head Cast, Arm-pit Cast, Basic Swing. Do not continue unless athletes have mastered the basic skills. Alternate with BOTH arms!

Snatch to Torch Position and yield to Back Position (the 2nd half of the Head Cast movement). Immediately follow with a side step, turning the torso 90° while simultaneously executing an explosive Arm-Pit Cast. Allow follow through into a Basic Swing. Park the Clubbell®. Perform two-repetition sets.

Complete a total of 4–5 sets, stopping well short of fatigue or failure. This program stimulates neurological development, primarily. Make the rest periods 2 minutes in length. Between sets, practice serves for technique and power.

FIELD HOCKEY TEAMS
4X/week for pre-season conditioning cycles

Begin with a pre-cycle of honing the following basic exercises: Inward Pendulums, Backward Circles, and Pre-swing Cleans. Do not continue unless athletes have mastered the basic skills.

Sprint 10 yards and execute 8 very slow Backward Circles; Spring 10 yards back and execute 8 slow Inward Pendulums; Sprint 10 yards laterally and execute 16 EXPLOSIVE Pre-swing Cleans. This is the first set.

Perform 3 sets, and each time divide the reps by two: 8/8/16 on the 1st set, 4/4/8 on the 2nd set, and 1/1/4 on the 3rd set. Also, multiply the sprint distance on each set by two: 10 yards on the 1st set, 20 on the 2nd set, 40 on the 3rd set. Begin with a 30 second rest period and add 30 seconds each set.

VOLLEYBALL PLAYERS
3X/week for transitional pre-season conditioning cycle.

Begin with a pre-cycle honing of the following basic exercises: Snatch to Torch Position, Extended Snatch, Clean to Order, Inward Pendulum, Arm-pit Cast, and Head Cast. Do not continue unless athletes have mastered the basic skills.

Session 1: Using one Clubbell® held in the striking arm, begin from a dead-hang position. Execute Snatches to top position, extending off the heel to ball of foot. Park the Clubbell®. Immediately Clean the Clubbell® with the striking arm completely to Back Position and execute an explosive Head Cast to a leverage hold. That is one repetition. Complete 20 sets of 2 in 15 minutes. Between sets execute one net block.

Session 2: Use Extended Snatches (standing on appropriate benches) to maximize jump depth. Exchange Session 1's dead-hang for a normal (with swing) Snatch. This time only extend to the heel and don't go up to ball of foot. Immediately Clean the Clubbell® with the striking arm completely to Back Position and execute an explosive Arm-pit Cast. Allow the inertia to taper off gradually with a full Basic Swing. That is one repetition. Complete 20 sets of 2 in 15 minutes.

Session 3: Do double Clubbell® alternating Inward Pendulums (while the other remains in order) with a Side Step. Follow a 5 X 5 protocol with 2-minute rest periods. Rest-pauses are acceptable. Between sets execute one serve.

GOLF PLAYERS
5X/week for pre-season conditioning cycles, or 2X/week in the competitive season

Begin with a pre-cycle honing of the following basic exercises: Inward Pendulum, Backward Circle, Head Cast and Shield Cast. Do not continue unless athletes have mastered the basic skills. Alternate with BOTH arms!

Snatch or Clean and Torch Press the Clubbell® to top position. Perform a Backward Circle all the way around to top position again, and then yield to the behind the head portion of the Shield Cast. Immediately follow with an Inward Pendulum, ending in top-position. Yield and Park the Clubbell®. Perform only SINGLE repetition sets!

Complete a total of 4–5 sets, stopping well short of fatigue or failure. This program stimulates neurological development, primarily. Make the rest periods 2 – 5 minutes in length. Between sets, hit two long shots for technique and power.

BIBLIOGRAPHY

Ackland, Jon and Reid, Brett. "Overtraining" *The Power to Perform*.

Alter, Joseph, Ph.D. *The Wrestler's Body: Identity and Ideology in North India*. 1992

Alter, Joseph, Ph.D. *Iron Game History*, October 1995

Author unknown: *How to Be Healthy, A Complete Course of Physical Exercises with Instruction for Dumb Bells, Club Swinging and Ju Jitsu*. 1913, 77 diagrams

Amateur Athletic Union of the United States. Constitution, By-Laws, General and Athletic Rules, Chapter X. Club-Swinging.

AG Spalding and Bros 1890 *Australian Calisthenics Federation Manual*. Club swinging section pp42–55, photos revised 1993

Beale, Alfred M. *Calisthenics and Light Gymnastics for Home and School*. Excelsior Publishing House, New York 1888

Beck, Charles. *A Treatise on Gymnastiks, Taken Chiefly from the German of F. L. Jahn*, Northampton Massachusetts; Simeon Butler, 1828.

Benedict, George H. *Manual of Boxing, Club Swinging and Manly Sports*. 1886

Black Belt Magazine. "Gama the Lion," *Black Belt Magazine*; Summer 1963

Brookfield, John. *Mastery of Hand Strength*.

Bornstein M. *Indian Clubs and Other Exercises*. 1880

Bornstein M. *Manual of Instruction in the Use of Dumb-bell, Indian Club, and Other Athletic Exercise*. 1889

Bott, Jenny. *Modern Rhythmic Gymnastics*. Club swinging section pp66–70. EP Sport Series, EP Publishing Limited, UK1981

Bompa, Tudor Ph.D. *Periodization*.

Boyd, John, Col. *Patterns of Conflict*.

Burrows, Tom W. *Club Swinging as Applied to Health, Development, Training and Display*. 1906

Burrows, Tom W (The World's Champion). *Text-Book of Club Swinging*. Health and Strength Ltd, London, 1908, 1922, 1935, pp80, 20 illustrations, 16 diagrams.

Chek, Paul, "The Inner Unit: A New Frontier In Abdominal Training"; *IAAF Technical Quarterly: New Studies in Athletics*, April 1999

Cobbett, Colonel GTB and Jenkin AF. *Indian Clubs*. G Bell and Sons, London, 1921 pp118

Davies, John. "Complex Training" *Testosterone Magazine* Issue 215 testosterone.net

Dempsey, Jack. "How I Got and Keep My Fighting Muscles" *Muscle Builder* Magazine, Macfadden Publication, FEB 1925

Dick, William *Dick's Dumb-bell and Indian Club Exercises* New York: Dick and Fitzgerald Publishers 1887

Draper, Dave. *Six Keys to Successful Bodybuilding*.

Draper, Dave. *Brother Iron, Sister Steel* (On Target Publications. 2001)

Fillary, Roger and Waldron, Gil "Bodybuilding and Muscle Control in India" (*Eugene Sandow and the Golden Age of Iron Men: www.sandowplus.co.uk*)

Frolov, Vladimir, MD. *Endogenous Respiration*.

Gardiner, Benjamin. *Indian Club Swinging*. Providence Freeman 1884

Griffin, Charles Eldridge. *How to Be a Club Swinger: As a means of physical culture the Indian clubs stand preeminent among the varied apparatus of gymnastics now in use: a complete self-instructor by which any person can learn the healthy exercise and become a professional*. New York 1897

Hackenschmidt, George. *The Way to Live*

Harrison. *Indian Clubs, Dumb-bells and Sword Exercises* 2nd ed. London: Dean and Son, no date

Hartle, Mike, D.C., "Sledgehammer GPP" *Intensity Magazine*. Volume 1, Issue 34; June 04, 2002

Hatfield, Frederick, Ph.D., FISSA, *How They Train: Conditioning Methods of World Champion Boxer Evander Holyfield,* Sportscience News Sep-Oct 1997

Hill, Gus and Burrows, Tom. *Club Swinging*. New York, Fox 1913

Hoffman, Alice J. *Indian Clubs*. Harry N Abrams N.Y. USA 1996

Hoffman, Bob. *Simplified System of Swing Bar Training*. 1943

Hoyman, Dr Annelis. *Rhythmic Gymnastics (Indian clubs)*. Last of a series of four manuals on rhythmic gymnastics with hand apparatus. Kimbo Music Publishing Co 1968 pp35 "

International Jugglers Association. *Swingers discover excitement in two-club twirl.* Includes 4 pictures of Allan Jacobs. IJA Newsletter, Feb 1980

International Jugglers Association. *Picture shows "an Anaheim, CA women's gym class circa 1906–7 posing with clubs for swinging".* IJA Newsletter March 1981

International Jugglers Association. *Full page picture of Allan Jacobs, 1983 IJA Champion and text.* IJA Juggler's World, Sept 1983 pp 6–7

Jacobs, Allan. Video. Club Swinging. Maverick Media / IJA Productions, US 1990. Reviewed in Kaskade Magazine, Sept 1991: issue 23 pp32 by Gabi Keast

Jesse, John. Wrestling Physical Conditioning Encyclopedia (Athletic Press: 1970

Jillings, Anna. Modern Club Swinging and Pole Spinning. 1994, Butterfingers, Bath, UK, pp99, 116 diagrams. * "Swingers Rejoice" review, Kaskade Magazine, June 1994: issue 34, pp15 by Gabi Keast

Jillings, Anna. The Snake: Club Swinging part III. Kaskade Magazine Dec 1993: issue 32, pp34–36 *

Jillings, Anna. *Fantastic Fire Swingers.* Review of the fire show at Leeds EJC 1993. The Catch Magazine, Dec 1993 — Feb 1994, issue 6, vol 1. pp40

Jones AK. Indian Club Exercises and Drills. 1901

Jowett, George. Jowett Institute Course in Muscle Building and Physical Culture. New York: 1927

Jowett, George. Molding A Mighty Grip. New York

Justa, Steve. Rock, Iron, Steel: The Book of Strength. Ironmind Enterprises, Inc.; pages 70–73

Judd, Leslie James. Indian Club Swinging. Graduation Thesis, International Young Men's Christian Association College, Springfield, Mass, USA June 1920, pp13

Kubrik, Brooks. Dinosaur Training: Lost Secrets of Strength and Development.

Keast, Gabi. Club Swinging parts I and II. Kaskade Magazine Issues 27/28 September and December 1992, pp23–25 and 33–35 *

Kehoe, Simon D. Indian Club Exercise, with Explanatory Figures and Positions Photographed for Life. Perk and Snyder 1861, 1866, 1882

Lawton, WJ Henri. Champion Club Swinging Series, 1898

Lemaire, EF. Indian clubs and how to use them: a new and complete method for learning to wield light and heavy clubs graduated from the simplest to the most complicated exercises. London 1889

Lewis, Dio, MD. The New Gymnastics for Men, Women and Children. James R Osgood and Co., Boston 12th edition 1873

Lewis, Dio, MD, in Exercises with Clubs Boston; Tickner and Fields, 1882

Leistner, Ken, Ph.D. "Perspective on Strength" THE STEEL TIP Vol. 1, No. 2, February 1985.

Lord, Charles E. Indian Club Exercises etc. 4th edition 1902

Massue. *Rückblick auf die Benutzung der Keule in der rhytmischen Sportgymnastik. Charakteristik der Keulengymnastik und verschiedene Bewegungen werden dargestellt*. In: Revue de l',ducation physique 22, 1980

Miller, Frank Edward. *Indian club swinging*. New York Saalfield 1900

Moss, Alfred Staff Sergeant. *Simple Indian Club Exercises*. Health and Strength, London 1909 Reprint, Athletic Publications, London 1936, 1942, 1943, 1952, pp 31

Raiport, Grigori MD, Ph.D. *Red Gold: Peak Performance Techniques of the Russian and East German Olympic Victors* (Los Angeles, Jeremy Tarcher, Inc. 1988)

Rauchfuss, M. *Ergebnisse trainingsbegleitender Untersuchungen zum Erlernen des Keulenjonglierens in der rhythmischen Sportgymnastik*. In: Theorie und Proxi Leistungssport, Leipzig — 24 1986

Richter, Ben. *Book of Club Swinging*. 1994, Circusstuff, Fife, UK pp 92 * Reviewed in Kaskade Magazine Issue 36, Winter 1994 pp 26 by Gabi Keast *

Schäfer, Dirk. *Keulenschwingen*. Forthcoming, Germany, November 1996, ISBN 3-89535-437-6. (info: Karolingerring 40, 50678 Cologne Tel/Fax: 0221 3318151)

Schatz, William Jackson. *Club Swinging for Physical Education and Recreation: a book for information about all forms of Indian club swinging used in gymnasiums and by individuals*. Originally published Boston: American Gymnasia 1908. Reprinted by Brian Dubé Inc, New York 1990

Schatz, William Jackson. *Elementary Club Swinging for Normal Classes*. Philadelphia Wright, 1913

Schlüter, Heinrich. *Die schwingende und fliegen de Keule*: 15 Minuten Keulengymnastik. In: Turnen und Sport: Fachzeitschrift fur Turnen, Gymnastik, Spiel und Sport — Celle 54, 1980

Shelburne, Dave. *George Roth hungered for the Olympics: the 1932 winner in Indian clubs was motivated by more than competition*. Daily News, Dec 17 1983, 2 pgs

Siff, Mel, Ph.D. *Facts and Fallacies of Fitness* MyoDynamics.com.

Spielman, Ed. *The Spiritual Journey of Joseph Greenstein*.

Sports Illustrated. George Roth, USA. *Olympic medal winner at club swinging in 1932*. 2 pgs, pics of 1932 and 1984, July 18 1984

Sonnon, Scott. *Flow-Fighting and the Flow-State Performance Spiral: Peak Performance in Combat Sports*

Stecher, WA ed. *Gymnastics*, chapter by Froehlich, Fred W, *Exercises with Clubs*. Lee and Shepardard, Boston 1895.

Summers, Kit. *Juggling with Finesse*. Club swinging section pp 180–186. Finesse Press, San Diego 1987, 1988, 1990

Thomas, Ed. Ed.D. "*Treasures in the Attic*" <u>Tae Kwon Do Times</u>. January 2002

Todd, Jan, Ph.D. "*From Milo to Milo: A History of Barbells, Dumbbells, and Indian Clubs*" <u>Iron Game History</u>, Volume 3 Number 6

Trall, RIT, MD. <u>The Illustrated Family Gymnasium</u>. Fowler and Wells, New York 1857

Tsatsouline, Pavel. <u>Beyond Stretching</u>.

Tsatsouline, Pavel. <u>Power to the People</u>.

Verkhoshansky, Yuri, Ph.D., <u>SUPERTRAINING : Special Strength Training for Sporting Excellence</u> MyoDynamics.com.

Walker, Donald. <u>Manly Exercises</u> 1837

Walker, Donald. <u>Exercises for Ladies; calculated to preserve and improve beauty and to prevent and correct personal defects, inseparable from constrained or careless habits: founded on Physiological Principals</u>. Thomas Hurst, London 2nd edition 1837

Warman, Edward B. <u>Indian Club Exercises</u>. 1909

Weaver, George. <u>The Enrichment of Life</u>.

Webster, David <u>Bodybuilding: An Illustrated History</u>. New York: Arco Publishing, 1982; pages 123–124

Wheelwright, Samuel T. <u>A New System of Instruction in the Indian Club Exercise</u>. E I Horsman, New York 1871

Whelan, Bob. "*John Grimek was the Man*" <u>Hardgainer Magazine</u> Issue 59 MAR-APR 1999

Willoughby, David. <u>The Super Athletes</u>.

Yessis, Michael, Ph.D. <u>Secrets of Soviet Sports Fitness and Training</u>. Arbor House, New York, 1987

Zatsiorsky, Vladimir, Ph.D. <u>Science and Practice of Strength Training</u>.

Photographer: Wesley Buckingham • Contributed by D. Cody Fielding